Introduction to Identity-Based Encryption

For a listing of recent titles in the *Artech House Information Security and Privacy Series,* turn to the back of this book.

Introduction to Identity-Based Encryption

Luther Martin

ARTECH HOUSE
BOSTON | LONDON
artechhouse.com

Library of Congress Cataloging-in-Publication Data
A catalog record for this book is available from the U.S. Library of Congress.

British Library Cataloguing in Publication Data
A catalogue record for this book is available from the British Library.

ISBN-13: 978-1-59693-238-8

Cover design by Yekaterina Ratner

685 Canton Street
Norwood, MA 02062

10 9 8 7 6 5 4 3 2 1

Contents

Preface

The content of this book roughly parallels the content of a series of talks that I gave at the Voltage Security "brown-bag" seminar, the randomly occurring series of talks that technologists at Voltage gave to others in the company, talks that attempted to explain what was going on in the east side of the building, the side where people often came to work late, routinely worked until the early morning, and always drank too much coffee. Thus the material is aimed at a typical Silicon Valley engineer—a person who probably has an undergraduate degree in computer science and has been working for a few years. And although they have usually been exposed to a fair amount of discrete math, abstract algebra, and cryptography in the past, they have forgotten the details of most of it, but can recall it again if reminded of the basic facts. This type of person also seems to like being shown concrete examples of how things work to clarify new concepts; and I've tried to follow this model with this book, trying to give readers a good idea of how identity-based encryption algorithms work. So by reading this book you can almost experience a bit of what it's like to be at a Silicon Valley start-up, but without free food or the stress of wondering how long your company will be able to survive. The topic of the talks was identity-based encryption, or "IBE" as it is commonly known.

The years since 2001, when Dan Boneh and Matt Franklin wrote the paper "Identity-Based Encryption from the Weil Pairing," have been interesting ones, at least to those in the field of cryptography. The techniques that they described in this paper started what could probably be called a revolution in the field, and their paper has been cited at a higher rate than experienced by either of the two other ground-breaking papers in public-key cryptography, "A Method for Obtaining Digital Signatures and Public-Key Cryptosystems" by Ron Rivest, Adi Shamir, and Len Adleman, and "New Directions in Cryptography" by Whitfield Diffie and Martin Hellman. The paper by Boneh and Franklin might be considered the beginning of pairing-based cryptography in the same way that Christopher Columbus might be given credit for discovering the New World; they might not have been the first to actually accomplish something, but their accomplishments were almost certainly the most significant.

What makes the new field of pairing-based cryptography interesting depends on your point of view. It certainly allows for the construction of interesting cryptographic primitives that were unknown before the use of pairings, and identity-based encryption is one of the most important of these. Identity-based encryption is in turn interesting because it allows for the implementation of systems that are simpler and easier to use than the alternatives, and it is probably this rather than any other benefits that has led to the rapid acceptance of the technology. In the few years since its first commercial availability in 2003, the rapid rate of adoption of identity-based encryption has led to the situation in which there are currently almost as many users of the technology as there are users of traditional public-key infrastructure technologies, and at the current rate of adoption, the number of users of identity-based encryption will soon outnumber those of competing technologies. So if you are a user of information security technology, the technology should be interesting to you, for you may see it sooner than you might have expected, and this book is designed to give such people a way to understand the technology that is quicker and easier than reading the academic papers on the subject.

The number of users of encryption has increased dramatically in recent years, driven by the increasingly stringent regulatory environment in which businesses now operate, and using encryption is an easy way to convince your auditors that you are taking data security and privacy seriously enough for them to approve of your overall data security and data privacy program. This has increased interest in both encryption in general and in particular encryption technologies like identity-based encryption, which provide an easy way to comply with data privacy laws while staying within your budget and not causing support nightmares for your IT organization. Unfortunately, the only way to learn about identity-based encryption until now has been to read research papers on the topic, a requirement that makes the topic inaccessible to most people, even those with potential uses for the technology. With any luck, this book will bridge that gap a bit and make the technology more accessible.

1

Introduction

This book describes a public-key encryption technology called identity-based encryption (IBE), and tries to answer a few of the commonly asked questions about it. These include the following:

1. What is IBE and how does it differ from other public-key technologies?
2. Why should I care about IBE?
3. Why should I believe that IBE schemes are secure?
4. What are some of the techniques that have been used to create practical and secure IBE schemes?
5. How can I efficiently implement IBE schemes?

The answers to the first two of these questions are relatively simple, and are contained in this chapter. The other three require a significant level of background before they can be answered. Chapters 2, 3, and 4 of this book provide a framework for understanding the answers to the more complex questions. Chapters 5 and 6 provide an answer to the third question. Chapters 7 through 11 collectively provide an answer to the fourth question. Chapter 12 provides some answers to the fifth question.

1.1 What Is IBE?

IBE is a public-key encryption technology that allows a user to calculate a public key from an arbitrary string. We usually think of this string as representing an identity of some kind, but it is usually useful to use more than just an identity to calculate such a public key. For example, to avoid a user having the same IBE key forever, it is useful to include some information in this string about the validity period of the key. Or, to ensure that a user will receive different keys from different IBE systems, it may be useful to include information in this string that is unique to a particular IBE implementation, perhaps a URL that identifies a server that is used in the implementation of each of the different IBE systems. Because the string used to calculate a key almost always contains more than just an identity, it may be more accurate to use the term *identifier-based encryption* instead, but this term is not widely used to describe the technology. The ability to calculate keys as needed gives IBE systems different properties than those of traditional public-key systems, and these properties provide significant practical advantages in some situations. So although there are probably few situations in which it is impossible to solve any problem with traditional public-key technologies that can be solved with IBE, the solutions that use IBE may be much simpler to implement and much less expensive to support than alternatives.

In implementations of a traditional public-key system that uses digital certificates to manage public keys, a public-private key pair is generated randomly by either a user, or an agent working on behalf of a user, in which the public key contains all of the parameters needed for using it in cryptographic calculations. Random generation of keys is not strictly required by the public-key algorithms that are used in such systems, but is required by the existing standards that define the use of such algorithms. After it is created, the public key, along with the identity of the owner of the key, is digitally signed by a certificate authority (CA) to create a digital certificate that is then used to transport and manage the key. The owner of the private key then receives a copy of the certificate and a copy of the certificate is stored in a certificate repository that is accessible by others who might need to get a user's key. In applications where it may be necessary to recover private keys that are lost or unavailable in some way, the private keys are also securely archived by a key recovery agent. If an agent created the private key on behalf of a user, like often happens when keys are centrally generated so that copies can be archived to allow the recovery of lost or otherwise unavailable keys, the owner of the key also receives the private key from the CA. This is shown in Figure 1.1.

In a traditional public-key system, the identity of a user is usually carefully verified before a digital certificate is issued to him, a process that is typically relatively expensive. The process of generating public-private key pairs can also be computationally expensive. Generating two 512-bit prime numbers that are suitable for use in creating a 1,024-bit RSA private key is certainly feasible, but generating larger primes gets progressively more expensive. Creating two 7,680-bit primes that are suitable for use in creating a 15,360-bit RSA private key is not an operation that widely used computers can easily perform, yet such

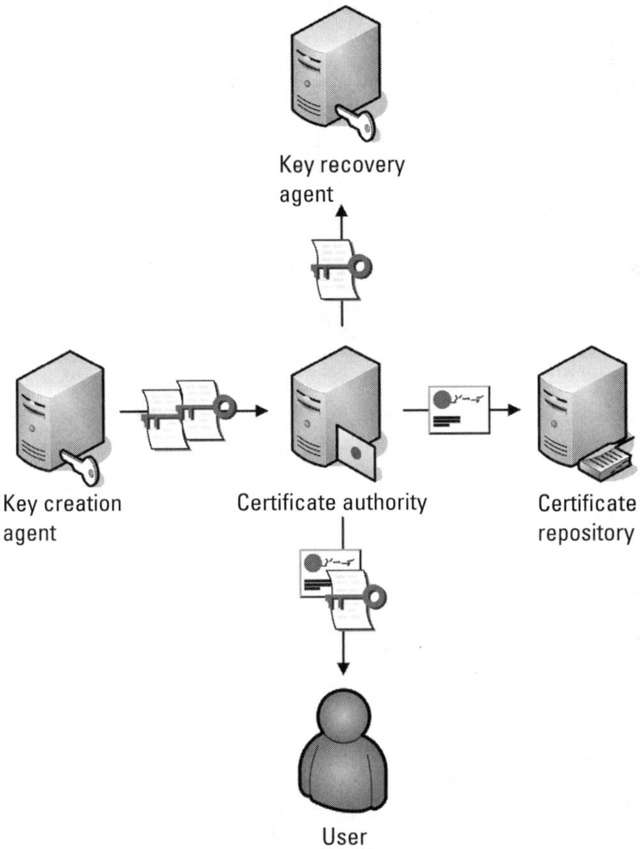

Figure 1.1 Generation of keys in a traditional public-key system.

keys are needed to securely transport the 256-bit AES keys that are used today. Because generating keys and verifying users' identities can be expensive, digital certificates are often issued with fairly long validity periods, often between one and three years. Because of the relatively long validity period of the public keys managed by digital certificates, it is often necessary to check the key in a certificate for validity before using it. This is shown in Figure 1.2. There have been many solutions proposed for validating public keys, but the existing technologies to do this are still relatively unproven and have practical difficulties when used for a large number of users.

To use a public key that is contained in a digital certificate, a user queries the public repository where the certificate can be found and retrieves the certificate. Because a public key may be valid for quite a while, it is often necessary to check such a public key for validity before using it. This may be by checking a list of invalid certificates or by querying an online service that returns the

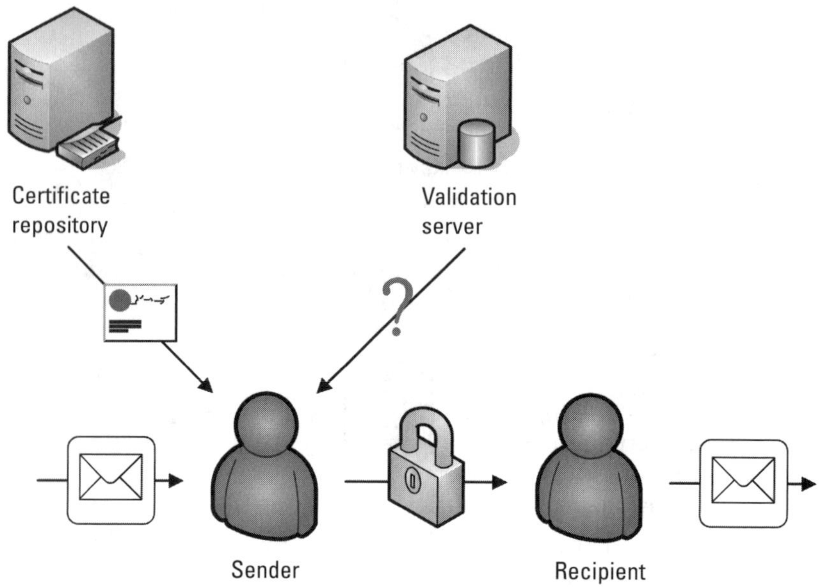

Figure 1.2 Validation and use of a public key in a traditional public-key system.

validity status of a certificate. After any necessary validity checking is done, the user then uses the public key to encrypt information to the owner of the public key. Because the recipient has the private key that corresponds to the public key, he is able to decrypt this information. This is shown in Figure 1.2.

IBE was first mentioned by Adi Shamir in 1984 [1], when he described a rough outline of the properties that such a system should have and how it could be used, although he was unable to find a secure and feasible technology that worked as he described. He seemed to see the advantages of IBE to be related to its ease of use relative to other technologies when he described IBE in this way:

> An identity-based scheme resembles an ideal mail system: If you know somebody's name and address you can send him messages that only he can read, and you can verify the signatures that only he could have produced. It makes the cryptographic aspects of the communication almost transparent to the user, and it can be used effectively even by laymen who know nothing about keys or protocols.

An IBE system has similarities to traditional public-key systems, but is also quite different in other ways. While traditional public keys contain all of the parameters needed to use the key, to use an IBE system, a user typically needs to get a set of public parameters from a trusted third party. With these parameters, a user can then calculate the IBE pubic key of any user and use it to encrypt information to that user. This process is shown in Figure 1.3.

The recipient of IBE-encrypted information then authenticates in some way to a private key generator (PKG), a trusted third party that calculates the IBE private key that corresponds to a particular IBE public key. The PKG typically uses secret information called a *master secret*, plus the user's identity, to calculate such a private key. After this private key is calculated, it is securely distributed to the authorized user. This is shown in Figure 1.4. These differences are summarized in Table 1.1.

In a traditional public-key scheme, we can summarize the algorithms involved in the creation and use of a public-private key pair as key generation, encryption, and decryption. Two additional algorithms, certification and key validation, are often used in many implementations of such schemes. To fully specify the operation of such a scheme we need to define the operation of each of these algorithms. In the key generation step, one key of the public-private key pair is generated randomly and the other key in the pair is calculated from it. After this, the public key and the identity of its owner is digitally signed by a CA to create a digital certificate. Encryption is performed using the public key contained in this certificate. Decryption is performed using the private key that corresponds to the public key.

In an IBE scheme there are also four algorithms that are used to create and use a public-private key pair. These are traditionally called setup, extraction,

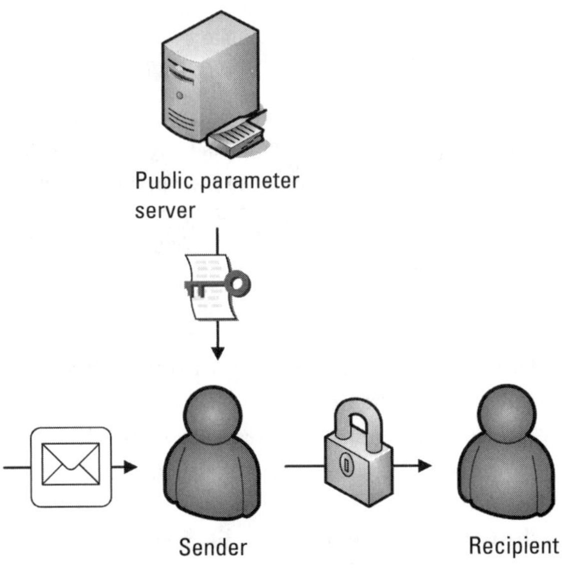

Figure 1.3 Encrypting with an IBE system.

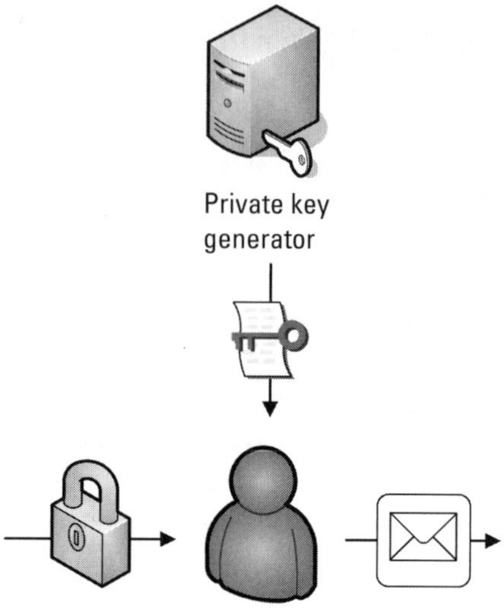

Figure 1.4 Decrypting with an IBE system.

Table 1.1
Comparison of Properties of IBE and Traditional Public-Key Systems

IBE	Traditional Public-Key Systems
Public parameters are distributed by a TTP	All required parameters are part of a public key
PKG master secret is used to calculate private keys	CA private key is used to create digital certificates
Private keys generated by PKG	Private keys are generated randomly
Public keys can be calculated by any user	Public keys calculated from private keys and transported in a digital certificate
Keys typically short-lived	Keys typically valid for long periods
Only encryption	Digital signatures plus encryption

encryption, and decryption. Setup is the algorithm with which the parameters needed for IBE calculations are initialized, including the master secret that a PKG uses to calculate IBE private keys. Extraction is the algorithm for calculating an IBE private key from the parameters established in the setup step, along with the identity of a user, and uses the master secret of the PKG to do this. Encryption is performed with an IBE public key that is calculated from the parameters from the setup step and the identity of a user. Decryption is performed with an IBE private key that is calculated from a user's identity and the private key of the PKG. These steps are summarized in Table 1.2. The discussions of IBE schemes in the subsequent chapters will describe the operation of IBE schemes in terms of these four parts: the algorithms that implement the setup, extraction, encryption, and decryption steps.

There are five main objectives that an information security solution can meet: providing confidentiality, integrity, availability, authentication, and nonrepudiation. Confidentiality keeps information secret from those not authorized to see it. Integrity ensures that information has not been altered by unauthorized or unknown means. Availability ensures that information is in the place required by a user at the time that the information is required and in the form that a user needs it. Authentication is the ability to verify the identity of a user. Nonrepudiation prevents the denial of previous commitments or actions. The use of cryptography can support most of these objectives; the use of IBE can support only one of these objectives. This is summarized in Table 1.3.

Encryption of data is an easy way to provide confidentiality. In a well-designed system, decrypting encrypted data is infeasible to anyone not possessing the correct decryption key. Digital signatures provide solutions for the other

Table 1.2
Four Algorithms Comprising an IBE Scheme

Step	Summary
Setup	Initialize all system parameters.
Extraction	Calculate IBE private key from PKG master secret and an identity using system parameters.
Encrypt	Encrypt information using an IBE public key calculated from system parameters and an identity.
Decrypt	Decrypt information using an IBE private key calculated from PKG master secret and an identity.

Table 1.3
Applicability of Different Encryption Technologies in Attaining Information Security Goals

Security Goal	IBE	Traditional Public-Key Technologies
Confidentiality	Yes	Yes
Integrity	No	Yes
Availability	No	Yes
Authentication	No	Yes
Nonrepudiuation	No	No

objectives of information security. They provide a way to provide integrity, because modifying digitally signed data while keeping the signature valid is as computationally infeasible as defeating the underlying cryptography that is used to create the signature. They can also provide a technical basis for nonrepudiation, although defining exactly what nonrepudiation means is fairly difficult. Not all written signatures are legally binding, after all, and we should expect the same limitations to the nonrepudiation provided by digital signatures. For all practical purposes, nonrepudiation seems to be an unattainable goal for existing information security technologies. Digital signatures also provide a way to authenticate users; a user creating a valid digital signature needs to either have possession of the private key used to create the signature or to have defeated the cryptography used to create the signature. So using digital signatures to authenticate users can also help prevent denial-of-service attacks, which increases the availability of data.

IBE provides an easy solution that provides for the confidentiality of data. It does not provide integrity, availability, authentication, and nonrepudiation. These are more easily provided by digital signatures using keys that are created and managed by a traditional public-key system. As we will see, however, the advantages that IBE provides make it a very good solution for some problems, and a hybrid solution that used IBE for encryption and a traditional public-key system to provide digital signatures may be a solution that combines the best features of each technology.

1.2 Why Should I Care About IBE?

IBE is an interesting technology because other public-key algorithms have encountered practical difficulties in use. In particular, implementations of traditional public-key technologies have gained a reputation for being difficult and expensive, at least when they are used by people; the most successful application of public-key technology has been in the widespread use of SSL, which requires minimal interaction with a user when it is used to authenticate a server and to encrypt communications with the same server. Applications that require a user to mange or use public keys have not been as successful.

A classic study in 1999 by Alma Whitten and J. D. Tygar that was popularized by the paper "Why Johnny Can't Encrypt" [2], found that 75% of users were unable to use a public-key-based system to send an encrypted e-mail. Usability of public-key technology seems to have increased since this study, but apparently not enough. The title alone of the 2006 paper "Why Johnny Still Can't Encrypt" [3] indicates that the technology is still too difficult for many users: none of the six test subjects in this second study were able to encrypt e-mail. Poor usability causes high-support costs for users of the technology, and has probably been one of the major factors hindering the widespread adoption of public-key technology. Dan Geer even conjectured that high costs are unavoidable when using any type of cryptography [4]:

> Both symmetric cryptosystems, like Kerberos, and asymmetric cryptosystems, like RSA, do the same thing—that is to say they do key distribution—but the semantics are quite different. The fundamental security-enabling activity of a secret key system is to issue fresh keys at low latency and on demand. The fundamental security-enabling activity of an asymmetric key system is to verify the as-yet-unrevoked status of a key already in circulation, again with low latency and on demand. This is key management and it is a systems cost; a secret key system like Kerberos has incurred nearly all its costs by the moment of key issuance. By contrast, a public key system incurs nearly all its costs with respect to key revocation. Hence, a rule of thumb: The cost of key issuance plus the cost of key revocation is a constant, just yet another version of "You can pay me now or you can pay me later.

Geer's conjecture tells us that we should expect any use of cryptography to be expensive. Because there are many cases where the use of encryption is desirable, a new type of encryption technology that avoids some of the problems associated with traditional public-key technologies is inherently interesting, and this is one of the promises of IBE. IBE may not offer any new capabilities that traditional public-key technologies cannot provide, but it allows for the creation of solutions that would be very difficult and expensive to implement with earlier technologies. In particular, these solutions seem to violate Geer's principle that using encryption has to have a high cost.

Key validation, or checking to make sure that a particular key is valid at some point in its lifetime, can be an expensive and difficult process, particularly when validating uses of a key that took place in the past. Suppose that you are doing digitally signed and encrypted electronic transactions and you need to verify whether or not a particular transaction had a valid signature at some point in the past, like when the transaction took place two years ago. The validity of a digital certificate can change during its lifetime as it is temporarily suspended or revoked, so it is necessary to be able to reconstruct the validity of the key managed by any certificate at any point in the key's lifetime to be able to answer such questions. Doing so requires being able to reconstruct the state of the system that manages the validity of keys, which is a complex and difficult problem.

To avoid the practical difficulties of key validation, IBE systems typically use short-lived keys. So if an IBE key is valid for only one day, then we assume that it is valid for that entire day, and there is no provision for revoking or suspending a key during that period. This may not provide the same level of precision as the ability to immediately revoke or suspend a key, but it makes the validation of such keys trivial. This, in turn, lets us build simpler and less expensive systems. The ability to quickly and easily calculate keys makes short-lived keys in IBE practical, where they are often impractical, although not impossible, to use in a system based on traditional PKI technology.

Key recovery, the capability to restore a lost or otherwise-unavailable key, is an essential feature for commercially successful encryption technology. In practice, most key recovery is apparently performed when passwords protecting access to keys are lost or forgotten [5] instead of the scenario in which the owner of a key is not present, yet there is an immediate need for information encrypted with his key. In traditional public-key systems, key recovery is typically implemented through having a TTP generate keys on behalf of a user and securely archiving a copy of the user's private key that can be used for key recovery as needed. Such key recovery systems require securely storing archival copies of all private keys and carefully controlling access to the archive of these keys.

IBE systems, on the other hand, calculate keys as needed, so there is no need for archiving keys at all. The only information that needs to be backed-up is the master secret that is used by the PKG to calculate IBE private keys. This simpler process makes IBE systems simpler and easier in many applications than traditional public-key technologies, and can make the cost of supporting and maintaining an IBE system much less than the cost of supporting and maintaining a system with the same capabilities that is based on traditional public-key technology. It also provides IBE systems with some capabilities that can be fairly difficult to implement with traditional public-key technologies.

The ability to calculate public and private keys as needed is a subtle difference between IBE and traditional public-key technologies, but one that provides many useful properties. In particular, it is not necessary to enroll a user before encrypting information to them. Therefore, it is easy to IBE-encrypt information to a user that does not exist yet and rely on the future user to properly authenticate before he can decrypt the information. If a validity period is part of an identity, it is possible to encrypt information that can only be decrypted at some point in the future, for example. Or, in a response to a natural disaster, responders may want to securely communicate with other responders, but they may not know with whom they will need to communicate before a disaster happens. Because it is impractical to pre-enroll every potential responder to every type of disaster, a technology that allows encrypting information to users before they are enrolled can be useful in circumstances like this. IBE provides a useful way to accomplish this.

E-mail messaging has become fairly dangerous. The e-mail messages received by a typical user include annoying unsolicited commercial e-mail, but also include computer viruses as well as messages that are part of organized efforts to acquire sensitive personal information, bank account numbers or credit card numbers. To combat this growing threat, many organizations implement filtering on both incoming and outgoing e-mail messages to protect users from such malicious messages. Organizations may also want to search outgoing messages for sensitive information and process it in some way that ensures that no sensitive material is sent unencrypted over a public network. Some organizations return the original message to the sender with a warning to encrypt such sensitive content in the future. Others want to automatically encrypt such messages. Using IBE, it is not difficult to scan even encrypted messages for unsuitable content. Delegate the authority to retrieve IBE private keys to a scanning process, and the scanning process can then request IBE keys on behalf of the owner of the private key, scan the decrypted message for unsuitable content, and reencrypt the message after it is scanned by using the recipient's IBE public key that it can easily calculate. This is shown below in Figure 1.5. It is possible to implement a similar solution using traditional public-key technologies, but it is typically much more complex and difficult to implement.

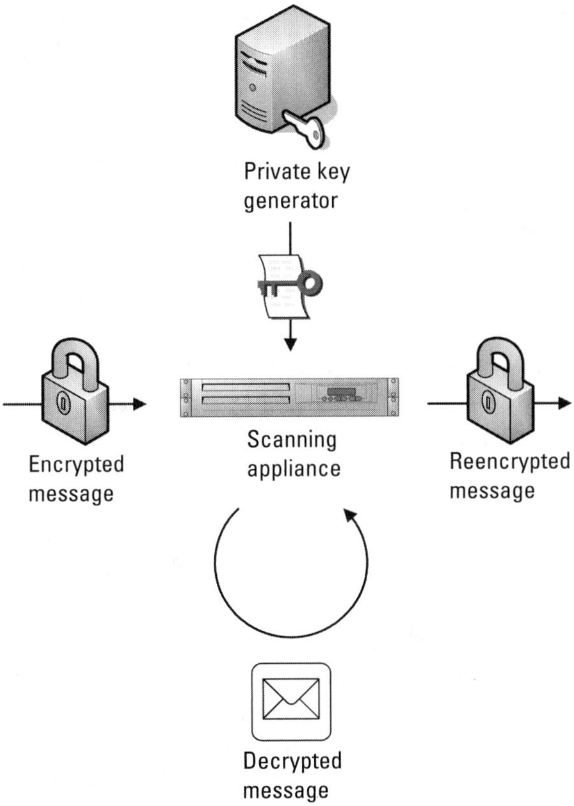

Figure 1.5 Scanning the content of IBE-encrypted e-mail.

Existing information security architectures focus on creating and maintaining a security perimeter. Inside the perimeter it is supposed to be relatively secure, and the perimeter is designed to keep threats away from the protected network. Trends in both the organization of businesses and the evolution of technology have made this model more and more difficult to implement.

One trend in the organization of businesses is the continuing integration of business partners to help all of the participants gain from the lower costs of tightly integrated operations. In the case of credit card processing, for example, the networks of the merchants who accept credit cards, the banks that issue credit cards, and the credit card companies themselves are now tightly integrated to make the processing of credit card transactions more efficient. In situations like this, it can sometimes be difficult to determine exactly where the network perimeter is, which makes it very difficult to create and maintain a security architecture that relies on a strong security perimeter.

Wireless devices also broadcast data without regard for a logical security perimeter, and thus make it difficult to implement security that is based on enforcing such a perimeter because an eavesdropper can easily intercept wireless transmissions without having to physically connect to a network. Situations like these are leading to an alternative to a highly secure perimeter: a security architecture in which we protect the data that resides in the network instead of the network itself.

One way to implement a security architecture in which we protect data instead of the network is by using encryption, where we encrypt data so that only the authorized users can decrypt it. IBE can use any arbitrary data for an identity, including strings encoding roles. So it is possible to use IBE to encrypt sensitive medical records using "doctor" as part of an identity, for example, and then to require users to prove that they are authorized to access such data when they request the IBE private key needed to decrypt it.

Most organizations have some existing form of infrastructure in place to manage identities, even if it is as simple as the username/password combinations needed to login to their network. More complex systems exist that manage more general forms of identity, and these systems provide a common way to manage many different forms of identity information. Such systems provide an interesting possibility for use with IBE, in which many different sources of identity information could be combined and used to calculate IBE keys that could then enforce access to sensitive information in ways that correspond to the permissions that different combinations of identities might give. Just like an e-mail message can be encrypted to multiple recipients, any of which can decrypt it, we can use IBE to encrypt sensitive information that could be decrypted by someone satisfying any one of several possible combinations of existing identity information. As trends in both business and technology make protecting data with encryption more and more interesting, the properties of

IBE may make it particularly useful to solve the problems that this different model of security will present.

So it appears that the properties of IBE give systems that use the technology interesting properties and allow for the creation of solutions that may be easier to use and less expensive to support than solutions provided by traditional public-key technologies. On the other hand, IBE only provides the capability to encrypt and does not allow the creation of digital signatures. This means that a complete information security solution using IBE, one that provides confidentiality, integrity, availability, authentication, and nonrepudiation, may need to be a hybrid solution that uses both IBE and traditional public-key technologies to provide a solution that takes advantage of the strengths of each of the technologies. Such solutions may eventually reduce the cost of using encryption to the point where it will be used on a wide scale, violating Geer's principle that any use of encryption must be expensive. The promise of such solutions is what motivated the existing commercial applications of IBE and will probably also motivate future applications of the technology.

References

[1] Shamir, A., "Identity-Based Cryptosystems and Signature Schemes," *Proceedings of CRYPTO '84*, Santa Barbara, CA, August 19–22, 1984, pp. 47–53.

[2] Whitten, A., and J. Tygar, "Why Johnny Can't Encrypt: A Usability Evaluation of PGP 5.0," *Proceedings of the 8th USENIX Security Symposium*, Washington, D.C., August 23–26, 1999, pp. 169–184.

[3] Sheng, S., et al., "Why Johnny Still Can't Encrypt: Evaluating the Usability of Email Encryption Software," *Proceedings of the 2006 Symposium on Usable Privacy and Security*, Pittsburgh, PA, July 12–14, 2006.

[4] Geer, D., "Risk Management Is Where the Money Is," *Risks Digest*, Vol. 20, No. 6, 1998, pp. 1–9.

[5] Nielsen, R., "Observations from the Deployment of a Large Scale PKI," *Proceedings of the 4th Annual PKI R&D Workshop*, Gaithersburg, MD, August 19–21, 2005, pp. 159–165.

2

Basic Mathematical Concepts and Properties

This chapter contains a review of all of the necessary definitions needed in the following chapters in which we discuss IBE algorithms. It also provides a list of the notation that we will use in the following chapters and states without any proofs various facts that will be cited in following chapters. Proofs of the facts listed in this chapter maybe found in [1, 2].

2.1 Concepts from Number Theory

Number theory concerns the properties of the integers and their generalizations, and provides a foundation for the other concepts that follow in later sections.

The set of natural numbers $\{1, 2, 3, \ldots\}$ is denoted by the symbol $\mathbb{N}$.

The set of integers $\{\ldots, -3, -2, -1, 0, 1, 2, 3, \ldots\}$ is denoted by the symbol $\mathbb{Z}$.

The set of real numbers is denoted by the symbol $\mathbb{R}$.

The set of complex numbers is denoted by the symbol $\mathbb{C}$. Elements of $\mathbb{C}$ can be written as $a + bi$, where a and b are real numbers and $i^2 = -1$.

Definition If a and b are integers, then *a divides b* or a is a *divisor* of b if there exists an integer c such that $b = ac$. In this case we write $a \mid b$ and we say that a is a *factor* of b.

Example 2.1

(i) Note that $1{,}001 = 7 \cdot 11 \cdot 13$, so that $7 \mid 1{,}001$ and 7 is a factor of 1,001.

(iii) We can also write $1{,}001 = (-7) \cdot (-11) \cdot 13$, so -7 and -11 are also factors of 1,001.

Definition 2.1

An integer $p \geq 2$ is a *prime* if its only positive divisors are 1 and p.

Definition 2.2

A prime p is a *Solinas prime* if we can write $p = 2^a \pm 2^b \pm 1$ for some positive integers a and b. Such primes are useful in the efficient implementation of many IBE algorithms, in which we need to perform a double-and-add iteration on the binary expansion of a prime. If we use a Solinas prime in such algorithms, the low density of a Solinas prime of the form $p = 2^a + 2^b + 1$ will clearly minimize the number of operations needed to implement such an iteration. The cases where $p = 2^a \pm 2^b \pm 1$ can be similarly implemented very efficiently by representing p in nonadjacent form [3]. In the following we will always assume that a Solinas prime is of the form $p = 2^a + 2^b + 1$.

Example 2.2

(i) The prime $41 = 2^5 + 2^3 + 1$ is a Solinas prime.
(ii) The prime $29 = 2^5 - 2^2 + 1$ is a Solinas prime.

Definition 2.3

Let $F = \{p_1, p_2, \ldots, p_n\}$ be a set of primes. We say an integer n is F-smooth is all of the prime factors of n are elements of F.

Definition 2.4

A nonnegative integer d is the *greatest common divisor* of integers a and b if d is the largest positive integer that divides both a and b. This is denoted by $d = \gcd(a, b)$.

Example 2.3

(i) If $a = 1{,}001 = 7 \cdot 11 \cdot 13$ and $b = -286 = -2 \cdot 11 \cdot 13$, then $\gcd(a, b) = 11 \cdot 13 = 143$.
(ii) If $a = 11$ and $b = 13$, then $\gcd(a, b) = 1$.

2.1.1 Computing the GCD

The greatest common divisor of integers a and b can be computed by the following Algorithm 2.1, known as the *extended Euclidean algorithm*. In addition to gcd(a, b), this algorithm also returns integers x and y such that gcd$(a, b) = ax + by$.

Algorithm 2.1: extended_gcd
INPUT: integers a, b with $a \geq b$
OUTPUT: gcd(a, b), integers x and y such that gcd$(a, b) = ax + by$

1. If $b = 0$
2. $d \leftarrow a$, $x \leftarrow 1$, $y \leftarrow 0$, return (d, x, y)
3. $x_1 \leftarrow 0$, $x_2 \leftarrow 1$, $y_1 \leftarrow 1$, $y_2 \leftarrow 0$
4. While $b > 0$
5. $q \leftarrow \lfloor a/b \rfloor$, $r \leftarrow a - qb$, $x \leftarrow x_2 - qx_1$, $y \leftarrow y_2 - qy_1$
6. $a \leftarrow b$, $b \leftarrow r$, $x_2 \leftarrow x_1$, $x_1 \leftarrow x$, $y_2 \leftarrow y_1$, $y_1 \leftarrow y$
7. $d \leftarrow a$, $x \leftarrow x_2$, $y \leftarrow y_2$, return (d, x, y)

Definition 2.5

For integers a and b, if gcd(a, b) then we say that a and b are *relatively prime.*

Example 2.4

(i) If $a = 1{,}001$ and $b = 286$, then gcd$(a, b) = 77$, so a and b are not relatively prime.
(ii) If $a = 11$ and $b = 13$, then gcd$(a, b) = 1$, so a and b are relatively prime.

Definition 2.6

If a, b, and n are integers, then we say that a is *congruent to b modulo n* if n divides $(b - a)$ and we write $a \equiv b (\text{mod } n)$.

Example 2.5

(i) $7 \equiv 3 (\text{mod } 4)$ because $4 \mid (7 - 3)$.
(ii) $11 \equiv 3 (\text{mod } 4)$ because $4 \mid (11 - 3)$.
(iii) $-7 \equiv 2 (\text{mod } 3)$ because $3 \mid (-7 - 2)$.
(iv) $7 \equiv 11 (\text{mod } 4)$ because $4 \mid (7 - 11)$.

Property 2.1 (Chinese Remainder Theorem)

Let $n_1 n_2 \ldots n_k$ be integers that are pairwise relatively prime, that is, gcd$(n_i, n_j) = 1$ when $i \neq j$. Then the following system of congruences has a unique solution modulo the product $n = n_1 n_2 \ldots n_k$:

$$x \equiv a_1 \pmod{n_1}$$
$$x \equiv a_2 \pmod{n_2}$$
$$\vdots$$
$$x \equiv a_k \pmod{n_k}$$

Property 2.2 (Gauss' Algorithm)

The solution to the system of congruences given in Property 2.1 can be computed as

$$x = \sum_{i=1}^{k} a_i N_i M_i \bmod n \tag{2.1}$$

where

$$N_i = \frac{n}{n_i}$$

and

$$M_i = N_i^{-1} \bmod n_i$$

Gauss' algorithm can be written in a slightly different way that makes it easier to understand. In particular, note that we can also write (2.1) as

$$x = \sum_{i=1}^{k} a_i \cdot e_i \bmod n$$

where each e_i has the property that

$$e_i \equiv \begin{cases} 1 \pmod{n_i} \\ 0 \pmod{n_j},\ j \neq i \end{cases}$$

So we can think of Gauss' algorithm as being essentially an integer version of Lagrange interpolation, where we fit a polynomial to k points by creating a similar set of coefficients that are either 0 or 1 and thus force the desired behavior at the given points.

Example 2.6

Consider the following system of congruences:

$$x \equiv 2 \pmod 3 = a_1 \pmod{n_1}$$
$$x \equiv 3 \pmod 4 = a_2 \pmod{n_2}$$

Applying Gauss' algorithm, we find that

$$n = n_1 n_2 = 3 \cdot 4 = 12$$

$$N_1 = \frac{n}{n_1} = \frac{12}{3} = 4$$

$$N_2 = \frac{n}{n_2} = \frac{12}{4} = 3$$

$$M_1 = N_1^{-1} \bmod n_1 = 4^{-1} \bmod 3 = 1$$

$$M_2 = N_2^{-1} \bmod n_2 = 3^{-1} \bmod 4 = 3$$

so that

$$\begin{aligned} x &= (a_1 N_1 M_1 + a_2 N_2 M_2) \bmod 12 \\ &= (2 \cdot 4 \cdot 1 + 3 \cdot 3 \cdot 3) \bmod 12 \\ &= (2 \cdot 4 + 3 \cdot 9) \bmod 12 \\ &= (8 + 27) \bmod 12 = 35 \bmod 12 = 11 \bmod 12 \end{aligned}$$

In this example we can also think of Gauss' algorithm as finding integers e_1 and e_2 such that we have

$$x = (2 \cdot e_1 + 3 \cdot e_2) \bmod 12$$

Gauss' algorithm then finds $e_1 = 4$ and $e_2 = 9$, where we have

$$e_1 = 4 \equiv \begin{cases} 1 \pmod 3 \\ 0 \pmod 4 \end{cases}$$

and

$$e_2 = 9 \equiv \begin{cases} 0 \pmod 3 \\ 1 \pmod 4 \end{cases}$$

Definition 2.7

For a positive integer n, $\phi(n)$ denotes the number of integers less than n that are relatively prime to n. This function is called *Euler's phi function*.

Property 2.3

If m and n are relatively prime then $\phi(mn) = \phi(m)\,\phi(n)$.

Example 2.7

(i) $\phi(7) = 6$ because each of the integers 1, 2, 3, 4, 5, and 6 are relatively prime to 7.

(ii) $\phi(p) = p - 1$ for any prime p because 1, 2, 3, . . . , $p - 1$ are all relatively prime to p.

(iii) $\phi(77) = \phi(7)\,\phi(11) = 6 \cdot 10 = 60$.

Property 2.4 (Fermat's Little Theorem)

Let p be a prime and a be any integer. Then we have that

$$a^p \equiv a(\text{mod } p)$$

If a is relatively prime to p, then we also have that

$$a^{p-1} \equiv 1\,(\text{mod } p)$$

Example 2.8

(i) For $p = 5$ and $a = 2$, we have that $a^p = 2^5 = 32 \equiv 2(\text{mod } 5)$.

(ii) For $p = 5$ and $a = 2$, we have that $a^{p-1}\ 2^4 = 16 \equiv 1(\text{mod } 5)$.

(iii) For $p = 5$ and $a = 10$, we have that $a^p = 10^5 = 100{,}000 \equiv 0(\text{mod } 5) \equiv 10(\text{mod } 5)$.

(iv) For $p = 5$ and $a = 10$, we have that $a^{p-1}\ 2^4 = 10{,}000 \equiv 0(\text{mod } 5) \not\equiv 1(\text{mod } 5)$.

Property 2.5 (Euler's theorem)

Let n be an integer and a be an integer relatively prime to n. Then we have that

$$a^{\phi(n)} \equiv 1\,(\text{mod } n)$$

Example 2.9

(i) With $n = 3 \cdot 5 = 15$, we have $\phi(n) = 8$ and that $2^8 = 256 \equiv 1(\text{mod } 15)$.

(ii) With $n = 5 \cdot 7$, we have that $\phi(n) = 24$ and that $5^{24} \equiv 1 \pmod{35}$.

(iii) With $n = 11 \cdot 13 = 143$, we have that $\phi(n) = 120$ and that $11^{120} \equiv 1 \pmod{143}$.

Definition 2.8

We use $\mathbb{Z}_n$ to denote the set of integers $\{0, 1, \ldots, n - 1\}$.

We can perform arithmetic on elements of $\mathbb{Z}_n$ by reducing a sum or product to the remainder that is left after dividing by n, which we call *reducing modulo n*. In $\mathbb{Z}_n$ we have $a + b = c$ when $(a + b) \equiv c \pmod{n}$. Even though we define $\mathbb{Z}_n$ to only include the integers from 0 through $n - 1$, it is often convenient to think of $n - 1$ as being -1, even though -1 is not really an element of $\mathbb{Z}_n$.

Example 2.10

(i) In $\mathbb{Z}_{12}$ we have that $9 + 6 = 3$, or $9 + 6 \equiv 3 \pmod{12}$.

(ii) In $\mathbb{Z}_9$ we have that $3 \cdot 3 = 0$, or $3 \cdot 3 \equiv 0 \pmod 9$.

As Table 2.1 shows, not every element of $\mathbb{Z}_5$ has a square root in $\mathbb{Z}_5$. In particular, 0, 1, and 4 have square roots in $\mathbb{Z}_5$ while 2 and 3 do not. This motivates the following definitions.

Definition 2.9

A nonzero element $a \in \mathbb{Z}_n$ is called a *quadratic residue* modulo n if there exists some $x \in \mathbb{Z}_n$ with $x^2 \equiv a \pmod{n}$. If no such x exists, we say that a is a *quadratic nonresidue* modulo n.

Example 2.11

(i) From Table 2.1 we see that 0, 1, and 4 are quadratic residues modulo 5.

(ii) From Table 2.1 we see that 2 and 3 are quadratic nonresidues modulo 5.

Table 2.1
Multiplication in $\mathbb{Z}_5$

*	0	1	2	3	4
0	0	0	0	0	0
1	0	1	2	3	4
2	0	2	4	1	3
3	0	3	1	4	2
4	0	4	3	2	1

Legendre symbols are a notation that indicates whether or not an integer is a quadratic residue.

Definition 2.10

Let p be an odd prime and a an integer. Then the Legendre symbol $\left(\frac{a}{p}\right)$ is defined to be

(i) 0 if p divides a.

(ii) +1 if a is a quadratic residue modulo p.

(iii) −1 if a is a quadratic nonresidue modulo p.

Property 2.6

Let a and b be integers and p and q be odd primes. Then Legendre symbols have the following properties:

(i) $\left(\frac{a}{p}\right) \equiv a^{(p-1)/2} \pmod{p}$

(ii) $\left(\frac{ab}{p}\right) = \left(\frac{a}{p}\right)\left(\frac{b}{p}\right)$

(iii) If $a \equiv b \pmod{p}$ then $\left(\frac{a}{p}\right) = \left(\frac{b}{p}\right)$

(iv) $\left(\frac{2}{p}\right) = (-1)^{(p^2-1)/8}$

(v) $\left(\frac{p}{q}\right) = \left(\frac{q}{p}\right)(-1)^{(p-1)(q-1)/4}$

Property 2.6(i) tells us that −1 is a quadratic residue modulo p if $p \equiv 1 \pmod{4}$ and that −1 is a quadratic nonresidue modulo p if $p \equiv 3 \pmod{4}$. If −1 is a quadratic nonresidue modulo p, then we have that

$$\left(\frac{-a}{n}\right) = \left(\frac{a}{n}\right)\left(\frac{-1}{n}\right) = -\left(\frac{a}{n}\right)$$

so that either a is a quadratic residue or $-a$ is a quadratic residue. In particular, this is true when $p \equiv 3 \pmod{4}$.

Property 2.6(v) tells us that

$$\left(\frac{p}{q}\right) = \left(\frac{q}{p}\right)$$

unless both p and q are congruent to 3 modulo 4, in which case we have that

$$\left(\frac{p}{q}\right) = -\left(\frac{q}{p}\right)$$

Example 2.12

(i) $\left(\frac{6}{3}\right) = 0$ because 3 divides 6

(ii) $\left(\frac{3}{7}\right) = 3^{(7-1)/2} = 3^3 = 27 \equiv -1 \pmod 7$

(iii) Because 3 and 7 are both congruent to 3 modulo 4, we have that $\left(\frac{7}{3}\right) = -\left(\frac{3}{7}\right) = +1$

We can generalize the definition of Legendre symbols to get Jacobi symbols, which are defined for composite denominators as follows.

Definition 2.11

Let a be an integer and n be a positive odd integer with

$$n = \prod_{i=1}^{k} p_i^{a_i} = p_1^{a_1} p_2^{a_2} \ldots p_k^{a_k}$$

Then the Jacobi symbol

$$\left(\frac{a}{n}\right)$$

is defined to be

$$\left(\frac{a}{n}\right) = \prod_{i=1}^{k} \left(\frac{a}{p_i}\right)^{a_i} = \left(\frac{a}{p_1}\right)^{a_1} \left(\frac{a}{p_2}\right)^{a_2} \ldots \left(\frac{a}{p_k}\right)^{a_k}$$

where each of the factors

$$\left(\frac{a}{p_i}\right)^{a_i}$$

is a Legendre symbol as defined in Definition 2.10.

Property 2.7

Let a, b be integers and $n \geq 3$ and $m \geq 3$ be odd integers. Then Jacobi symbols have the following properties.

(i) $\left(\frac{a}{n}\right)$ can be either 0, +1 or −1

(ii) $\left(\frac{a}{n}\right) = 0$ if $\gcd(a, n) \neq 1$

(iii) $\left(\frac{ab}{n}\right) = \left(\frac{a}{n}\right)\left(\frac{b}{n}\right)$

(iv) $\left(\frac{a}{mn}\right) = \left(\frac{a}{m}\right)\left(\frac{a}{n}\right)$

(v) If $a \equiv b \pmod{n}$, then $\left(\frac{a}{n}\right) = \left(\frac{b}{n}\right)$

(vi) $\left(\frac{1}{n}\right) = +1$

(vii) $\left(\frac{-1}{n}\right) = (-1)^{(n-1)/2}$

(viii) $\left(\frac{2}{n}\right) = (-1)^{(n^2-1)/8}$

(ix) $\left(\frac{m}{n}\right) = \left(\frac{n}{m}\right)(-1)^{(m-1)(n-1)/4}$

Example 2.13

(i) $\left(\frac{15}{21}\right) = 0$ because $\gcd(15, 21) \neq 1$

(ii) $\left(\frac{2}{11}\right) = (-1)^{(11^2-1)/8} = (-1)^{15} = -1$

(iii) $\left(\frac{7}{11}\right) = \left(\frac{11}{7}\right)(-1)^{(11-1)(7-1)/4} = \left(\frac{11}{7}\right)(-1)^{15} = -\left(\frac{11}{7}\right)$

Property 2.8

If p and q and distinct odd primes and $n = pq$, then $a \in \mathbb{Z}_n^*$ is a quadratic residue modulo n if and only if a is a quadratic residue modulo p and a is a quadratic residue modulo p.

2.1.2 Computing Jacobi Symbols

Suppose that n is an odd integer and we can write $a = 2^k b$ where b is an odd integer. Then we have that

$$\left(\frac{a}{n}\right) = \left(\frac{2^k b}{n}\right) = \left(\frac{2^k}{n}\right)\left(\frac{b}{n}\right) = \left(\frac{2}{n}\right)^k\left(\frac{b}{n}\right)$$

$$= \left(\frac{2}{n}\right)^k\left(\frac{n}{b}\right)(-1)^{(b-1)(n-1)/4}$$

$$= \left(\frac{2}{n}\right)^k\left(\frac{n \bmod b}{b}\right)(-1)^{(b-1)(n-1)/4}$$

This gives us the following algorithm for computing Jacobi symbols. Note that it is not necessary to know the factorization of n to do this.

Algorithm 2.2: JacobiSymbol
INPUT: odd integer $n \geq 3$, integer a with $0 \leq a < n$
OUTPUT: Jacobi symbol (a/n)

1. If $a = 0$, return 0
2. If $a = 1$, return 1
3. Write $a = 2^k a_1$ where a_1 is odd
4. If k is even, then $s \leftarrow 1$
5. Else if $n \equiv 1 \pmod 8$ or $n \equiv 7 \pmod 8$, then $s \leftarrow 1$
6. Else if $n \equiv 3 \pmod 8$ or $n \equiv 5 \pmod 8$, then $s \leftarrow -1$
7. $n_1 \leftarrow n \bmod a_1$
8. Return $s \cdot JacobiSymbol(n_1, a_1)$

2.2 Concepts from Abstract Algebra

Abstract algebra provides the framework for defining the differences and similarities between different algebraic structures. The real numbers and the integers are fundamentally alike in some ways and different in other ways, for example, and the framework of abstract algebra provides a way to describe these properties and generalize them to other structures. In particular, structures that are suitable for use in computers have finite-length representations, so we want to understand the properties of structures that behave much like the real numbers yet are finite instead of infinite.

Definition 2.12

A *binary operation* on a set S is a function $f: S \times S \rightarrow S$, or a function that takes two input values and produces a single output value. Addition and multiplication of real numbers are examples of binary operations.

Definition 2.13

A *group* $(G, *)$ is a set G and a binary operation $*$ on G that has the following properties:

(i) $a * (b * c) = (a * b) * c$ for all a, b, c in G (associativity).

(ii) There is a special element of G called the *identity* element which we write as e. This identity element satisfies $a * e = e * a = a$ for all a in G.

(iii) Each element a of G has an *inverse* that we write as a^{-1}, also an element of G, such that $aa^{-1} = a^{-1}a = e$.

We say that G is a group *under* the operation $*$ if $(G, *)$ is a group. We will also somewhat inaccurately say that a set G is a group without listing the group operation if the operation is clear from the context of the discussion, so we might say that "the integers are a group," for example, even though it is somewhat inaccurate.

Example 2.14

(i) The integers $\mathbb{Z}$ under addition are a group. In this case, the integer 0 acts as the identity element.

(ii) The integers $\mathbb{Z}$ under multiplication are not a group because not all integers have multiplicative inverses that are also in $\mathbb{Z}$. The multiplicative inverse of 3 is not an integer, for example.

(iii) The natural numbers $\mathbb{N}$ under addition are not a group because the natural numbers lack an additive identity, that is, $0 \in \mathbb{N}$.

(iv) The nonzero real numbers under multiplication form a group. In this case, the real number 1 acts as the identity element.

(v) $\mathbb{Z}_n$ is a group under addition but may not be a group under multiplication; $\mathbb{Z}_n$ is a group under multiplication if and only if n is prime.

(vi) The set $V = \{0, 1, 2, 3\}$ along with the operation shown in Table 2.2 is a group. In this group, every element is its own inverse.

Definition 2.14

If $(G, *)$ is a group, then the number of elements in the set G is called the *order* of the group. This can be either finite or infinite.

Definition 2.15

A group $(G, *)$ with the additional property that $a * b = b * a$ for all a and b in G is called an *Abelian* group.

Table 2.2
Operations in the Group V

*	0	1	2	3
0	0	1	2	3
1	1	0	3	2
2	2	3	0	1
3	3	2	1	0

Example 2.15

(i) The integers under addition are an Abelian group.

(ii) The set of all 2×2 invertible matrices with real entries is a group under matrix multiplication, but not an Abelian group because matrix multiplication is not commutative.

If a group is Abelian we often write the group operation as + instead of * and using + to denote a group operation is usually reserved for Abelian groups. Writing $a * b \neq b * a$ is fine, because not all groups are Abelian, but if you write $a + b \neq b + a$ it will make many mathematicians uncomfortable.

Definition 2.16

If $(H, *)$ and $(G, *)$ are groups and H is a subset of G, then we say H is a *subgroup* of G. Note that this means that the subgroup must have the group structure with respect to the same operation that defines the group structure in G.

Example 2.16

(i) The even integers under addition are a subgroup of the integers under addition.

(ii) The odd integers under addition are not a subgroup of the integers under addition.

(iii) The group $V = \{0, 1, 2, 3\}$ of Example 2.14(vi) has three subgroups of order 2: $H_1 = \{0, 1\}$, $H_2 = \{0, 2\}$, and $H_3 = \{0, 3\}$.

Definition 2.17

Let $(G, *)$ be a group with identity element e and $g \in G$. The smallest positive integer n such that

$$\underbrace{g * g * \ldots * g}_{n \text{ times}} = g^n = e$$

is called the *order* of the element g. If no such integer exists then we say that the order of g is infinite.

Example 2.17

(i) In the group $(\mathbb{Z}_7, +)$ the order of the element 2 is 7.
(ii) In the group $(\mathbb{Z}_6, +)$ the order of the element 2 is 3.
(iii) In the group $(\mathbb{Z}, +)$ the order of the element 1 is infinite.

Property 2.9 (Lagrange's theorem)

The order of any element of a group divides the order of the group.

Property 2.10

Let G be a group of order n and p a prime. If $p \mid n$ but $p^2 \nmid n$, then G has a unique subgroup of order p. In some IBE systems we need to map an identity to a point of prime order, and knowing that this mapping will map the identity to an element of a particular subgroup is useful.

Example 2.18

(i) The group $\mathbb{Z}_{132}$ has order $132 = 2^2 \cdot 3 \cdot 11$ and thus has a unique subgroup of order 11. Given any element of $g \in \mathbb{Z}_{132}$, we can find an element of the subgroup of order 11 by calculating

$$\left(\frac{132}{11}\right)g = 12 \cdot g$$

(ii) The group V of Example 2.14(vi) is of order 4 but has three different subgroups of order 2.

Definition 2.18

A group $(G, *)$ is *cyclic* if there exists a $g \in G$ such that for any $h \in G$ there exists an integer i such that we can write $h = g^i$. Such an element g is called a *generator* of G and we write $G = \langle g \rangle$ to indicate this.

Example 2.19

(i) If p is a prime, then any nonzero element of $\mathbb{Z}_p$ generates the group $\mathbb{Z}_p$ and the group $\mathbb{Z}_p$ is cyclic.
(ii) Both 1 and 5 generate $\mathbb{Z}_6$, while 2, 3, 4 do not generate $\mathbb{Z}_6$.

Definition 2.19

If G is a group with identity element 0, then we use the notation G^* to denote the nonzero elements of G.

Definition 2.20

Let G be a group generated by g. For any $a \in G$, we say that the *discrete logarithm* to the base g of a is α if we have that α is the smallest positive integer such that $a = g^{\alpha}$.

Example 2.20

(i) In the group $G = (\mathbb{Z}_n, +)$, we have that $G = \langle 1 \rangle$, and that the discrete logarithm of $k = k \cdot 1$ to the base 1 is k.
(ii) In the group $G = (\mathbb{Z}_{11}^*, \times)$, we have that $G = \langle 2 \rangle$, and that the discrete logarithm of $6 \equiv 2^9 \pmod{11}$ to the base 2 is 9.

In some cases, we will have two groups that behave exactly the same way, but are labeled differently in some way. In a trivial case, we could write one version of the integers in an italic font and another version in bold font and notice that these two versions behave exactly the same way if we ignore this slight difference. So while we could not add an italic 2 to a bold font 2, for example, we can easily map the two sets to each other by making the necessary font change. The desire to find a way to define how two structures have the same properties but with changed names motivates the following definition.

Definition 2.21

Let f be a function from a group $(G, +)$ to a group $(H, \oplus)$. Then f is a *homomorphism* of groups if we have that $f(a + b) = f(a) \oplus f(b)$ for all a and b in G. A homomorphism of groups is a function that preserves some of the structure of a group but not necessarily all of the structure.

Definition 2.22

Let f be a homomorphism from a group $(G, +)$ to a group $(H, \oplus)$. Then f is an *isomorphism* of groups if it has the following properties:

(i) For every a and b in G, if $f(a) = f(b)$ then $a = b$.
(ii) For each $h \in H$ there exists a $g \in G$ with $h = f(g)$.

When these properties hold, we say that the groups $(G, +)$ and $(H, \oplus)$ are *isomorphic* and write $G \cong H$ to indicate this. An isomorphism is a function that preserves all of the structure of a group, and groups that are isomorphic are essentially identical, differing only in the way that their elements are written.

Definition 2.23

An *endomorphism* is a homomorphism from a group $(G, +)$ to $(G, +)$, that is, from a group to itself.

Example 2.21

(i) If e is the identity element of a group $(G, +)$, then the function $f(g) = e$ for any $g \in G$ is a homomorphism of groups, where the range of f implicitly lies in the trivial group containing just the element e. This is not an isomorphism because it fails property (i) of Definition 2.20.

(ii) The mapping f where $f(n) = 2n$ is a group homomorphism from the integers under addition to the even integers under addition because $f(a + b) = 2(a + b) = 2a + 2b = f(a) + f(b)$. This mapping f also satisfies properties (i) and (ii) of Definition 2.22, so it is also an isomorphism.

(iii) The real numbers under addition are isomorphic to the positive real numbers under multiplication, with an isomorphism given by $f(x) = e^x$.

(iv) Complex conjugation, that is, $f(a + bi) = a - bi$, is an endomorphism of the complex numbers under addition.

Definition 2.24

A *field* $(F, +, *)$ is a set F and a two binary operations $+$ and $*$ on F that have the following properties for all a, b, c in F.

(i) $(F, +)$ is an Abelian group.

(ii) Let F^* denote the set of elements of F not equal to the identity element for the operation $+$. Then $(F^*, *)$ is an Abelian group. We think of F^* as being the nonzero elements of F.

(iii) $a * (b + c) = a * b + a * c$ (distributivity).

Note that only two operations are defined in a field, which we think of as addition and multiplication. Subtraction and division are not defined, so when $(F, +, *)$ is a field and a and b are elements of F, when we write $a - b$ we really mean $a + (-b)$ where $-b$ is the inverse of b under the operation $+$ and when we write a/b we really mean ab^{-1} where b^{-1} is the inverse of b under the operation $*$.

Example 2.22

(i) $(\mathbb{R}, + \cdot)$ is a field. Property (ii) of Definition 2.24 tells us that all real numbers except zero need to have a multiplicative inverse. Zero is excluded so that we do not have to worry about the possibility of dividing by zero, which is undefined.

(ii) If p is a prime, $(\mathbb{Z}_p, +, \cdot)$ is a field.

(iii) The set of polynomials with real coefficients with the operations of addition and multiplication of polynomials is a field.

(iv) The set of all polynomials with real coefficients with addition and multiplication performed modulo the polynomial $x^2 + 1$ is a field.

(v) If p is a prime, the set of all polynomials with coefficients from $\mathbb{Z}_p$ with the operations of polynomial addition and multiplication is a field.

As with groups, we will somewhat inaccurately say that the set F is a field without listing the field operations if the operations are clear from the context of the discussion.

Definition 2.25

If $(F, +, *)$ is a field, then the number of elements in the set F is called the *order* of the field. This can be infinite or finite. We write $\mathbb{F}_q$ for a finite field with q elements.

Definition 2.26

If $(F, +, *)$ is a field and n is the smallest positive integer such that

$$\underbrace{x + x + \ldots + x}_{n \text{ times}} = nx = 0$$

for all $x \in F$ is called the *characteristic* of the field. If no such integer exists, then we say that the field has *characteristic zero*.

Example 2.23

(i) If p is a prime, then the field $\mathbb{F}_p$ has characteristic p.

(ii) The field of real numbers has characteristic zero.

(iii) If p is a prime, the field of polynomials with coefficients from $\mathbb{F}_p$ is a field of characteristic p. This field is infinite, yet has characteristic p.

Definition 2.27

A *homomorphism* of fields is function that preserves some of the structure of a field. Let f be a function from a field $(K, +, *)$ to a field $(F, \oplus, \otimes)$. Then f is a *homomorphism* of fields if we have that

$$f(a + b) = f(a) \oplus f(b)$$

and

$$f(a * b) = f(a) \otimes f(b)$$

for all a and b in K.

Definition 2.28

An *isomorphism* of fields is a function that preserves all of the structure of a field. Let f be a homomorphism from a field $(K, +, *)$ to a field $(F, \oplus, \otimes)$. Then f is an isomorphism of fields if it has the following properties:

(i) For every a and b in K, if $f(a) = f(b)$ then $a = b$.

(ii) For each $b \in F$ there exists a $a \in K$ with $b = f(a)$.

When these properties hold, we say that the fields $(K, +, *)$ and $(F, \oplus, \otimes)$ are *isomorphic* and write $K \cong F$ to indicate this. An isomorphism is a function that preserves all of the structure of a field, and fields that are isomorphic are essentially identical, differing only in the way that their elements are written.

Example 2.24

The field of complex numbers is isomorphic to the field of polynomial with real coefficients modulo the polynomial $x^2 + 1$, and we can write an isomorphism f between the two fields explicitly as $f(a + bi) = a + bx$.

Property 2.11

Any field with a finite number of elements has a number of elements equal to p^n for some prime p and some natural number n. All finite fields with the same number of elements are isomorphic, so we can talk about *the* finite field $\mathbb{F}_q$, even if there may be different ways to represent the elements of this field.

Definition 2.29

If $(K, +, *)$ and $(F, +, *)$ are fields and K is a subset of F, then we say K is a *subfield* of F. Note that this means that the subfield K has to have the field structure with respect to the same operations that defines the field structure in F.

Definition 2.30

If K is a subfield of a field F, then we say that F is an *extension field* of K.

Example 2.25

(i) The complex numbers are an extension field of the real numbers and the real numbers are a subfield of the complex numbers.

(ii) The field $\mathbb{F}_q$ is not a subfield of the real numbers. Although the elements of $\mathbb{F}_q$ are a subset of the real numbers if q is a prime, the operations defined on $\mathbb{F}_q$ are different from those defined in the real numbers, so $\mathbb{F}_q$ cannot be a subfield of the real numbers. In $\mathbb{F}_3$, for example, we have that $2 + 2 = 1$, which is different than the fact that $2 + 2 = 4$ in the real numbers. A more careful description of $\mathbb{F}_3$ might write its elements as $\hat{0}$, $\hat{1}$, and $\hat{2}$ and its operation as $\oplus$ to make this explicit.

Definition 2.31

If F is an extension field of K, then F is a vector space of dimension k over K for some positive integer k. The value of k is called the *degree* of the extension. The degree of an extension may be either finite or infinite. If k is finite then we can write a typical element of F as $\alpha = (x_1, x_2, \ldots, x_k)$ where each $x_i \in K$.

Example 2.26

(i) The complex numbers are an extension field of degree 2 of the real numbers and we can write a complex number $z = x + iy$ as $z = (x, y)$ to emphasize the fact that complex numbers can be considered vectors with real coordinates.

(ii) Polynomials with real coefficients are an extension field of infinite degree of the real numbers.

(iii) Let $v \in \mathbb{F}_q$ and α be a solution to the equation $x^d - v = 0$ with $\alpha^n \neq v$ for $n < d$. So if α is a sixth root of v, for example, then it is not a cube root or square root. Then the smallest extension to $\mathbb{F}_q$ in which $x^d - v = 0$ has a solution is $\mathbb{F}_{q^d}$.

(iv) Suppose that F_3 is a finite field that is an extension of degree k_2 of the finite field F_2 and that F_2 is a finite field that is an extension of degree k_1 of the finite field F_1. Then by writing an element of F_3 in terms of the basis of F_2 and then writing the basis of F_2 in terms of the basis of F_1 we see that F_3 is an extension of degree $k_1 k_2$ of the finite field F_1.

Suppose that if $q = p^n$ for some prime p and that $\mathbb{F}_q$ is an extension of $\mathbb{F}_p$. Because $\mathbb{F}_q$ is a vector space of dimension n over $\mathbb{F}_p$, elements of $\mathbb{F}_q$ must look like $a = (a_0, \ldots, a_{n-1})$ where $a_i \in \mathbb{F}_p$ for each $0 \leq i \leq n - 1$. We can add two such vectors in the obvious way, so that if $b = (b_0, \ldots, b_{n-1})$, then $a + b = (a_0 + b_0, \ldots, a_{n-1} + b_{n-1})$. We can also define $-a$ in the obvious way, where $-a = (-a_0, \ldots, -a_{n-1})$. Such operations supply the group structure under the operation of addition that the definition of a field requires. Because $\mathbb{F}_q$ is a vector space of dimension n over $\mathbb{F}_p$, we can talk about elements of $\mathbb{F}_q$ being linearly independent, which has the same meaning as in linear algebra.

Definition 2.32

Elements of $\mathbb{F}_{q^k}$ x and y are *linearly independent* if for all $a, b \in \mathbb{F}_q$ we have that $a \cdot x + b \cdot y = 0$ implies that $a = 0$ and $b = 0$.

Example 2.27

(i) In $\mathbb{F}_{11^2}$ (0, 1) and (1, 0) are linearly independent.

(ii) In $\mathbb{F}_{11^2}$ (0, 1) and (0, 2) are not linearly independent because $(0, 1) + 5 \cdot (0, 2) \equiv (0, 0) \pmod{11}$.

To make $\mathbb{F}_q$ a field, however, we also need to be able to multiply such vectors and to be able to find their multiplicative inverses. One way to do this is to identify the components of a vector with coefficients of a polynomial and then multiply vectors as if they were the polynomials created in this way. So we identify $a = (a_0, \ldots, a_{n-1})$ with the polynomial $f(x) = a_0 + a_1 x + \ldots + a_{n-1} x^{n-1}$.

Definition 2.33

If F is a field, we write $F[x]$ for the set of all polynomials in the variable x with coefficients from F.

Example 2.28

(i) $(3 + 2i)x^2 + (1 + i)x + 1 \in \mathbb{C}[x]$

(ii) $7x^2 + 2x + 1 \in \mathbb{F}_{11}[x]$

Definition 2.34

If F is a field and $f(x) \in F[x]$, then we write $F[x]/(f(x))$ for the set of polynomials in $F[x]$ reduced modulo the polynomial $f(x)$.

Example 2.29

(i) In $\mathbb{R}[x]/(x^2 + 1)$ we do calculations modulo the polynomial $x^2 + 1$, so that $x^2 + 1 \equiv 0$ or that $x^2 \equiv -1$. So we can write that $x^3 = x \cdot x^2 \equiv x(-1) = -x \pmod{x^2 + 1}$ and that $x^4 = x^2 \cdot x^2 \equiv (-1)(-1) = 1 \pmod{x^2 + 1}$, for example.

(ii) In $\mathbb{F}_5[x]/(x^2+1)$ we have that $(x+2)(x+3) = x^2+5x+6 \equiv 0 \pmod{x^2+1}$.

Definition 2.35

If F is a field and $f(x) \in F[x]$ then we say that $f(x)$ is *irreducible* over F if it cannot be written as the product of two polynomials in $F[x]$ of positive degree.

Example 2.30

(i) Over the real numbers, the polynomial x^2+1 is irreducible.

(ii) Over the complex numbers, the polynomial $x^2+1 = (x+i)(x-i)$ is not irreducible.

(iii) Over the real numbers, the polynomial $x^2-1 = (x+1)(x-1)$ is not irreducible.

(iv) Over $\mathbb{F}_5$, the polynomial $x^2+1 = (x+2)(x+3)$ is not irreducible.

Property 2.12

If F is a field and $f(x) \in F[x]$ is irreducible, then $F[x]/(f(x))$ is a field.

Example 2.30

(i) $F = \mathbb{R}[x]/(x^2+1)$ is a field. In this case, F is isomorphic to the complex numbers. If we multiply $x^2 \cdot x^2 = x^4$ in $\mathbb{R}[x]/(x^2+1)$, we can reduce the result modulo x^2+1 by noting that $x^2+1 \equiv 0 \pmod{x^2+1}$ so that $x^2 \equiv -1 \pmod{x^2+1}$, and we find that $x^4 = x^2 \cdot x^2 \equiv (-1)(-1) \pmod{x^2+1} \equiv 1 \pmod{x^2+1}$.

(ii) $F = \mathbb{R}[x]/(x^2-1)$ is not a field. Note that both $x+1 \in F^*$ and $x-1 \in F^*$ but $(x+1)(x-1) \equiv 0 \pmod{x^2-1} \notin F^*$ so that F^* is not a group as required by the definition of a field.

(iii) If p is a prime and -1 is a quadratic nonresidue modulo p then we cannot find $\sqrt{-1}$ modulo p so we cannot factor x^2+1 as $\left(x+\sqrt{-1}\right)\left(x-\sqrt{-1}\right)$. Thus x^2+1 is irreducible and $F = \mathbb{Z}_p[x]/(x^2+1)$ is a field. This field has p^2 elements and can be written $\mathbb{F}_{p^2}$. We can think of elements of $\mathbb{F}_{p^2}$ as being either vectors of the form (a_0, a_1), as polynomials $a_0 + a_1 x$, or as complex numbers $a_0 + a_1 i$.

(iv) Because -1 is a quadratic nonresidue modulo 11, $F = \mathbb{Z}_{11}[x]/(x^2+1)$ is a field with $11^2 = 121$ elements. Both $a = (3, 7) = 3+7i$ and $b = (4, 5) = 4+5i$ are elements of F. We can multiply a and b to get $ab = (3, 7)(4, 5) = (3+7i)(4+5i) = -23+43i \equiv (10+10i) \pmod{11} = (10, 10)$. Because $(6+9i)(4+5i) = -21+$

$66i \equiv 1 \pmod{11}$ we see that $b^{-1} = 6 + 9i$ so that we can calculate $a/b = ab^{-1} = (3 + 7i)(6 + 9i) = -45 + 69i \equiv (10 + 3i) \pmod{11}$, so in F we have that

$$\frac{(3, 7)}{(4, 5)} = (3, 7)(4, 5)^{-1} = (10, 3)$$

(v) Because 2 is a quadratic nonresidue modulo 5, $x^2 + 2$ is irreducible over $\mathbb{F}_5$ and $F = \mathbb{Z}_5[x]/(x^2 + 2)$ is a field with $5^2 = 25$ elements. We can write elements of F as $a + b\sqrt{2}$, for example.

So if $q = p^n$, by finding an irreducible polynomial of degree n over $\mathbb{F}_p$, we can create a representation of $\mathbb{F}_q$ as $\mathbb{F}_p[x]/(f(x))$, where we can do calculations in $\mathbb{F}_p$ by identifying elements of $\mathbb{F}_q$ with polynomials in $\mathbb{F}_p[x]$ and performing calculations modulo $f(x)$.

Note that we can find multiplicative inverses of elements of $\mathbb{F}_q$ by using the extended Euclidean algorithm (Algorithm 2.1). If we can identify an element $\alpha \in \mathbb{F}_q$ with the polynomial $p(x)$, then we must have $\gcd(p(x), f(x)) = 1$. Thus we can use the extended Euclidean algorithm to find polynomials $a(x)$ and $b(x)$ such that we have $a(x)p(x) + b(x)f(x) = 1$.

In $\mathbb{F}_p[x]/(f(x))$ we have that $b(x)f(x) = 0$, so that $a(x)p(x) = 1$, so that $a(x)$ is the inverse of $p(x)$, and the field element corresponding to $a(x)$ is the inverse of α in $\mathbb{F}_q$.

Definition 2.36

Let F be a finite field and $\alpha \in K$ where K is an extension of F. Then we write $F[\alpha]$ to indicate all sums of the form $\Sigma x_i \alpha^i$ where $x_i \in F$ and where all but a finite number of the coefficients x_i are zero.

Example 2.31

(i) For the real numbers $\mathbb{R}$ and $i^2 = -1$, we have that $\mathbb{R}[i]$ is all finite sums of the form $\Sigma x_k i^k$. We can use the properties that $i^3 = -i$, $i^4 = 1$, and so forth, to reduce any sum of this form to a single complex number $a + bi$, so elements of $\mathbb{R}[i]$ are just the complex numbers.

(ii) Let α be a root of the irreducible polynomial $f(x) = x^3 + x + 1$. Then $\mathbb{R}[\alpha]$ is all finite sums of the form $\Sigma x_k \alpha^k$. For any power of α greater than or equal to α^3 we can use the property that $x^3 + x + 1 = 0$ so that $x^3 = -(x + 1)$ to reduce sums of this form to value of the form $x_2 \alpha^2 + x_1 \alpha + x_0$, so $\mathbb{R}[\alpha]$ is an extension of degree 3 of

$\mathbb{R}$ and is isomorphic to $\mathbb{R}[x]/(x^3 + x + 1)$. A similar observation shows that we can find a way to represent the finite field $\mathbb{F}_{q^k}$ as sums of powers of the root of an irreducible polynomial of degree k over $\mathbb{F}_q$.

Property 2.13

If $\mathbb{F}_{q^k}$ is a finite field then $\mathbb{F}_{q^k}^*$ is a cyclic group of order $q^k - 1$. In particular, if $a \in \mathbb{F}_{q^k}^*$ then $a^{q^k - 1} = 1$.

Definition 2.37

The *algebraic closure* of a field F is an extension to F in which all elements of $F[x]$ have roots. So if $f(x)$ is a polynomial with coefficients from the field F, then all solutions to the equation $f(x) = 0$ are elements of the algebraic closure of F. We write the algebraic closure of F as $\overline{F}$. A field F with $F = \overline{F}$ is called *algebraically closed.*

Example 2.32

(i) The real numbers are not algebraically closed because the polynomial $f(x) = x^2 + 1 = (x + i)(x - i)$ does not have roots that lie in the real numbers.

(ii) The Fundamental Theorem of Algebra tells us that the algebraic closure of the real numbers is the complex numbers, or that any polynomial with real coefficients has all of its roots in the complex numbers.

(iii) The complex numbers are the algebraically closed because any polynomial with complex coefficients has roots that lie in the complex numbers.

(iv) If p is a prime, then the algebraic closure of $\mathbb{F}_p$ is an infinite field that is the union of the fields $\mathbb{F}_{p^n}$ for each $n \in \mathbb{N}$.

Definition 2.38

For sets X and Y we define the *Cartesian product* of X and Y to be

$$X \times Y = \{(x, y) \mid x \in X, y \in Y\}$$

The Cartesian product can be similarly defined for groups, with the group operations being applied to each component of the Cartesian product. So if $(G, \bullet)$ and $(H, \circ)$ are groups, then we can define a group operation $\odot$ on $G \times H$ in which the group operations of $(G, \bullet)$ and $(H, \circ)$ are applied componentwise to the elements of $G \times H$, so that

$$(g_1, h_1) \odot (g_2, h_2) = (g_1 \bullet g_2, h_1 \circ h_2)$$

We use the notation $G \oplus H$ to denote the group $(G \times H, \odot)$ formed in this way.

Example 2.33

Let V be the group defined in Example 2.14(vi). This is isomorphic to the group $\mathbb{Z}_2 \oplus \mathbb{Z}_2$, as Table 2.3 shows.

Property 2.14 (Lagrange interpolation)

Let F be a field, $x_1, x_2, \ldots, x_{n+1}$ be distinct elements of F and $y_1, y_2, \ldots, y_{n+1}$ be elements of F. Then there is a unique polynomial $f(x) \in F[x]$ of degree no more than n such that $f(x_i) = y_i$ for each $1 \leq i \leq n + 1$. This polynomial can be written as

$$f(x) = \sum_{i=1}^{n+1} e_i(x) y_i$$

where each $e_i(x)$ has the property that

$$e_i(x_j) = \begin{cases} 1, j = i \\ 0, j \neq i \end{cases}$$

and is defined by

$$e_i(x) = \sum_{j \neq i} \frac{x - x_i}{x_j - x_i}$$

Example 2.34

(i) The result of using Lagrange interpolation on $n + 1$ points may result in a polynomial of degree less than n. This may happen, for example, if the points all satisfy a polynomial of degree less than n.

Table 2.3
Operations in the Group $\mathbb{Z}_2 \oplus \mathbb{Z}_2$

+	(0, 0)	(0, 1)	(1, 0)	(1, 1)
(0, 0)	(0, 0)	(0, 1)	(1, 0)	(1, 1)
(0, 1)	(0, 1)	(0, 0)	(1, 1)	(1, 0)
(1, 0)	(1, 0)	(1, 1)	(0, 0)	(0, 1)
(0, 0)	(1, 1)	(1, 0)	(0, 1)	(0, 0)

(ii) Suppose that we have the following points and we want to use Lagrange interpolation to find a polynomial that fits the three points

$$(x_1, y_1) = (0, 1)$$
$$(x_2, y_2) = (1, 0)$$
$$(x_3, y_3) = (2, 1)$$

We first find the polynomials $e_i(x)$ as

$$e_1(x) = \frac{(x - x_2)(x - x_3)}{(x_1 - x_2)(x_1 - x_3)} = \frac{(x - 1)(x - 2)}{(0 - 1)(0 - 2)} = \frac{(x - 1)(x - 2)}{2}$$
$$e_2(x) = \frac{(x - x_1)(x - x_3)}{(x_2 - x_1)(x_2 - x_3)} = \frac{(x - 0)(x - 2)}{(1 - 0)(1 - 2)} = \frac{x(x - 2)}{1}$$

and

$$e_3(x) = \frac{(x - x_1)(x - x_2)}{(x_3 - x_1)(x_3 - x_2)} = \frac{(x - 0)(x - 1)}{(2 - 0)(2 - 1)} = \frac{x(x - 1)}{2}$$

so that we find that

$$\begin{aligned} f(x) &= e_1(x)y_1 + e_2(x)y_2 + e_3(x)y_3 \\ &= \left(\frac{x(x - 2)}{2}\right)1 + (x(x - 1))0 + \left(\frac{x(x - 1)}{2}\right)1 \\ &= \left(\frac{(x - 1)(x - 2)}{2}\right)1 + (x(x - 1))0 + \left(\frac{x(x - 1)}{2}\right)1 \\ &= x^2 - 2x + 1 \end{aligned}$$

References

[1] LeVeque, L., *Fundamentals of Number Theory*, Mineola, NY: Dover Books, 1977.

[2] Herstein, I., *Abstract Algebra*, New York: Wiley, 2001.

[3] Blake, I., G. Seroussi, and N. Smart, *Elliptic Curves in Cryptography*, Cambridge, U.K.: Cambridge University Press, 1999.

3

Properties of Elliptic Curves

Many IBE algorithms rely on the properties of certain functions on elliptic curves called *pairings*. This chapter describes the basic properties of elliptic curves that will be used in following chapters to understand properties of pairings and how to calculate them. Further detail on the connection between elliptic curves and elliptic functions can be found in [1]; additional detail on the algebraic structure of groups of points on elliptic curves can be found in [2]; further details on the efficient implementation of algorithms involving points on elliptic curves can be found in [3].

3.1 Elliptic Curves

Elliptic curves arise naturally in the study of elliptic functions, functions that are doubly periodic in the complex plane, or having two different complex periods, say ω_1 and ω_2 for an elliptic function f such that $f(z+\omega_1) = f(z+\omega_2) = f(z)$. They are also related to arc length integrals on ellipses, which explains the source of their name. The properties of elliptic curves that are mentioned below follow from the properties of the Weierstrass $\wp$ (an old German "P") function. In particular, for periods ω_1 and ω_2, the $\wp$ function is defined to be the infinite sum

$$\wp(z) = \frac{1}{z^2} + \sum_{\omega \neq 0} \left(\frac{1}{(z-\omega)^2} - \frac{1}{\omega^2} \right)$$

where the sum ranges over all sums of integer multiples of the periods $\omega = n_1\omega_1 + n_2\omega_2$ except 0. The set of such sums of the form $\omega = n_1\omega_1 + n_2\omega_2$ defines a lattice of points in the complex plane as shown in Figure 3.1.

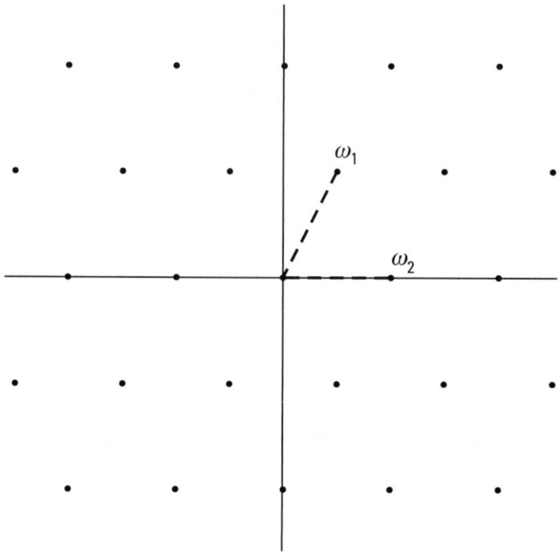

Figure 3.1 Lattice in the complex plane.

If we look more closely at one period of this lattice, like the one shown in Figure 3.2, we can imagine cutting the picture from the page and connecting the edges of this region that differ by either the period ω_1 (the dashed lines in Figure 3.2) or the period ω_2 (the solid lines in Figure 3.2), to get the torus shown in Figure 3.3. So we can imagine that the doubly periodic nature of

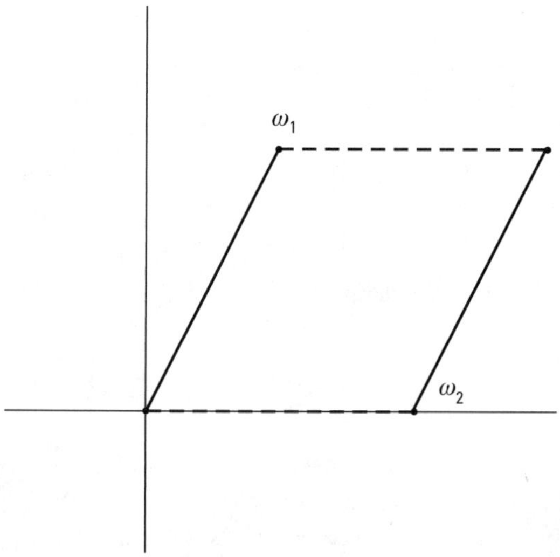

Figure 3.2 Closer look at one period of a lattice.

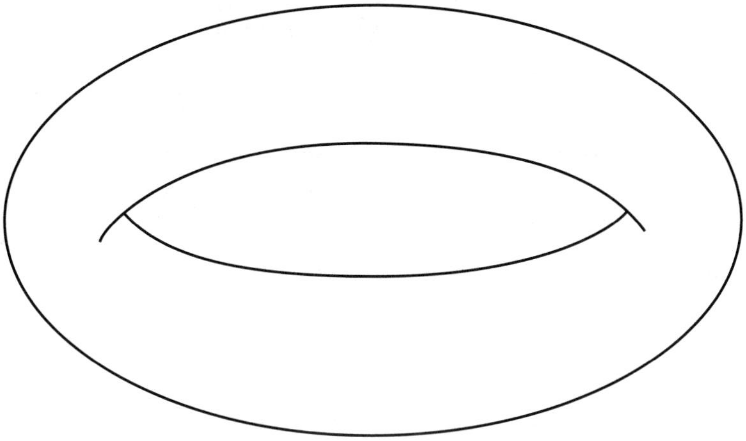

Figure 3.3 Torus formed from a single period of a lattice.

such a lattice means that it reduces operations in the complex plane to operations on the surface of a torus.

The $\wp$ function also satisfies the following differential equation:

$$(\wp'(z))^2 = 4(\wp(x))^3 - g_2\wp(z) - g_3$$

where g_2 and g_3 are constants that depend on the periods of the $\wp$ function. Identifying $\wp'(z)$ with y and $\wp(z)$ with x we get that x and y satisfy

$$y^2 = 4x^3 - g_2x - g_3$$

in which we can change variables to get

$$y^2 = x^3 + ax + b$$

This is analogous to noticing that the trigonometric functions cos t and $\cos' t = \sin t$ satisfy the differential equation

$$(\cos t)^2 + (\cos' t)^2 = 1$$

and then identifying cos t with x and sin t with y to get the familiar form of a circle:

$$x^2 + y^2 = 1$$

The $\wp$ function also satisfies the following identity:

$$\det\begin{pmatrix} \wp(z_1) & \wp'(z_1) & 1 \\ \wp(z_2) & \wp'(z_2) & 1 \\ \wp(z_1+z_2) & -\wp'(z_1+z_2) & 1 \end{pmatrix} = 0 \tag{3.1}$$

Recall that we have

$$\det\begin{pmatrix} x_1 & y_1 & 1 \\ x_2 & y_2 & 1 \\ x_3 & y_3 & 1 \end{pmatrix} = 0$$

exactly when the three points (x_1, y_1), (x_2, y_2), and (x_3, y_3), are collinear. So if we identify $P_1 = (x_1, y_1)$ with $(\wp(z_1), \wp'(z_1))$, $P_2 = (x_2, y_2)$ with $(\wp(z_2), \wp'(z_2))$, and $P_3 = (x_3, -y_3)$ with $(\wp(z_1+z_2), -\wp'(z_1+z_2))$, then we see that the points P_1, P_2, and P_3 are collinear because the determinant (3.1) is zero, suggesting a way to define adding points on a elliptic curve in which we find $P_1 + P_2$ by first finding the third collinear point on the curve $P_3 = (x_3, -y_3)$ and then defining $P_1 + P_2$ to be (x_3, y_3).

Definition 3.1

An *elliptic curve* is the set of points satisfying an equation of the form $y^2 = x^3 + ax + b$ where the coefficients a and b are elements of a field F with the characteristic of F is not equal to 2 or 3. We write E/F to indicate this and say that the elliptic curve is *over* the field. Such a curve is said to be in *Weierstrass normal form*. We can think of the points on an elliptic curve as being either points in a set or as rational functions of x and y, and can freely change between the two points of view as needed.

The requirement that the characteristic of F be greater then 3 is not strictly required for an elliptic curve, but this restriction limits us to the elliptic curves of interest in the discussion of IBE in this book. If the characteristic of the field over which an elliptic curve is defined is equal to 2 or 3, alternative forms other than the Weierstrass normal form need to be used. In particular, the algorithm for adding points on an elliptic curve in Weierstrass normal form uses the constants 2 and 3, which makes it behave badly over a field of characteristic 2 or 3, so alternate forms are needed in these cases.

Over a field of characteristic 2 the following alternative can be used:

$$y^2 + ay = x^3 + bx^2 + cxy + dx + e$$

and over a field of characteristic 3 the following alternative can be used:

$$y^2 = x^3 + ax^2 + bx + c$$

Elliptic curves for which the cubic has repeated roots turn out to have undesirable properties from the cryptographic point of view, so it is useful to be able to identify which curves these are. To determine this, we can find the roots of the cubic part of an elliptic curve in Weierstrass normal form by factoring $x^3 + ax + b = 0$ into $(x - x_1)(x - x_2)(x - x_3)$ using the rarely used cubic formula to get

$$x_1 = -\frac{\left(\frac{2}{3}\right)^{1/3} a}{\left(-9b + \sqrt{3}\sqrt{4a^3 + 27b^2}\right)^{1/3}} + \frac{\left(-9b + \sqrt{3}\sqrt{4a^3 + 27b^2}\right)^{1/3}}{2^{1/3}3^{2/3}}$$

$$x_2 = \frac{\left(1 + i\sqrt{3}\right)a}{2^{2/3}3^{1/3}\left(-9b + \sqrt{3}\sqrt{4a^3 + 27b^2}\right)^{1/3}} + \frac{\left(1 - i\sqrt{3}\right)\left(-9b + \sqrt{3}\sqrt{4a^3 + 27b^2}\right)^{1/3}}{2^{4/3}3^{2/3}}$$

$$x_3 = \frac{\left(1 - i\sqrt{3}\right)a}{2^{2/3}3^{1/3}\left(-9b + \sqrt{3}\sqrt{4a^3 + 27b^2}\right)^{1/3}} + \frac{\left(1 + i\sqrt{3}\right)\left(-9b + \sqrt{3}\sqrt{4a^3 + 27b^2}\right)^{1/3}}{2^{4/3}3^{2/3}}$$

Using these values for the roots of the cubic we find that

$$(x_1 - x_2)^2(x_1 - x_3)^2(x_2 - x_3)^2 = -(4a^3 + 27b^2) \tag{3.2}$$

so that we have a repeated root whenever $-(4a^3 + 27b^2) = 0$. For historical reasons connected to the classical study of elliptic functions, $-16(4a^3 + 27b^2)$ is used instead of $-(4a^3 + 27b^2)$ to characterize this behavior of an elliptic curve, but the additional constant factor does not change which curves have repeated roots and which do not.

Definition 3.2

The *discriminant* of an elliptic curve in Weierstrass normal form $y^2 = x^3 + ax + b$ is the quantity $\Delta = -16(4a^3 + 27b^2)$.

Property 3.1

Elliptic curves over the real numbers for which the discriminant $\Delta < 0$ have two components, as shown in Figure 3.4, which corresponds to all of the roots

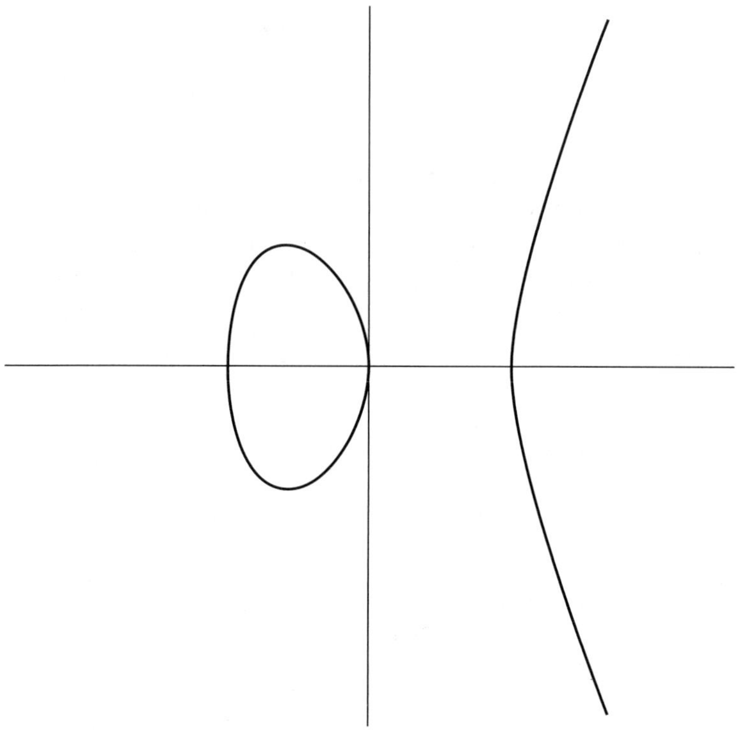

Figure 3.4 Graph of the elliptic curve $y^2 = x^3 - 4x$ for which $\Delta < 0$.

of (3.2) being real (i.e., no imaginary component). Elliptic curves over the real numbers for which the discriminant $\Delta > 0$ have one component, as shown in Figure 3.5, which corresponds to two of the roots of the cubic in (3.2) having nonzero imaginary part so that they do not appear on the x-axis of a graph of the curve.

Definition 3.3

An elliptic curve for which the discriminant $\Delta = 0$ is called *singular*. An elliptic curve for which the discriminant $\Delta \neq 0$ is called *nonsingular*. Note that an elliptic curve may be nonsingular over one field and singular over another. Note that this definition of the discriminant is always even so it is always zero in a field of characteristic 2. In this case, the Weierstrass normal form needs to be replaced with a different form for which the discriminant is not always zero.

Example 3.1

(i) The elliptic curve $y^2 = x^3 + x + 1$ is nonsingular over the real numbers because it has discriminant $\Delta = -16(31) = -496$.

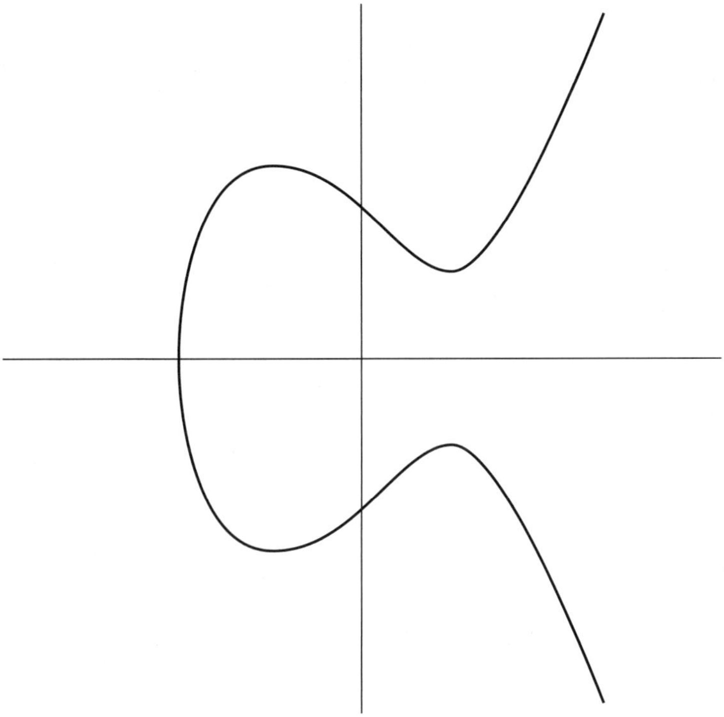

Figure 3.5 Graph of the elliptic curve $y^2 = x^3 - 3x + 3$ for which $\Delta > 0$.

(ii) The elliptic curve $y^2 = x^3 + x + 1$ is singular over a field of characteristic 31 because it has discriminant $\Delta = -16(31)$ so that $\Delta \equiv 0 \pmod{31}$.

Graphs of singular elliptic curves over the real numbers are shown in Figures 3.6 and 3.7. Figure 3.6 shows an elliptic curve for which the cubic has two repeated roots. This type of elliptic curve is said to have a *cusp* at the repeated root. Figure 3.7 shows an elliptic curve for which the cubic has three repeated roots. This type of elliptic curve is said to have a *node* at the repeated root. Many discussions of elliptic curves restrict the meaning of the term to only nonsingular curves, a convention that we will also follow hereafter. We will see in a Chapter 5 that cryptographic algorithms using arithmetic on singular elliptic curves are extremely weak compared to those using arithmetic on nonsingular curves.

3.2 Adding Points on Elliptic Curves

We can define a geometric way to add points on an elliptic curve that is based on (3.1). We do this in the following steps. To add points P_1 and P_2, construct

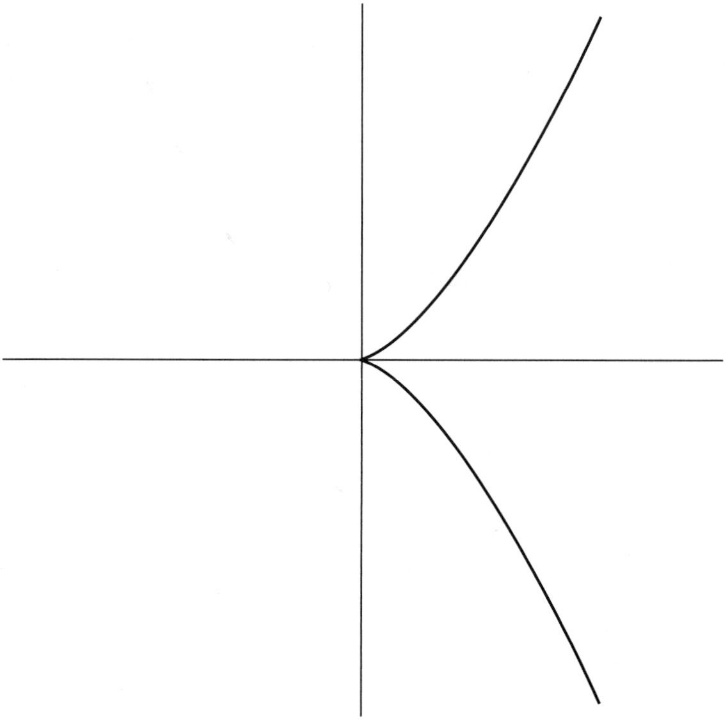

Figure 3.6 Graph of the singular elliptic curve $y^2 = x^3$, an example of a cusp.

the line through P_1 and P_2 and find the third point where it intersects the elliptic curve. To add a point to itself, use the line tangent to the curve through the point instead. Reflect this third point across the x-axis to get the sum of the points $P_1 + P_2$. These steps are shown in Figure 3.8 for the elliptic curve $y^2 = x^3 + 1$. In Figure 3.5, the line u represents the line through P_1, P_2 and $-(P_1 + P_2)$ and v represents the vertical line through $-(P_1 + P_2)$ and $P_1 + P_2$, and the same lines u and v will be important in constructing the Tate pairing that we discuss in Chapter 4. We also consider the point at infinity to be on an elliptic curve, and write this special point as O, and we have that $P + O = P$ for any point on an elliptic curve, so that the point at infinity acts much like the number 0 does in the real numbers.

If we have two points on an elliptic curve, $P_1 = (x_1, y_1)$ and $P_2 = (x_2, y_2)$, we can write the sum of the points $P_1 + P_2 = P_3 = (x_3, y_3)$. There are two ways to find P_3: one if $P_1 \neq P_2$ and another if $P_1 = P_2$. If $P_1 \neq P_2$ then we can find the slope of the line through P_1 and P_2 as

$$m = \frac{y_2 - y_1}{x_2 - x_1} \tag{3.3}$$

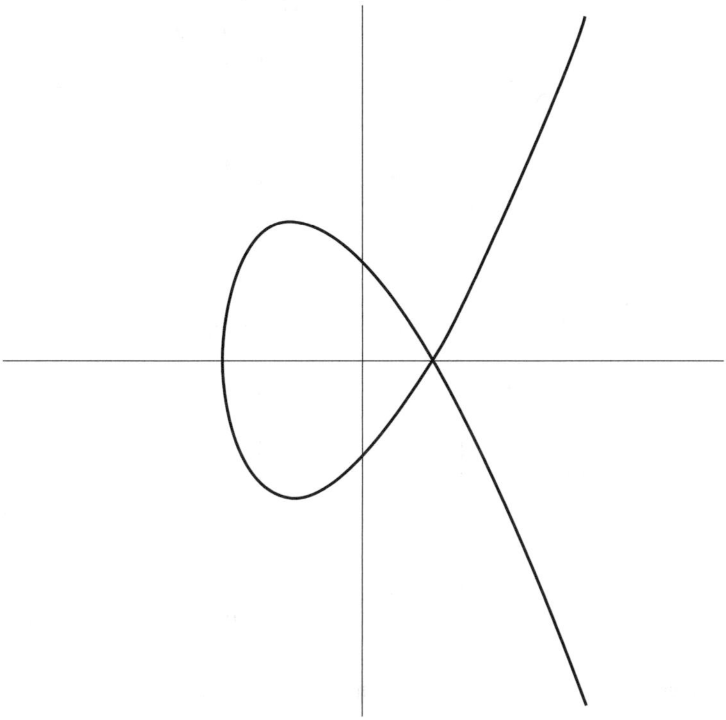

Figure 3.7 Graph of the singular elliptic curve $y^2 = x^3 - 3x + 2$, an example of a node.

If $P_1 = P_2$ then we can find the slope of the line through P_1 from

$$m = \frac{3x_1^2 + a}{2y_1} \tag{3.4}$$

Note that (3.3) shows why we restricted an elliptic curve to being defined over fields with characteristic other than 2 or 3. In either of these two cases, a characteristic of either 2 or 3 makes the expression (3.3) inadequate where multiplying by 2 or 3 is equivalent to multiplying by 0, so alternate forms for elliptic curves are needed other than the Weierstrass normal form.

If we write the line through P_1 and P_2 as $y = mx + \beta$, then this line intersects the elliptic curve when

$$(mx + \beta)^2 = x^3 + ax + b$$

or that

$$x^3 + ax + b - (mx + \beta)^2 = 0$$

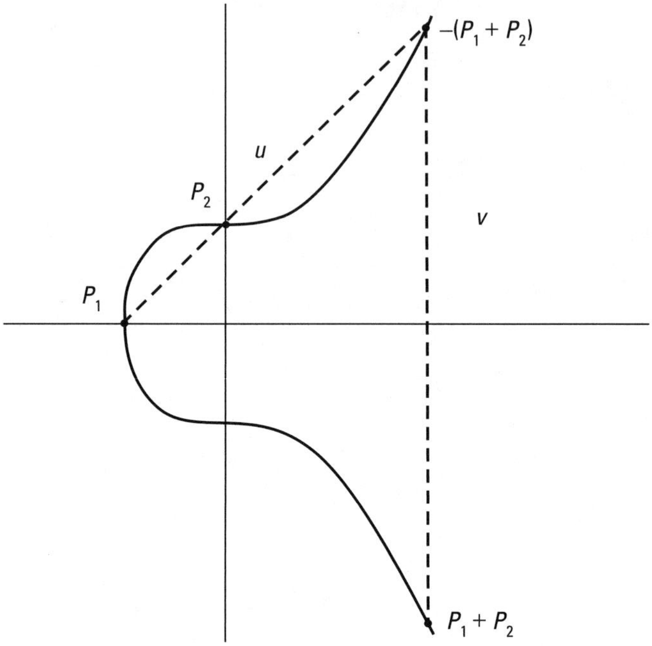

Figure 3.8 Addition of points on an elliptic curve.

or

$$x_3 - m^2x^2 + (a - 2m\beta)x + (b - \beta^2) = 0$$

Recall that for a monic polynomial or degree n the sum of its roots of the polynomial is the negative of the coefficient of the x^{n-1} term. In this case, the sum of the roots must be m^2, so that

$$x_1 + x_2 + x_3 = m^2$$

or that

$$x_3 = m^2 - x_1 - x_2 \qquad (3.5)$$

Because the point $(x_3, -y_3)$ is on the line $y = mx + \beta$ we have

$$\begin{aligned} -y_3 &= mx_3 + \beta \\ &= mx_3 + (y_1 - mx_1) \\ &= m(x_3 - x_1) + y_1 \end{aligned}$$

so that

$$y_3 = m(x_1 - x_3) - y_1 \tag{3.6}$$

Example 3.2

(i) The points $P_1 = (-1, 0) = (x_1, y_1)$ and $P_2 = (0, 1) = (x_2, y_2)$ are on the elliptic curve $y^2 = x^3 + 1$ over the real numbers. In this case we can find $P_3 = (x_3, y_3) = P_1 + P_2$ by finding

$$m = \frac{y_2 - y_1}{x_2 - x_1} = \frac{1 - 0}{1 - (-1)} = 1$$

so that

$$x_3 = m^2 - x_1 - x_2 = 1^2 - (-1) - 0 = 2$$

and

$$y_3 = m(x_1 - x_3) - y_1 = 1(-1 - 2) = 0 = -3$$

so that $P_3 = (2, -3)$.

(ii) The points $P_1 = (0, 1) = (x_1, y_1)$ and $P_2 = (2, 8) = (x_2, y_2)$ are on the elliptic curve $y^2 + x^3 + 1$ over $\mathbb{F}_{11}$. In this case we can find $P_3 = (x_3, y_3) = P_1 + P_2$ by finding

$$m = \frac{y_2 - y_1}{x_2 - x_1} = \frac{8 - 1}{2 - 0} = \frac{7}{2} = 7 \cdot 2^{-1} = 7 \cdot 6 = 56 \equiv 1 \pmod{11}$$

so that

$$x_3 = m^2 - x_1 - x_2 = 1^2 - 0 - 2 \equiv 10 \pmod{11}$$

and

$$y_3 = m(x_1 - x_3) - y_1 = 1(0 - 10) \equiv 0 \pmod{11}$$

so that $P_3 = (10, 0)$.

(iii) Let $P_1 = (x, y_1)$ and $P_2 = (x, y_2)$ be points on any elliptic curve. Because the x-coordinates of these two points are identical, their sum will always be O, the point at infinity, so that $P_1 + P_2 = O$.

3.2.1 Algorithm for Elliptic Curve Point Addition

The following algorithm describes the process for adding points on an elliptic curve.

Algorithm 3.1:
INPUT: $P_1 = (x_1, y_1)$, $P_2 = (x_2, y_2)$, points on an elliptic curve $y^2 = x^3 + ax + b$
OUTPUT: $P_3 = P_1 + P_3$

1. If $x_1 = x_2$ return O
2. If $P_1 = P_2$ then
3. If $y_1 = 0$ return O
4. Else $m \leftarrow \dfrac{3x_1^2 + a}{2y_1}$
5. Else $m \leftarrow \dfrac{y_2 - y_1}{x_2 - x_1}$
6. $x_3 \leftarrow m^2 - x_1 - x_2$
7. $y_3 \leftarrow m(x_1 - x_3) - y_1$
8. Return $P_3 = (x_3, y_3)$

Example 3.3

We find that we have the following six points on the curve $E/\mathbb{F}_5 : y^2 = x^3 + 1$ (see Table 3.1).

Table 3.1
Points on the Curve
$E/\mathbb{F}_5 : y^2 = x^3 + 1$

Point	**(x, y)**
$\hat{P}_1$	(0, 1)
$\hat{P}_2$	(0, 4)
$\hat{P}_3$	(2, 2)
$\hat{P}_4$	(2, 3)
$\hat{P}_5$	(4, 0)

Table 3.2
Addition of Points on the Curve $y^2 = x^3 + 1$ over $\mathbb{F}_5$

+	O	$\hat{P}_1$	$\hat{P}_2$	$\hat{P}_3$	$\hat{P}_4$	$\hat{P}_5$
O	O	$\hat{P}_1$	$\hat{P}_2$	$\hat{P}_3$	$\hat{P}_4$	$\hat{P}_5$
$\hat{P}_1$	$\hat{P}_1$	$\hat{P}_2$	O	$\hat{P}_4$	$\hat{P}_5$	$\hat{P}_3$
$\hat{P}_2$	$\hat{P}_2$	O	$\hat{P}_1$	$\hat{P}_5$	$\hat{P}_3$	$\hat{P}_4$
$\hat{P}_3$	$\hat{P}_3$	$\hat{P}_4$	$\hat{P}_5$	$\hat{P}_2$	O	$\hat{P}_1$
$\hat{P}_4$	$\hat{P}_4$	$\hat{P}_5$	$\hat{P}_3$	O	$\hat{P}_1$	$\hat{P}_2$
$\hat{P}_5$	$\hat{P}_5$	$\hat{P}_3$	$\hat{P}_4$	$\hat{P}_1$	$\hat{P}_2$	O

and that adding points on the curve obeys the rules in Table 3.2.

3.2.2 Projective Coordinates

Dealing with O, the point at infinity on an elliptic curve can be troublesome using affine coordinates, the usual (x, y) coordinates that we use to define the Weierstrass normal form of an elliptic curve. One easy way to handle this point is through the use of projective coordinates. Projective coordinates encode a point (x, y) with two coordinates in three coordinates (x, y, z) where (x, y, z) represents any point of the form $(x/z, y/z)$. Such projective coordinates are called *standard projective coordinates.* In particular, we can represent a point on an elliptic curve $P = (x, y)$ as $(x, y, 1)$ and the point at infinity can be represented by $(0, 1, 0)$. We can also easily convert from projective coordinates (x, y, z) where $z \neq 0$ into affine coordinates $(x/z, y/z)$.

In addition to being an easy way to handle the point at infinity, projective coordinates are often useful in performing computations on elliptic curves because it is possible to add two points on an elliptic curve using projective coordinates without performing any divisions, which are typically very expensive computationally in finite fields. Finally, because many different values of z can be used to represent the same affine point (x, y), so it is possible to use random values of z to encode such points, this will provide an additional level of protection against side-channel attacks, attacks on an implementation of a cryptographic algorithm that seek to find information about the cryptographic key being used through physical measurements of an operating device and its environment.

In cryptographic applications where we may want to perform operations in $\mathbb{F}_q$ for fairly large values of q, determining the inverse of an element of $\mathbb{F}_q$ can be fairly expensive relative to multiplications in $\mathbb{F}_q$, and using projective coordinates will often provide a performance advantage over using affine coordinates. Note that there are other forms of projective coordinates that may also be useful for elliptic curve arithmetic. These forms of projective coordinates require different procedures for adding points than the technique presented below. In particular, *Jacobian projective coordinates* encode an affine point $(x/z^2, y/z^3)$ as the projective point (x, y, z), and *Chudnovsky projective coordinates* encode an affine point $(x/z^2, y/z^3)$ as the projective point (x, y, z, z^2, z^3) [4]. Each type of projective coordinates requires a different number of field operations to add or double points, which is summarized in Table 3.3. The choice of the most efficient projective coordinate system will depend on the application. If only point additions need to be performed, it is more efficient to use standard projective coordinates. If only point doublings need to be performed, it is more efficient to use Chudnovsky projective coordinates. In most cases, it is more efficient to use Jacobian projective coordinates. Point doubling operations can be further optimized if the coefficient $a = -3$ in the Weierstrass normal form of an elliptic curve.

3.2.3 Adding Points in Jacobian Projective Coordinates

If we have points in Jacobian coordinates $P_1 = (x_1, y_1, z_1)$ and $P_2 = (x_2, y_2, z_2)$ and want to find $P_3 = (x_3, y_3, z_3) = P_1 + P_2$, then we can convert to the projective point to affine coordinates where $Q_1 = \left(x_1/z_1^2, y_1/z_1^3\right)$ and $Q_2 = \left(x_2/z_2^2, y_2/z_2^3\right)$, find the sum $Q_3 = \left(x_3/z_3^2, y_3/z_3^3\right) = Q_1 + Q_2$ using (3.3), (3.5), and (3.6), and then convert Q_3 to the projective P_3. This is summarized in the following algorithm. Note that this algorithm is independent of the coefficients a and b in the elliptic curve $y^2 = x^3 + ax + b$.

Algorithm 3.2: JacobianAdd
INPUT: $P_1 = (x_1, y_1, z_1)$, $P_2 = (x_2, y_2, z_2)$ on an elliptic curve $y^2 = x^3 + ax + b$ over a field F. All operations are performed in the field F and the point at infinity is represented as (0, 1, 0).
OUTPUT: $P_3 = (x_3, y_3, z_3) = P_1 + P_2$

Table 3.3
Field Operations Needed to Implement Elliptic Curve Operations in Different Coordinate Systems Where n Field Multiplications and m Field Squarings Is Indicated by the Notation $nX + mS$ and I Indicates That an Inversion Is Also Required

Coordinate System	Point Addition	Point Doubling
Jacobian	$12M + 4S$	$4M + 6S$
Standard	$12M + 2S$	$7M + 5S$
Chudnovsky	$11M + 3S$	$5M + 6S$
Affine	$I + 2M + 2S$	$I + 2M + 1S$

1. $u_1 \leftarrow x_1 \cdot z_2^2$
2. $u_2 \leftarrow x_2 \cdot z_1^2$
3. $s_1 \leftarrow y_1 \cdot z_2^3$
4. $s_2 \leftarrow y_2 \cdot z_1^3$
5. If $u_1 = u_2$
6. If $s_1 \neq s_2$
7. Return (0,1,0)
8. Else
9. Return JacobianDouble(x_1, y_1, z_1)
10. $h \leftarrow u_2 - u_1$
11. $r \leftarrow s_2 - s_1$
12. $x_3 \leftarrow r^2 - h^3 - 2 \cdot u_1 \cdot h^2$
13. $y_3 \leftarrow r \cdot (u_1 \cdot h^2 - x_3) - s_1 \cdot h^3$
14. $z_3 \leftarrow h \cdot z_1 \cdot z_2$
15. Return (x_3, y_3, z_3)

3.2.4 Doubling a Point in Jacobian Projective Coordinates

If we have a point in Jacobian coordinates $P_1 = (x_1, y_1, z_1)$ and want to find $P_2 = (x_2, y_2, z_2) = P_1 + P_1 = 2P_1$, then we can convert to the projective point to affine coordinates where $Q_1 = \left(x_1/z_1^2, y_1/z_1^3\right)$ find the sum $Q_2 = \left(x_2/z_2^2, y_2/z_2^3\right) = Q_1 + Q_1 = 2Q_1$ using (3.3), (3.5), and (3.6), and then convert Q_2 to the projective P_2. This is summarized in the following algorithm.

Algorithm 3.3: JacobianDouble
INPUT: $P_1 = (x_1, y_1, z_1)$, on an elliptic curve $y^2 = x^3 + ax + b$ over a field F. All operations are performed in the field F.
OUTPUT: $P_2 = (x_2, y_2, z_2) = P_1 + P_1$

1. If $y_1 = 0$
2. Return (0,1,0)
3. $s \leftarrow 4 \cdot x_1 \cdot y_1^2$
4. $m \leftarrow 3 \cdot x_1^2 + a \cdot z_1^4$
5. $x_2 \leftarrow m^2 - 2 \cdot s$
6. $y_2 \leftarrow m \cdot (s - x_2) - 8 \cdot y_1^4$
7. $z_2 \leftarrow 2 \cdot y_1 \cdot z_1$
8. Return (x_2, y_2, z_2)

3.3 Algebraic Structure of Elliptic Curves

Points on an elliptic curve provide a structure that we can define in the terminology of abstract algebra.

Definition 3.4

If E is an elliptic curve over a field F then we write $E(F)$ to indicate the set of points on E along with the operation of adding points described in Algorithm 3.1.

Property 3.2

If F is a field and E is an elliptic curve then $E(F)$ is a group. The point at infinity acts as the identity element for this group. Note that there is only one operation defined for $E(F)$, which we are thinking of as addition, so it is impossible to multiply or divide elements of $E(F)$. Thus, $E(F)$ cannot be a field, which requires two operations that we think of as being addition and multiplication.

Definition 3.5

Multiplication of a point P on an elliptic curve by an integer n is the result of adding a point to itself n times, so that

$$nP = \underbrace{P + P + \ldots + P}_{n \text{ times}}$$

Definition 3.6

Let $P \in E(F)$ for some elliptic curve E/F. We say that the *order of a point* is n if n is the smallest positive integer such that $nP = O$.

Definition 3.7

If E is an elliptic curve over a field F and n is a positive integer, we write $E(F)[n]$ for the set of points of order n in $E(F)$. If the field F is clear from the context, this can be abbreviated to $E[n]$. $E(F)[n]$ is a subgroup of $E(F)$. The points in $E(F)[n]$ are also called the *n-torsion points* of the curve E.

Definition 3.8

We write $\#E(F)$ to indicate the order of the group $E(F)$, which is the number of points on an elliptic curve E over a field F, including the point at infinity, O. Determining the value of $\#E(F)$ for an arbitrary elliptic curve is a nontrivial problem.

Example 3.4

From Table 3.2 we see that for the elliptic curve $y^2 = x^3 + 1$ we have that $\#E(\mathbb{F}_5) = 6$.

Definition 3.9

If E is an elliptic curve over $\mathbb{F}_q$ and we have $\#E(\mathbb{F}_q) = q + 1 - t$, then t is called the *trace of Frobenius*, or simply the *trace*.

We should expect to have approximately $q + 1$ points on an elliptic curve $E/\mathbb{F}_q$. The equation $y^2 = x^3 + ax + b$ has a solution when $x^3 + ax + b$ is a quadratic residue modulo q, which should happen roughly half the time. In each of these cases, we get a pair of square roots, so we should expect a random elliptic curve to have approximately q finite points plus the point at infinity, for a total of $q + 1$ points. Hasse's theorem tells us that an elliptic curve $E/\mathbb{F}_q$ has to have approximately $q + 1$ points on it, and that the trace tells us roughly how far from this expected behavior a particular curve is.

Property 3.3 (Hasse's theorem)

For an elliptic curve $E/\mathbb{F}_q$, the trace of Frobenius satisfies the inequality $|t| \leq 2\sqrt{q}$. Thus the number of points on an elliptic curve over $\mathbb{F}_q$ is approximately $q + 1$.

Definition 3.10

If E is an elliptic curve over $\mathbb{F}_q$ and we have $\#E(\mathbb{F}_q) = q$, then we say that E is *anomalous*. We will see in Chapter 5 that anomalous curves should be avoided for some cryptographic applications.

Definition 3.11

Let p be the characteristic of $\mathbb{F}_q$ and E be an elliptic curve over $\mathbb{F}_q$ and t be the trace of E. If p divides t then we say that the elliptic curve E is *supersingular*. A curve that is not supersingular is said to be *ordinary*. Note that the concepts of singular and supersingular are very different and should not be confused.

Property 3.4

If $E : y^2 = f(x)$ is an elliptic curve over $\mathbb{F}_q$ then E is *supersingular* exactly when the coefficient of x^{p-1} in

$$(f(x))^{\frac{p-1}{2}}$$

is zero [2].

Example 3.5

A particular elliptic curve can be either supersingular or ordinary, depending on what field it is defined over.

(i) If p is a prime with $p \geq 5$, then the elliptic curve $y^2 = x^3 + 1$ over $\mathbb{F}_p$ is supersingular when the coefficient of x^{p-1} in $(x^3 + 1)^{(p-1)/2}$

is zero. If $p \equiv 2 \pmod 3$ then this coefficient is zero and the curve is supersingular. When $p \equiv 1 \pmod 3$, then this coefficient is the binomial coefficient $\binom{(p-1)/2}{(p-1)/3}$ which is nonzero, so the curve is ordinary.

(ii) If p is a prime with $p > 2$, then the elliptic curve $y^2 = x^3 + x$ over $\mathbb{F}_p$ is supersingular when the coefficient of x^{p-1} in $(x^3 + x)^{(p-1)/2}$ is zero. If $p \equiv 3 \pmod 4$ then this coefficient is zero and the curve is supersingular. When $p \equiv 1 \pmod 4$, then this coefficient is the binomial coefficient $\binom{(p-1)/2}{(p-1)/4}$ which is nonzero, so the curve is ordinary.

(iii) If p is a prime with $p \equiv 11 \pmod{12}$, then both $y^2 = x^3 + 1$ and $y^2 = x^3 + x$ are supersingular over $\mathbb{F}_p$.

(iv) If p is a prime with $p \equiv 1 \pmod{12}$, then both $y^2 = x^3 + 1$ and $y^2 = x^3 + x$ are ordinary over $\mathbb{F}_p$.

Points on an elliptic curve form a group, but we need the structure of a field to perform the calculations that some IBE algorithms require. To do this, we want to embed an elliptic curve group in a finite field. In many cases, this will result in a finite field that is too large to be practical for computations.

Definition 3.12

Let $E/\mathbb{F}_q$ be an elliptic curve and n be an integer such that $n \mid \#E(\mathbb{F}_q)$. If k is the smallest positive integer such that $n \mid (q^k - 1)$ then k is called the *embedding degree* of E with respect to n. If $n = \#E(\mathbb{F}_q)$ then we can abbreviate this to saying that k is the embedding degree of E.

If k is the embedding degree of $E/\mathbb{F}_q$, we can think of $\mathbb{F}_{q^k}$ as being an extension of $\mathbb{F}_q$ in which $E(\mathbb{F}_q)$ is a subgroup of $\mathbb{F}^*_{q^k}$. This gives us the ability to multiply points, an operation that we cannot perform in an elliptic curve group, where only the operation of addition is defined.

Example 3.6

Let $E/\mathbb{F}_{11}$ be the elliptic curve $y^2 = x^3 + 1$. Because $\#E(\mathbb{F}_{11}) = 12$ divides $11^2 - 1 = 120$, we have that the embedding degree of E is $k = 2$.

The embedding degree of most elliptic curve groups is very high. This means that it is impractical to do calculations in the extension field $\mathbb{F}_{q^k}$, where we need to perform operations on k-tuples of coordinates, each of which is an element of $\mathbb{F}_q$. The following property gives an estimate for the chances of the embedding degree being low enough to make calculating discrete logarithms in $\mathbb{F}_{q^k}$ possible in polynomial time, which happens with the index calculus algorithm [5] when $k \leq (\log q)^2$. Note that this may still be far from being practical to implement.

Property 3.5 (Balasubramanian and Koblitz) [6]

Let q be a randomly chosen prime with $M/2 \leq q \leq M$ and $E/\mathbb{F}_q$ a randomly chosen elliptic curve. If $\#E(\mathbb{F}_q) = p$ for some prime p, then the probability that $p \mid (q^k - 1)$ for some $k \leq (\log q)^2$ is less than

$$\frac{c(\log M)^9(\log \log M)^2}{M}$$

for some constant c.

Example 3.7

(i) Ignoring the constant c, and using a 256-bit q (so that $M = 2^{257}$) and a 256-bit p, which are reasonable parameters for an IBE system, we find that the probability of having $p \mid (q^k - 1)$ for some $k \leq (\log q)^2$ is less than approximately 2×10^{-56}, or 2^{-185}.

(ii) An embedding degree $k \leq (\log q)^2$ can still be very impractical. For $q = 2^{256}$ we have $(\log q)^2 = 31{,}487$, and performing calculations in an extension field of degree 31,487 is almost certainly impractical.

The following property makes supersingular curves both useful as well as good to avoid in cryptographic applications, depending on the way in which the curve is being used. This will be discussed in detail in Chapter 5. A small embedding degree makes some elliptic curve cryptographic algorithm vulnerable to some cryptanalytic attacks, and it is necessary to select parameters of algorithms that use such curves carefully to avoid such weaknesses.

Property 3.6

If $E/\mathbb{F}_q$ is a supersingular curve with $q = p^n$ and trace t, then Table 3.4 lists the possible classes of supersingular curves [7]. In particular, any supersingular

Table 3.4
Classification of Supersingular Curves

Class	Trace t	Embedding Degree k	Comments
1	0	2	$E(F_q) \cong \mathbb{Z}_{q+1}$
2	0	2	$E(F_q) \cong \mathbb{Z}_{(q+1)/2} \oplus \mathbb{Z}_2$ and $q \equiv 3 \pmod 4$
3	q	3	n even
4	$2q$	4	$p = 2$, n odd
5	$3q$	6	$p = 3$, n odd
6	$4q$	1	n even

curve has embedding degree $k \leq 6$, and for $E/\mathbb{F}_q$ with $q > 3$ we have that the only three possible cases are $k = 1$, $k = 2$, and $k = 3$.

Definition 3.13

If E/F is an elliptic curve in Weierstrass normal form $y^2 = x^3 + ax + b$, we say that an elliptic curve E'/F in Weierstrass normal form $y^2 = x^3 + a'x + b'$ is *isomorphic* over F if there exists $u \in F^*$ with $a' = u^4 a$ and $b' = u^6 b$.

This definition is motivated by the isomorphism of the underlying lattice in the complex plane that is defined by the integer multiple of the two periods of the Weierstrass $\wp$ function $\{\omega_1, \omega_2\}$. Such a lattice with periods $\{\omega_1, \omega_2\}$ is isomorphic to another lattice if both periods differ by the same constant, or the second lattice is defined by integer multiples of periods $\{c \cdot \omega_1, c \cdot \omega_2\}$ for some $c \in \mathbb{R}$. Isomorphic elliptic curves come from the $\wp$ function defined on such isomorphic lattices.

The discriminant as defined in Section 3.1.2 only tells us when the cubic part of an elliptic curve has no repeated roots, and there can be many nonisomorphic elliptic curves with the same discriminant. A different quantity is needed to distinguish between isomorphic curves.

Definition 3.14

The *j-invariant* of an elliptic curve E in Weierstrass normal form is given by

$$j(E) = \frac{2^8 3^3 a^3}{4a^3 + 27b^2}$$

Note that the j-invariant and the discriminant are related by

$$j(E) = \frac{-2^{12} 3^3 a^3}{\Delta} = \frac{-1{,}728\,(4a)^3}{\Delta}$$

Property 3.7

Two elliptic curves that are isomorphic over F have the same j-invariant and elliptic curves over F with the same j-invariant are isomorphic over the algebraic closure $\overline{F}$.

Example 3.8

(i) Any elliptic curve E of the form $y^2 = x^3 + b$ has $j(E) = 0$. Such curves are sometimes referred to as "$j = 0$" curves.

(ii) Any elliptic curve E of the form $y^2 = x^3 + ax$ has $j(E) = 1{,}728$. Such curves are sometimes referred to as "$j = 1{,}728$" curves.

(iii) For $j \in \mathbb{F}_q, j \neq 0, j \neq 1{,}728$, let

$$k = \frac{j}{1{,}728 - j}$$

Then $E/\mathbb{F}_q : y^2 = x + 3kc^2x + 2kc^3$ has j-invariant j for $c \in \mathbb{F}_q$.

The observation that j-invariant does not change under the change of variables $a \to v^2a$ and $b \to v^3b$ leads to the following definition.

Definition 3.15

Let $E/\mathbb{F}_q : y^2 = x^3 + ax + b$ be an elliptic curve and $v \in \mathbb{F}_q^*$ be a quadratic nonresidue in $\mathbb{F}_q^*$. Then $E'/F : y^2 = x^3 + v^2ax + v^3b$ is called the *quadratic twist* of E. In this case, E is isomorphic to E' over an extension of degree 2 to $\mathbb{F}_q$ but not over $\mathbb{F}_q$ itself.

Example 3.9

Over $\mathbb{F}_5$ we have that $v = 2$ is a quadratic nonresidue so that $E' : y^2 = x^3 + 4x + 3$ is the quadratic twist of $E : y^2 = x^3 + x + 1$.

3.3.1 Higher Degree Twists

For some curves $E/\mathbb{F}_q$ it is possible to create twists other than the quadratic twist. In these cases we have $E' : y^2 = x^3 + a'x + b'$ where $a' = v^{4/d}a$ and $b' = v^{6/d}b$, and v is a root of degree d but not a root of less than degree d over F (so a fourth root is a fourth root but not a square root, for example), which we can call a *twist of degree d*. Such twists are isomorphic to E over $\mathbb{F}_{q^d}$, an extension of degree d to $\mathbb{F}_q$. The possible twists, both quadratic and of higher degree, are summarized in Tables 3.5 and 3.6. In each of these cases, we must also have that $q \equiv 1(\text{mod } d)$ for such a twist to exist.

We will see in Chapter 4 that mappings $\varphi_d : E' \to E$, where d is the degree of a twist, are useful in creating structures that are useful for implementing

Table 3.5
Elliptic Curves and Their Twists

Degree of Twist d	Form of E	Form of E'
2	$y^2 = x^3 + ax + b$	$y^2 = x^3 + v^2ax + v^3b$
3	$y^2 = x^3 + b$	$y^2 = x^3 + vb$
4	$y^2 = x^3 + ax$	$y^2 = x^3 + vax$
6	$y^2 = x^3 + b$	$y^2 = x^3 + vb$

Table 3.6
Points on Twists of Elliptic Curves

Degree of Twist d	Typical Point on E	Corresponding Point on E'
2	(x, y)	$(vx, v^{3/2}y)$
3	(x, y)	$(v^{1/3}x, v^{1/2}y)$
4	(x, y)	$(v^{1/2}x, v^{3/4}y)$
6	(x, y)	$(v^{1/3}x, v^{1/2}y)$

pairing-based algorithms. Changing to this point of view is easy, and results in the mappings shown in Table 3.7. Note that these mappings increase the dimension of their output by a factor of d, so that if the inputs are elements of some $\mathbb{F}_d$ then the outputs are elements of some $\mathbb{F}_{q^d}$.

Example 3.10

(i) We have that $E'/\mathbb{F}_{11} : y^2 = x^3 + 10$ is the quadratic twist of $E/\mathbb{F}_{11} : y^2 = x^3 + 1$ created using the quadratic nonresidue $v = 10$ so that $i^2 = v$. In this case we have that the point $(2, 3) \in E(\mathbb{F}_{11})$ while $(v \cdot 2, v^{3/2} \cdot 3) = (10 \cdot 2, 10i \cdot 3) = (9, 8i) \in E'(\mathbb{F}_{11})$.

(ii) For the quadratic twist $E'/\mathbb{F}_{11} : y^2 = x^3 + 10$ created from $E/\mathbb{F}_{11} : y^2 = x^3 + 1$ using the quadratic nonresidue $v = 10$ so that $i^2 = v$, we have that $\phi_2(x, y) = (v^{-1}x, v^{-3/2}y) = (10 \cdot x, i \cdot y)$. So for $Q = (9, 8i) \in E'(\mathbb{F}_{11})$ we have that $\phi_2(Q) = (10 \cdot 9, i \cdot 8i) = (2, 3)$.

Definition 3.16

Let $E/\mathbb{F}_q$ be an elliptic curve and n be an integer relatively prime to q, and P a point of order n in $E(\mathbb{F}_q)$. A *distortion map* with respect to (or for) P is an

Table 3.7
Mappings $\phi_d : E' \rightarrow E$

Degree of Twist d	$\phi_d : E' \rightarrow E$
2	$\phi_2(x, y) = (v^{-1}x, v^{-3/2}y)$
3	$\phi_3(x, y) = (v^{-1/3}x, v^{-1/2}y)$
4	$\phi_4(x, y) = (v^{-1/2}x, v^{-3/4}y)$
6	$\phi_6(x, y) = (v^{-1/3}x, v^{-1/2}y)$

endomorphism ϕ that maps the point P to a point $\phi(P)$ that is linearly independent from P. Another useful point of view is that such a distortion map is a nonrational endomorphism.

Useful distortion maps for curves over $\mathbb{F}_q$ where q is either a prime p or a power of a prime p^2 are summarized in Table 3.8.

Example 3.11

(i) For a curve of the form $E/\mathbb{F}_p : y^2 = x^3 + a$ where p is a prime with $p \equiv 3 (\text{mod } 4)$, it is possible to write a distortion map for E as $\phi(x, y) = (\xi x, y)$ where

$$\xi = \frac{p-1}{2}(1 + 3^{(p+1)/4} i) \tag{3.7}$$

For such a ξ we have that

$$\xi^3 = \left(\frac{p-1}{2}\right)^3 \left(1 + 3(3^{(p+1)/4} i) + 3(3^{(p+1)/4} i)^2 + (3^{(p+1)/4} i)^3\right) \tag{3.8}$$

$$= \left(\frac{p-1}{2}\right)^3 \left(1 - 3^{(p+3)/2} + i(3^{(p+5)/4} - 3^{(3p+3)/4})\right)$$

which we want to be equal to 1.

From Euler's theorem we have that

$$3^{p-1} \equiv 1 (\text{mod } p)$$

Table 3.8
Useful Distortion Maps

Field	Curve	Distortion Map	#E
$\mathbb{F}_p$	$y^2 = x^3 + ax$	$\phi(x, y) = (-x, iy)$	$p + 1$
$\mathbb{F}_p$	$y^2 = x^3 + ax$	$\phi(x, y) = (\xi x, y)$ $\xi \neq 1, \xi^3 = 1$	$p + 1$
$\mathbb{F}_{p^2}$	$y^2 = x^3 + ax$ $a \in \mathbb{F}_p$	$\phi(x, y) = \left(\omega \frac{x^p}{r^{(2p-1)/3}}, \frac{y^p}{r^{p-1}}\right)$ $r^2 = a, r \in \mathbb{F}_{p^2}$ $\omega^3 = r, \omega \in \mathbb{F}_{p^6}$	$p^2 - p + 1$

so that

$$3^{p-1} \equiv 3^{3(p-1)} (\text{mod } p)$$

and thus

$$3^{(p-1)+6} \equiv 3^{3(p-1)+6} (\text{mod } p)$$

so that

$$3^{p+5} \equiv 3^{3p+3} (\text{mod } p)$$

and

$$3^{(p+5)/4} \equiv 3^{(3p+3)/4} (\text{mod } p)$$

and

$$3^{(p+5)/4} - 3^{(3p+3)/4} \equiv 0 (\text{mod } p)$$

so that the imaginary part of (3.8) is equal to zero.

Similarly, we have that

$$\frac{p+3}{2} = \frac{p-1+4}{2} = \frac{p-1}{2} + 2$$

so that

$$s \equiv \frac{1}{8}(1 - 3^2) (\text{mod } p) = 1 (\text{mod } p)$$

by Euler's theorem. Thus the real part of (3.8) is equal to 1, and (3.7) is indeed a cube root of 1 as needed.

(ii) For the elliptic curve $E/\mathbb{F}_{11} : y^2 = x^3 + 1$, let $\phi(x, y) = (\xi x, y)$, where $\xi = \left(\frac{11-1}{2}\right)(1 + 3^{(11+1)/2} i) \equiv 5(1 + 5i) (\text{mod } 11) = (5 + 3i) (\text{mod } 11)$ which has the properties that $\xi \neq 1$ and $\xi^3 = 1$. Then for $P = (2, 3)$ we have that $\phi(P) = ((5 + 3 \cdot i) \cdot 2, 3) = (10 + 6 \cdot i, 3)$, which is linearly independent from P. This ϕ is a distortion map on E for the point P.

(iii) For the elliptic curve $y^2 = x^3 + x$ over $\mathbb{F}_{11}$, let $\phi(x, y) = (-x, iy)$. Then for $P = (0, 1)$ we have $\phi(P) = \phi(0, 1) = (0, i)$ which is linearly independent from $P = (0, 1)$, making ϕ a distortion map with respect to P.

Distortion maps are useful in creating structures that are useful for implementing many IBE algorithms. This will be discussed in Chapter 4. Their application is essentially limited to supersingular curves, however, as the following two properties describe.

Property 3.8 (Verheul) [8]

Let $E/\mathbb{F}_q$ be a supersingular elliptic curve with $P \in E(\mathbb{F}_q)[n]$. If n is relatively prime to the characteristic of $\mathbb{F}_q$, then there always exists a distortion map with respect to P.

Property 3.9 (Verheul) [8]

Let $E/\mathbb{F}_q$ be an ordinary elliptic curve and let $P \in E(\mathbb{F}_q)[n]$. If n is relatively prime to the characteristic of $\mathbb{F}_q$ and $E[n] \not\subset E(\mathbb{F}_q)$, then there cannot exist a distortion map with respect to P.

3.3.2 Complex Multiplication

All elliptic curve groups have some endomorphisms: the multiplication-by-n maps of the form $f_n(P) = nP$. Some elliptic curve groups have additional endomorphisms that are not isomorphic to such multiplication-by-n maps. An elliptic curve with this property is said to have *complex multiplication*, which we can abbreviate as "CM." The term "complex multiplication" comes from the fact that in many cases, these endomorphisms act much like multiplication by a complex number. So we might have that $f(f(P)) = -D \cdot P$ for some $D > 0$, so that $f \circ f = -D$ or $f^2 = -D$ suggesting that f acts like multiplying by the imaginary number $\sqrt{-D}$. We will see in later chapters that there are techniques that work on curves with complex multiplication that can be used to generate elliptic curves suitable for IBE calculations.

Example 3.12

(i) Any supersingular elliptic curve has a distortion map, so all supersingular curves have complex multiplication.

(ii) The elliptic curve $y^2 = x^3 + x$ has an endomorphism given by f: $(x, y) \to (-x, iy)$ so that $(f \circ f)(P) = (f \circ f)(x, y) = (x, -y) = -P$. Thus, $f \circ f = f^2$ acts like multiplication by -1, so we can think of f as acting like multiplying by $\sqrt{-1}$.

(iii) The elliptic curve $y^2 = x^3 + 1$ has an endomorphism given by $f: (x, y) \rightarrow (\xi x, y)$ where $\xi^3 = 1$, $\xi \neq 1$. In this case, $(f \circ f \circ f)(P) = (\xi^2 x, y) = (x, y) = P$, or that $f \circ f \circ f = f^3$ acts like multiplication by 1, but $f \neq 1$, so we can think of f as acting like multiplying by the complex number ξ.

References

[1] Lang, S., *Elliptic Functions*, New York: Springer-Verlag, 1987.

[2] Silverman, J., *The Arithmetic of Elliptic Curves*, New York: Springer-Verlag, 1986.

[3] Blake, I., G. Seroussi, and N. Smart, *Elliptic Curves in Cryptography*, Cambridge, U.K.: Cambridge University Press, 1999.

[4] Chudnovsky, D., and G. Chudnovsky, "Sequences of Numbers Generated by Addition in Formal Group and New Primality and Factorization Tests," *Advances in Applied Mathematics*, Vol. 7, No. 4, 1986, pp. 385–434.

[5] Stinson, D., *Cryptography: Theory and Practice*, New York: Chapman and Hall, 2005.

[6] Balasubramanian, R., and N. Koblitz, "The Improbability That an Elliptic Curve Has Subexponential Discrete Log Problem Under the Menezes-Okamoto-Vanstone Algorithm," *Journal of Cryptology*, Vol. 11, No. 2, 1998, pp. 141–145.

[6] Stinson, D., *Cryptography: Theory and Practice*, New York: Chapman and Hall, 2005.

[7] Menezes, A., *Elliptic Curve Public Key Cryptosystems*, New York: Springer-Verlag, 1993.

[8] Verheul, E., "Evidence That XTR Is More Secure Than Supersingular Elliptic Curve Cryptosystems," *Journal of Cryptology*, Vol. 17, No. 4, 2004, pp. 277–296.

4

Divisors and the Tate Pairing

This chapter introduces divisors, which are then used to construct the Tate pairing. The Tate pairing in turn provides the basis for many IBE schemes, including the Boneh-Franklin, Bohen-Boyen, and Sakai-Kasahara schemes. The discussion of the Tate pairing here is designed to provide an overview of the pairing, its properties, and how to calculate it. Further detail of the properties of the Tate pairing can be found in [1, 2].

The Tate pairing by itself turns out to be unsuitable for cryptographic applications because it frequently returns the value 1, but by modifying one of the inputs to the Tate pairing using either a distortion map or a point on the twist of an elliptic curve, it is easy to overcome this limitation.

4.1 Divisors

The divisors discussed in this section are very different from those discussed in Chapter 2, but they unfortunately share the same name. In this context, a divisor is a way of characterizing a function f based only on its zeroes, where $f(x) = 0$, and poles, where $f(x) = \pm\infty$, like when dividing by zero. We say that a function $f(x)$ has a pole at infinity if $f(1/x)$ has a pole at $x = 0$, so that a polynomial of degree n has a pole of degree n at infinity. Similarly, we say that a function $f(x)$ has a zero at infinity if $f(1/x)$ has a zero at $x = 0$. For example, the function

$$f(x) = \frac{(x-1)^2}{(x+2)^3} = (x-1)^2(x+2)^{-3}$$

has a zero of order 2 at $x = 1$, a zero of order 1 at infinity, and a pole of order 3 at $x = -2$. Because a divisor characterizes a function based on its zeroes and poles, two functions that differ by a constant will have the same divisor.

4.1.1 An Intuitive Introduction to Divisors

We keep track of the zeroes and poles of a rational function f in what we call a divisor, which we write as $div(f)$. We write such a divisor as the sum of the points where f has a zero or pole weighted by the multiplicities of the zeroes and poles, with the convention that zeroes get positive weights according to their multiplicities and poles get negative weights according to their multiplicities. In the example above, we write $div(f) = 2(1) + (\infty) - 3(-2)$, to indicate that f has a zero of order 2 at $x = 1$, a zero or order 1 at infinity, and a pole of order 3 at $x = -2$. In general, if we can write

$$f(x) = \prod_i (x - x_i)^{a_i}$$

then we write

$$div(f) = \sum_i a_i (x_i)$$

The notation for divisors can be a bit tricky, and we will need to be able tell from the context that we dealing with divisors instead of numbers, so that we are not tempted to treat divisors as numbers, trying to simplify expressions like $2(1) - 3(-2)$ to get a number instead of a divisor.

Note that multiplying rational functions corresponds to addition of their divisors and division of rational functions corresponds to subtraction of their divisors. So if we have $f(x)$ as defined above and

$$g(x) = \frac{(x+2)^3}{(x+1)^4}$$

then

$$\begin{aligned} f(x)g(x) &= \frac{(x-1)^2}{(x+2)^3} \frac{(x+2)^3}{(x+1)^4} \\ &= \frac{(x-1)^2}{(x+1)^4} \end{aligned}$$

which corresponds to adding the divisors:

$$\begin{aligned} div(fg) &= div(f) + div(g) \\ &= 2(1) + (\infty) - 3(-2) + 3(-2) + (\infty) - 4(-1) \\ &= 2(1) + 2(\infty) - 4(-1) \end{aligned}$$

We can formalize this informal description of divisors with the following definitions.

Definition 4.1

A *formal sum* of a set S is series $\{s_0, s_1, s_2, \ldots\}$ of elements of S. A formal sum is often written using a placeholder, with the understanding that the placeholder is not to be evaluated.

Example 4.1

(i) A power series is a formal sum which we usually write as $a_0 + a_1x + a_2x^2 + \ldots$, where each $a_i \in S$ for some set S. We write a power series with the understanding that the placeholder x is not to be evaluated, and we could also write the same power series as $\{a_0, a_1, a_2, \ldots\}$.

(ii) If $P = \{P_1, P_2, \ldots P_n\}$ is a set of points on an elliptic curve, then $D = a_1(P_1) + a_2(P_2) + \ldots + a_n(P_n)$ is a formal sum of the elements of P. In this case, we understand that in D the points in the set P are just placeholders like the variable x in a power series, and are not to be evaluated.

Definition 4.2

Let E be an elliptic curve. A *divisor* on E is a formal sum of the form

$$D = \sum_{P \in E} n_P(P)$$

where each n_P is an integer and all but finitely many n_P are zero.

Example 4.2

For points P_1 and P_2 on an elliptic curve, $D = (P_1) + 2(P_2) - 3(O)$ is a divisor.

Definition 4.3

We say that a divisor D is a *principal divisor* if there is a rational function f such that $D = div(f)$. An equivalent definition is that a divisor D on an elliptic curve is principal if we can write

$$D = \sum_i a_i (P_i)$$

where $\sum a_i = 0$ and $\sum a_i P_i = O$, with the last sum using the addition of points on an elliptic curve. In particular, if P is a point of order n, then the divisor $n(P) - n(O)$ is a principal divisor.

Example 4.3

(i) Let P_1, P_2 and P_3 be points on an elliptic curve with $P_3 = P_1 + P_2$. Then $D = (P_1) + (P_2) + (-P_3) - 3(O)$ is a principal divisor.

(ii) Let P be a point on an elliptic curve of order n. Then $D = n(P) - n(O)$ is a principal divisor.

Definition 4.4

If E is an elliptic curve and

$$D = \sum_{P \in E} n_P (P)$$

is a divisor then the *support* of D is the set of all points P such that $n_P \neq 0$.

Example 4.4

For the divisor $D = (P_1) + (P_2) + (-P_3) - 3(O)$, the support of D is the set $\{P_1, P_2, -P_3, O\}$.

Definition 4.5

Let D_1 and D_2 be divisors. Then we say that D_1 and D_2 have *disjoint support* if the intersection of the support of D_1 and the support of D_2 is the empty set, or $D_1 \cap D_2 = \varnothing$.

Example 4.5

(i) The divisors $D_1 = (P_1) - (O)$ and $D_2 = (P_1 + R) - (R)$ have disjoint support as long as $\{P_1, O\} \cap \{P_1 + R, R\} = \varnothing$.

(ii) The divisors $D_1 = (P) - (O)$ and $D_2 = (Q) - (O)$ do not have disjoint support.

We can think of the divisors as keeping track of where the graph of an elliptic curve E intersects the graph of a function $f(x)$, or where $E = f(x)$, so they keep track of zeroes and poles of $E = f(x)$. In particular, we get a zero when $E = f(x)$, or when the function $f(x)$ crosses the elliptic curve E and we get a pole when $f(x)$ has a pole.

The functions u and v that appear in Figure 4.1 are very important in implementing operations on divisors, and in the following, u will always represent a line through two points $P_1 = (x_1, y_1)$ and $P_2 = (x_2, y_2)$ on an elliptic curve and v will always represent a vertical line that goes through $P_3 = (x_3, y_3)$, where $P_3 = P_1 + P_2$.

Suppose that we do not have the case where $P_1 + P_2 = O$ and neither $P_1 = O$ nor $P_2 = O$. Then we can write the point-slope form of a line through (x_1, y_1) as

$$y - y_1 = m(x - x_1)$$

or

$$y - y_1 = -mx + mx_1 = 0$$

which gives us an explicit way to find the line u. Similarly, the line v is given by

$$x - x_3 = 0$$

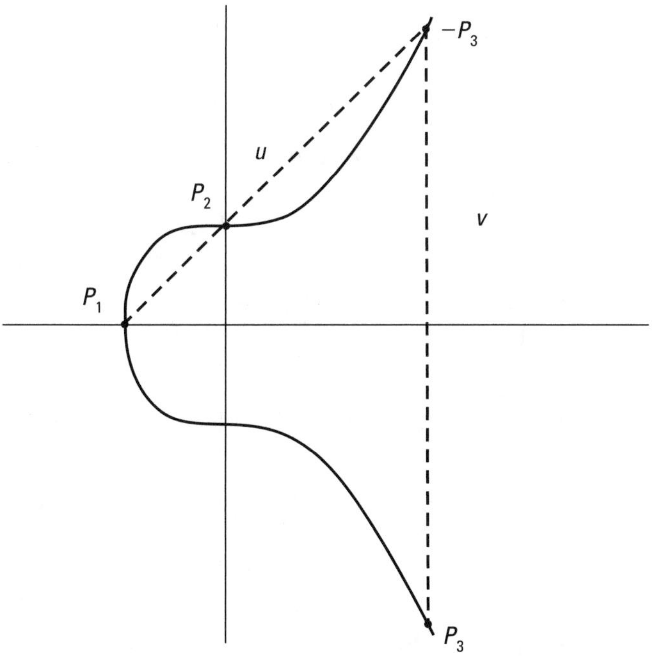

Figure 4.1 Illustration of the lines u and v in the addition of points on an elliptic curve.

If one of the two points is O, then u is the vertical line through the point that is not O, and if the point $(x_3, y_3) = O$ then v is the vertical line $x = 0$. These forms of the lines (x_1, y_1) and (x_1, y_1) are shown in Figure 4.2. The cases where either $P_1 = O$, $P_2 = O$, or $P_1 = P_2$ are shown in Algorithm 4.2, 4.3, and 4.4.

The particular points that we use to define the lines u and v should be clear from the context, so we will usually omit the points to keep the notation simpler. If we need to clarify which points are being used, we will write u_{P_1,P_2} or v_{P_3} to indicate the line through P_1 and P_2 or the vertical line through P_3, respectively. With this notation, u and v have the following divisors:

$$div(u) = (P_1) + (P_2) + (-P_3) - 3(O)$$
$$div(v) = (P_3) + (-P_3) - 2(O)$$

where we have now accounted for the poles that the lines u and v have at O.

Another useful fact is what we get when we subtract the divisor of u from the divisor of v:

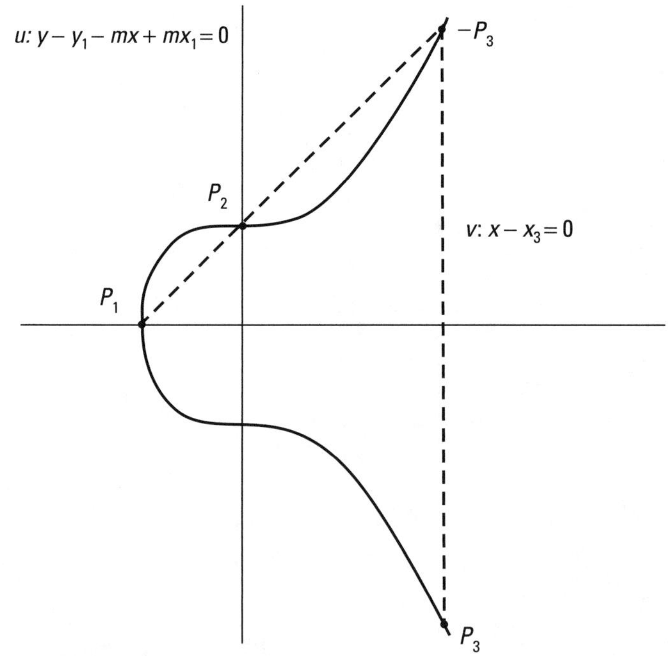

Figure 4.2 Forms of the lines u and v used to add divisors on an elliptic curve.

$$div(u) - div(v) = div(u/v) \quad (4.1)$$
$$= (P_1) + (P_2) + (P_3) - (O)$$

If we have two divisors of the form:

$$D_1 = (P_1) - (O) + div(f_1)$$
$$D_2 = (P_2) - (O) + div(f_2)$$

we can add the two divisors to get

$$D_1 + D_2 = (P_1) + (P_2) - 2(O) + div(f_1 f_2) \quad (4.2)$$

Solving for $(P_1) + (P_2)$ in (4.1) and substituting the result into (4.2) we find that

$$D_1 + D_2 = (P_3) - (O) + div(f_1 f_2 u/v) \quad (4.3)$$

So the divisors of the lines u and v provide a way to add two divisors and keep the result in the form $(P) - (O) + div(f)$.

To clarify how this works, we will now step through a calculation of the sum of two divisors, where the arithmetic is done on the curve $y^2 = x^3 + 1$ over $\mathbb{F}_5$, as is defined in Table 3.2.

In particular, we consider the divisor $D = (\hat{P}_2) - (O)$ and see what we get when we add it to itself. Using (4.3) and the fact that we can also write the divisor D as $div(1)$ we find that

$$D + D = (\hat{P}_2) - (O) + div(1) + (\hat{P}_2) - (O) + div(1)$$
$$= (\hat{P}_1) - (O) + div(u/v)$$

Now u is the line tangent to the elliptic curve at $\hat{P}_2$, and v is the line connecting $\hat{P}_2 + \hat{P}_2 = \hat{P}_1$ and $-(\hat{P}_2 + \hat{P}_2) = \hat{P}_2$. Solving for u and v we find that we have $y - 4 = 0$ for the line u, or $y + 1 = 0$ in $\mathbb{F}_5$. Similarly, we have $x = 0$ for the line v. Substituting these for u and v we get that

$$D + D = (\hat{P}_1) - (O) + div\left(\frac{y+1}{x}\right)$$

If we add the divisor D to this sum one more time we find that we are just left with the divisor of a rational function when the terms of the divisor involving points on the curve cancel each other when we reach

$3D = 3(\hat{P}_2) - 3(O)$ because $\hat{P}_2$ is a point of order 3. At the next step, the line u through $\hat{P}_1$ and $\hat{P}_2$ is the vertical line $x = 0$, since $x = 0$ is the common x coordinate that $\hat{P}_1$ and $\hat{P}_2$ share. We define the vertical line v through the point $\hat{P}_1 + \hat{P}_2 = O$ to be 1. Thus, we have

$$\begin{aligned}
3D &= 3(\hat{P}_2) - 3(O) \\
&= (\hat{P}_2 + \hat{P}_1) - (O) + div\left(\frac{y+1}{x}\frac{u}{v}\right) \\
&= (O) - (O) + div\left(\frac{y+1}{x}\frac{x}{1}\right) \\
&= div(y+1)
\end{aligned}$$

Definition 4.6

If D is a divisor of the form

$$D = \sum_i a_i(P_i)$$

then we define what it means to evaluate a rational function f at D by

$$f(D) = \prod_i f(P_i)^{a_i}$$

Example 4.6

(i) If $D = 2(P_1) - 3(P_2)$ then

$$\begin{aligned}
f(D) &= f(P_1)^2 f(P_2)^{-3} \\
&= \frac{f(P_1)^2}{f(P_2)^3}
\end{aligned}$$

(ii) If $P = (2, 3)$ and $Q = (0, 1)$ are points on $E/\mathbb{F}_{11}$ and D is the divisor $D = (P) - (Q)$ and f is the rational function $f(x, y) = y + 1$, then

$$f(D) = \frac{3+1}{1+1} = 4 \cdot 2^{-1} = 4 \cdot 6 \equiv 2 \pmod{11}$$

In many cases, it is possible to exchange the roles of a function f and a divisor D in expressions like $f(D)$. This is formalized in the following.

Property 4.1 (Weil Reciprocity)

Let f and g be rational functions defined on some field F. If $div(f)$ and $div(g)$ have disjoint support then we have that $f(div(g)) = g(div(f))$.

Example 4.7

Suppose that we have two rational functions f and g defined on $\mathbb{F}_{11}$ where

$$f(x) = \frac{x-2}{x-7}$$

and

$$g(x) = \frac{x-6}{x-5}$$

so that we have

$$div(f) = (2) - (7)$$

and

$$div(g) = (6) - (5)$$

then

$$f(div(g)) = \frac{f(6)}{f(5)} = \frac{7}{4} = 7 \cdot 3 = 10 \pmod{11}$$

and

$$g(div(f)) = \frac{g(2)}{g(7)} = \frac{5}{6} = 5 \cdot 2 = 10 \pmod{11}$$

Definition 4.7

Divisors D_1 and D_2 are *equivalent* if they differ by a principal divisor, that is, $D = D_1 - D_2$ is a principal divisor.

Example 4.8

(i) If f is a rational function, the divisors $(P) - (O)$ and $(P) - (O) + div(f)$ are equivalent.

(ii) We can see that $(P + R) - (R)$ is equivalent to $(P) - (O)$ by using the line u that goes through the points P, R and $-(P + R)$ and the line v that goes through the points $-(P + R)$ and $P + R$. Then we have that

$$div(u) = (P) + (R) + (-(P + R)) - 3(O)$$
$$div(v) = (-(P + R)) + (P + R) - 2(O)$$

so that

$$(P) - (O) = (P + R) - (R) + div(u/v)$$

So the difference between $(P + R) - (R)$ and $(P) - (O)$ is a principal divisor, since it is the divisor of the rational function u/v, and $(P + R) - (R)$ is equivalent to $(P) - (O)$.

4.2 The Tate Pairing

Now that we have defined divisors and how to manipulate them, we can define the Tate pairing and describe how to calculate it. The Tate pairing operates on pairs of points $P \in E(\mathbb{F}_q)[n]$ and $Q \in E(\mathbb{F}_{q^k})$, and produces a result in $\mathbb{F}^*_{q^k}$. We write $e(P, Q)$ for the Tate pairing of the points P and Q. For a point P of order n, to get $e(P, Q)$ we first find a rational function f_P so that $div(f_P)$ is equivalent to $n(P) - n(O)$ and then evaluate f_P at a divisor equivalent to $(Q) - (O)$. We can summarize this in the following.

Definition 4.8

Let $E/\mathbb{F}_q$ be an elliptic curve, $P \in E(\mathbb{F}_q)[n]$ and $Q \in E(\mathbb{F}_{q^k})$. Let f_P be a rational function with $div(f_P)$ equivalent to $n(P) - n(O)$ and A_Q be a divisor equivalent to $(Q) - (O)$ with the support of $div(f_P)$ and A_Q disjoint. Then the Tate pairing is defined to be $e(P, Q) = f_P(A_Q)$. This definition does not produce a unique value, and will include a constant that is an nth power of some element of $\mathbb{F}_{q^k}$.

It is not immediately obvious why the Tate pairing is well defined by this definition. So we should convince ourselves that this definition is actually independent of our choices for f_P and A_Q. In doing so, we will see why the Tate pairing is only defined up to multiplication by an nth power of some constant. In the following we will see that it is easy to get rid of this unwanted constant, leaving a unique value.

Note that f_P is defined up to a constant multiple. Applying the definition of evaluating a divisor at a function to such a constant multiple shows that this has no influence on the value of $f_P(A_Q)$, so it is independent of the choice of f_P.

Now suppose that D_1 and D_2 are both divisors equivalent to $(Q) - (O)$, say $D_1 = D_2 + div(g)$ for some rational function g. To be careful, we also need to assume that the support of $div(f_P)$ is disjoint from the support of $div(g)$. Then we have that

$$\begin{aligned} f_P(D_1) &= f_P(D_2 + div(g)) \\ &= f_P(D_2)\, f_P(div(g)) \\ &= f_P(D_2) g(div(f_P)) \text{ (by Weil reciprocity)} \\ &= f_P(D_2) g(n(P) - n(O)) \\ &= f_P(D_2) g((P) - (O))^n \end{aligned}$$

We can then abuse the notation of congruences slightly to write this as

$$f_P(D_1) \equiv f_P(D_2)$$

which we think of as meaning that $f_P(D_1) = f_P(D_2)$ up to a constant that is an nth power.

The examples of adding divisors above show how to find a divisor equivalent to $n(P) - n(O)$: we can add the divisor $(P) - (O)$ to itself n times by using the divisors $div(u)$ and $div(v)$ that we get from the lines through various points on the elliptic curve, and after reaching $n(P) - n(O)$ we will be left with a divisor of a rational function that we call f_P when all of the terms involving the point P disappear. To avoid the troubles with evaluating a function at the point at infinity that appears in $(Q) - (O)$, we can pick a random point R on our elliptic curve and evaluate f_P at $(Q + R) - (R)$ instead, which is equivalent to the divisor $(Q) - (O)$.

Because the point P is of order n, if we repeatedly add the divisor $(P) - (O)$ to get $n(P) - n(O)$ using the technique that is summarized in (4.3), we find that we end up with a divisor of a rational function that is the product of terms of the form u/v, where u is the line through two points (the points P_1 and P_2 in Figure 4.1, for example) on our elliptic curve and v is the vertical line that passes though the point that is the sum of the same two points (the point P_3 in Figure 4.1, for example).

Suppose that A_Q is a divisor of the form $(Q + R) - (R)$ that we get from a random $R \neq O$. Note that the requirement that the support of the divisors $n(P) - n(O)$ and A_Q are disjoint means that $Q + R \neq P$, and $R \neq P$. We exclude these cases because they either reduce the value of the pairing to zero by introducing a factor of zero in a calculation, or cause a division by zero error. An examination of Algorithms 4.2 through 4.4 should clarify the ways in which this can happen.

To give an example of how this works, we will use the same example that we used above to find $e(\hat{P}_2, \hat{P}_2)$. We found that $3(\hat{P}_2) - 3(O)$ is equivalent to the divisor $div(y + 1)$, so we have $f_{\hat{P}_2} = y + 1$. Next, we need a random point to add to $\hat{P}_2$, for which we pick $\hat{P}_4$, so we want to evaluate $f_{\hat{P}_2}$ at $(\hat{P}_2 + \hat{P}_4) - (\hat{P}_4) = (\hat{P}_3) - (\hat{P}_4)$, or we want to find $f_{\hat{P}_2}(\hat{P}_3)/f_{\hat{P}_2}(\hat{P}_4)$. Note that it is possible to pick a random point that causes division by zero, for example if we picked the point $\hat{P}_2$ in this example. If this happens, we can just pick another random point until we find one that works. Substituting the appropriate values from Table 3.2, we find that

$$\begin{aligned} e(\hat{P}_2, \hat{P}_2) &= \frac{f_{\hat{P}_2}(\hat{P}_3)}{f_{\hat{P}_2}(\hat{P}_4)} = \frac{3}{4} \\ &= 3 \cdot 4^{-1} = 2 \in \mathbb{F}_5 \end{aligned} \tag{4.4}$$

As mentioned above, the Tate pairing has an additional multiplicative factor of r^n for some $r \in \mathbb{F}_{q^k}$, so that we actually get $e(P, Q) = a \cdot r^n$ for when we calculate it. From Property 2.13 we have that for any $\xi \in \mathbb{F}_{q^k}$ we have that $\xi^{q^k - 1} = 1$, so if we raise $a \cdot r^n$ to the power $(q^k - 1)/n$ we get that

$$(a \cdot r^n)^{(q^k - 1)/n} = a^{(q^k - 1)/n} \cdot 1 = a^{(q^k - 1)/n}$$

so that such an exponentiation eliminates the extra multiplicative factor and leaves a unique result. Thus while $e(P, Q)$ is not unique, the additional exponentiation that gives us

$$e(P, Q)^{(q^k - 1)/n}$$

determines a unique value, and thus more suitable for many uses. The use of such an exponentiation to determine a unique value is called the *final exponentiation* and the unique value is called the *reduced pairing*.

Example 4.9

(i) Consider the case where we have $E/\mathbb{F}_{11} : y^2 = x^3 + x$ and $P = (5, 3) \in E(\mathbb{F}_{11})$ [3]. To find $f_P(x, y)$ we want to find the rational function so that $div(f_P)$ is equivalent to the divisor $3(P) - 3(O)$. We get this through a repeated application of (4.3).

We want to find

$$\begin{aligned}3(P) - 3(O) &= 3((P) - (O))\\ &= ((P) - (O)) + ((P) - (O)) + ((P) - (O))\end{aligned}$$

We can start calculating this by first finding

$$\begin{aligned}2(P) - 2(O) &= 2((P) - (O))\\ &= ((P) - (O)) + ((P) - (O))\end{aligned}$$

by

$$\begin{aligned}(P) - (O) + (P) - (O) &= (P) - (O) + div(1) + (P) - (O) + div(1)\\ &= (2P) - (O) + div(y + 2x + 9)\end{aligned}$$

Then

$$\begin{aligned}3(P) - 3(O) &= (2P) - (O) + div(y + 2x + 9) + (P) - (O) + div(1)\\ &= (3P) - (O) + div(y + 2x + 9)\\ &= (O) - (O) + div(y + 2x + 9)\\ &= div(y + 2x + 9)\end{aligned}$$

so that

$$f_P(x, y) = y + 2x + 9$$

If we have $Q = (7, 8)$ and $R = (10, 3)$, then $Q + R = (9, 10)$ and we evaluate f_P at $A_Q = (Q + R) - (R)$ we get

$$\begin{aligned}f_P((Q + R) - (R)) &= \frac{f_P(Q + R)}{f_P(R)} = \frac{4}{10}\\ &= 4 \cdot 10^{-1} = 4 \cdot 10 \equiv 7 \pmod{11}\end{aligned}$$

Thus $e(P, Q) = f_P(A_Q) = 7$.

(ii) Consider the case where we have $E/\mathbb{F}_{11} : y^2 = x^3 + 1$ and $P = (5, 4) \in E(\mathbb{F}_{11})$ [4]. Because P is of order 4, to find $f_P(x, y)$ we want to find the rational function so that $div(f_P)$ is equivalent to the divisor $4(P) - 4(O)$. We get this through a repeated application of (4.3).

We want to find

$$
\begin{aligned}
4(P) - 4(O) &= 4((P) - (O)) \\
&= ((P) - (O)) + ((P) - (O)) + ((P) - (O)) + ((P) - (O))
\end{aligned}
$$

We can start calculating this by first finding

$$
\begin{aligned}
2(P) - 2(O) &= 2((P) - (O)) \\
&= ((P) - (O)) + ((P) - (O))
\end{aligned}
$$

by

$$
\begin{aligned}
(P) - (O) + (P) - (O) &= (P) - (O) + div(1) + (P) - (O) + div(1) \\
&= (2P) - (O) + div\left(\frac{y + 3x + 3}{x + 1}\right)
\end{aligned}
$$

Then

$$
\begin{aligned}
3(P) - 3(O) &= (2P) - (O) + div\left(\frac{y + 3x + 3}{x + 1}\right) + (P) - (O) + div(1) \\
&= (3P) - (O) + div\left(\frac{(y + 3x + 3)^2}{(x + 1)(x + 6)}\right)
\end{aligned}
$$

And finally

$$
\begin{aligned}
4(P) - 4(O) &= (3P) - (O) + div\left(\frac{(y + 3x + 3)^2}{(x + 1)(x + 6)}\right) + (P) - (O) + div(1) \\
&= (4P) - (O) + div\left(\frac{(y + 3x + 3)^2}{x + 1}\right) \\
&= (O) - (O) + div\left(\frac{(y + 3x + 3)^2}{x + 1}\right) \\
&= div\left(\frac{(y + 3x + 3)^2}{x + 1}\right)
\end{aligned}
$$

so that

$$f_P(x, y) = \frac{(y + 3x + 3)^2}{x + 1}$$

If we have $Q = (5, 7)$ and $R = (9, 9)$, then $Q + R = (0, 1)$ and we evaluate f_P at $A_Q = (Q + R) - (R)$ we get

$$f_P((Q + R) - (R)) = \frac{f_P(Q + R)}{f_P(R)} = \frac{5}{8}$$

$$= 5 \cdot 8^{-1} = 5 \cdot 7 \equiv 2 \pmod{11}$$

Thus $e(P, Q) = f_P(A_Q) = 2$.

4.2.1 Properties of the Tate Pairing

As defined earlier, the Tate pairing has the following properties:

1. The Tate pairing is *nondegenerate*, that is, for each $P \in E(\mathbb{F}_q)[n]/\{O\}$ there is some $Q \in E(\mathbb{F}_{q^k})$ with $e(P, Q) \neq 1$.
2. The Tate pairing is *bilinear*, that is, for each $P, P_1, P_2 \in E(\mathbb{F}_q)[n]$ and $Q, Q_1, Q_2 \in E(\mathbb{F}_{q^k})$ we have $e(P_1 + P_2, Q) = e(P_1, Q)e(P_2, Q)$ and $e(P, Q_1 + Q_2) = e(P, Q_1)e(P, Q_2)$.

To convince ourselves that the Tate pairing is bilinear, we need to consider two separate cases.

To see that the Tate pairing is linear in its first parameter, let f_{P_1}, f_{P_2}, and $f_{P_1+P_2}$ be rational functions such that we have

$$div\left(f_{P_1}\right) = n(P_1) - n(O)$$

$$div\left(f_{P_2}\right) = n(P_2) - n(O)$$

and

$$div\left(f_{P_1+P_2}\right) = n(P_1 + P_2) - n(O)$$

Note that the divisor

$$D = (P_1 + P_2) - (P_1) - (P_2) + (O)$$

is a principal divisor so it is the divisor of some rational function, say

$$div(g) = D$$

then

$$div\left(f_{P_1+P_2}\right) - div(f_1) - div(f_2) = n(P_1 + P_2) - n(P_1) - n(P_2) - n(O)$$
$$= nD = ndiv(g) = div(g^n)$$

so that

$$div\left(f_{P_1+P_2}\right) = div(f_1) + div(f_2) + div(g^n)$$

so we can write

$$f_{P_1+P_2} = f_1 f_2 g^n$$

Thus

$$e(P_1 + P_2, Q) = f_{P_1+P_2}(A_Q) = f_{P_1}(A_Q) f_{P_2}(A_Q) g^n(A_Q)$$
$$= e(P_1, Q)\, e(P_2, Q) g^n(A_Q)$$

So if we are ignoring nth powers, we find that

$$e(P_1 + P_2, Q) = e(P_1, Q)\, e(P_2, Q)$$

as desired.

To see that the Tate pairing is bilinear in the second parameter, let $A_{Q_1+Q_2}$ be a divisor equivalent to $(Q_1 + Q_2) - (O)$, A_{Q_1} be a divisor equivalent to $(Q_1) - (O)$ and A_{Q_2} be a divisor equivalent to $(Q_1) - (O)$. Then $A_{Q_1+Q_2} - A_{Q_1} - A_{Q_2}$ is equivalent to

$$D = (Q_1 + Q_2) - (Q_1) - (Q_2) + (O)$$

which is a principal divisor. So $A_{Q_1+Q_2}$ is equivalent to $A_{Q_1} + A_{Q_2}$ because they differ by a principal divisor. Thus we can write

$$e(P, Q_1 + Q_2) = f_P\left(A_{Q_1+Q_2}\right)$$
$$= f_P\left(A_{Q_1} + A_{Q_2}\right) = f_P\left(A_{Q_1}\right) f_P\left(A_{Q_2}\right)$$
$$= e(P, Q_1)\, e(P, Q_2)$$

A mapping that is nondegenerate and bilinear and is also efficiently computable is called a *pairing*, and such mappings are the fundamental primitives from which many cryptographic algorithms are constructed. On the other hand, the Tate pairing also has the following property that limits its usefulness because it returns the value 1 in many cases.

Property 4.2 (Galbraith) [3]

Let $P \in E(\mathbb{F}_q)[n]\backslash\{O\}$ and n relatively prime to q. Then to have $e(P, P) \neq 1$, we must have $k = 1$.

So for an embedding degree $k > 1$ we have $e(P, P) = 1$, which also means that $e(aP, bP) = e(P, P)^{ab} = 1$ for integers a and b, so that the Tate pairing may not seem very useful at first. The following result provides insight into how to overcome this limitation.

Property 4.3 (Verheul) [4]

Let n be a prime, $P \in E(\mathbb{F}_q)[n]\backslash\{O\}$, $Q \in E(\mathbb{F}_{q^k})$ be linearly independent from P, and $k > 1$. Then we have that $e(P, Q)$ is nondegenerate.

So if we have $P \in E(\mathbb{F}_q)[n]$ and a nontrivial embedding degree, that is, we have $k > 1$, then one way to make sure that the Tate pairing $e(P, Q)$ is nondegenerate is to make sure that Q is linearly independent of P. One way to do this is to use a distortion map, so that instead of computing $e(P, Q)$, we compute $e(P, \phi(Q))$ instead, where ϕ is an appropriate distortion map. Another way is to compute $e(P, \phi_d(Q))$ where $Q \in E'$ is on the twist of the elliptic curve E and $\phi_d : E' \to E$ is the mapping defined in Section 3.3.1. In either case, we denote the resulting pairing by $\hat{e}(P, Q)$, where either $\hat{e}(P, Q) = e(P, \phi(Q))$ or $\hat{e}(P, Q) = e(P, \phi_d(Q))$ as appropriate and call such an $\hat{e}$ the *modified Tate pairing*.

Example 4.10

(i) (Distortion Map). From Example 4.1(ii), we have where $E/\mathbb{F}_{11} : y^2 = x^3 + 1$ and $P = (5, 4) \in E(\mathbb{F}_{11})\,[4]$, we get

$$f_P(x, y) = \frac{(y + 3x + 3)^2}{x + 1}$$

If we have $Q = (5, 7)$ and $R = (9, 9)$, then $Q + R = (0, 1)$ and we evaluate f_P at $A_Q = (Q + R) - (R)$ we get $e(P, Q) = f_P(A_Q) = 2 \in \mathbb{F}_{11}$, so that for the reduced Tate pairing we get

$$e(P, Q)^{(q^k - 1)/n} = 2^{(11^2 - 1)/4} = 2^{30} \equiv 1 \pmod{11}$$

In this case, $\phi(x, y) = (\xi x, y)$, where $\xi = 5 + 3 \cdot i$, is a distortion map for the point Q, and we find that $\phi(Q) = (3 + 4 \cdot i, 7)$ and that $\phi(Q) + R = (1 + 4 \cdot i, 5)$. Thus, we have that

$$f_P((\phi(Q) + R) - (R)) = \frac{f_P(\phi(Q) + R)}{f_P(R)}$$
$$= \frac{1 + 9i}{8} = 7 + 8i$$

so that for the reduced modified Tate pairing we get

$$e(P, \phi(Q))^{(q^k - 1)/n} = (7 + 8i)^{(11^2 - 1)/4} = (7 + 8i)^{30} \equiv 10 \pmod{11}$$

(ii) (Twist). We have that $E' : y^2 = x^3 + 10$ is the quadratic twist of $E/\mathbb{F}_{11} : y^2 = x^3 + 1$ that is created using the quadratic nonresidue $v = 10$. If $P = (5, 4) \in E(\mathbb{F}_{11})$ [4], then from Example 4.1(ii) we get

$$f_P(x, y) = \frac{(y + 3x + 3)^2}{x + 1}$$

In this case, we have

$$\phi_2(x, y) = (v^{-1}x, v^{-3/2}y) = (10 \cdot x, i \cdot y)$$

If we have $Q = (3, 2) \in E'$ and $R = (9, 9)$, then $\phi_2(Q) = (8, 2i)$ then $\phi_2(Q) + R = (5 + 8i, 8i)$. Thus we have that

$$f_P((\phi_2(Q) + R) - (R) = \frac{f_P(\phi_2(Q) + R)}{f_P(R)}$$
$$= \frac{4 + 8i}{6 + 8I} = 5i$$

so that for the reduced modified Tate pairing we get

$$e((P, \phi_2(Q))^{(q^k - 1)/n} = (5i)^{(11^2 - 1)/4} = (5i)^{30} \equiv 10 \pmod{11}$$

4.3 Miller's Algorithm

The technique that we used above to find a divisor equivalent to $n(P) - n(O)$, in which we iteratively find divisors equivalent to $(P) - (O)$, $2(P) - 2(O)$,

. . . , up to $n(P) - n(O)$ by a repeated application of (4.3) will certainly work, but it is extremely inefficient. In a typical cryptographic application, n is typically at least 2^{160}, so iterating in this way is impractical. Instead, the way we calculate $n(P) - n(O)$ is by the double-and-add technique, and finding a divisor equivalent to $n(P) - n(O)$ in this way is called *Miller's algorithm* [5]. Miller's algorithm is based on the observation that it is easy to generalize (4.3) to divisors

$$D_1 = (aP) - (O) + div(f_1)$$

and

$$D_2 = (bP) - (O) + div(f_2)$$

to find that

$$D_1 + D_2 = (a+b)P - (O) + div\left(f_1 f_2 \frac{u_{aP,\, bP}}{v_{(a+b)P}}\right)$$

We can formalize Miller's algorithm as follows. Pick an elliptic curve E on which all of the following calculations will be performed. Let $P \in E(\mathbb{F}_q)[n]$ and $Q \in E(\mathbb{F}_{q^k})$ with

$$n = \sum_{i=0}^{t} b_i 2^i \text{s}$$

so that $(b_i, \ldots, b_1, b_0)$ is the binary expansion of n. We start with $f = 1$, $S = P$, and R a random point on E. We then do a double-and-add iteration through the binary expansion of n, performing the doubling step at each iteration and the adding step if the bit we are at is a 1. This will let us build the rational function equivalent to $n(P) - n(O)$ out of the repeatedly doubled terms, and we evaluate each of these terms at $(Q + R) - (R)$ as we calculate them. We do this by the following algorithms.

Algorithm 4.1: TatePairing (Miller's algorithm for computing the Tate pairing)
INPUT: Elliptic curve $E : y^2 = x^3 + ax + b$, $P \in E[n]$ with $n = \sum_{i=0}^{t} b_i 2^i$, Q
OUTPUT: $e(P, Q)$

1. $f \leftarrow 1$, $t \leftarrow \lfloor \log_2 n \rfloor$, $S \leftarrow P$, $R \leftarrow$ a random point of E, $R \neq O$, $Q + R \neq O$

2. For $i \leftarrow t - 1$ down to 0
3. $f \leftarrow f^2 \dfrac{u_{S,S}(Q+R)\,v_{2S}(R)}{v_{2S}(Q+R)\,u_{S,S}(R)}$
4. $S \leftarrow 2S$
5. If $b_i = 1$
6. $f \leftarrow f \dfrac{u_{S,P}(Q+R)\,v_{S+P}(R)}{v_{S+P}(Q+R)\,u_{S,P}(R)}$
7. $S \leftarrow S + P$
8. Return f

Algorithm 4.2: v
INPUT: P, Q
OUTPUT: $v_P(Q)$

1. If $P = O$
2. Return 1
3. Return $x_Q - x_P$

Algorithm 4.3: tangent_u
INPUT: P, Q on an elliptic curve $E : y^2 = x^3 + ax + b$
OUTPUT: $u_{P,P}(Q)$

1. If $P = O$
2. Return 1
3. If $y_P = 0$
4. Return $v(P, Q)$
5. $m \leftarrow \dfrac{3x_P^2 + a}{2y_P}$
6. Return $y_Q - y_P - mx_Q + mx_P$

Algorithm 4.4: u
INPUT: P_1, P_2, Q
OUTPUT: $u_{P_1,P_2}(Q)$

1. If $P_1 = O$
2. Return $v(P_2, Q)$
3. If $P_2 = O$ or $P_1 + P_2 = O$
4. Return $v(P_1, Q)$

5. If $P_1 = P_2$
6. Return $tangent\_u(P_1, Q)$
7. $m \leftarrow \frac{y_{P_2} - y_{P_1}}{x_{P_2} - x_{P_1}}$
8. Return $y_Q - y_{P_1} - mx_Q + mx_{P_1}$

References

[1] Lang, S., *Elliptic Functions*, New York: Springer-Verlag, 1987.

[2] Silverman, J., *The Arithmetic of Elliptic Curves*, New York: Springer-Verlag, 1986.

[3] Galbraith, S., "Supersingular Curves in Cryptography," *Proceedings of Asiacrypt 2001*, Gold Coast, Australia, December 9–13, 2001, pp. 495–513.

[4] Verheul, E., "Evidence That XTR Is More Secure Than Supersingular Elliptic Curve Cryptosystems," *Journal of Cryptology*, Vol. 17, No. 4, 2004, pp. 277–296.

[5] Miller, V., "The Weil Pairing and Its Efficient Calculation," *Journal of Cryptology*, Vol. 17, No. 4, 2004, pp. 235–261.

5

Cryptography and Computational Complexity

The goal of this chapter is to provide a framework for quantifying the security provided by IBE algorithms. As with any method of communicating securely, believing that the security provided by IBE is adequate requires making certain assumptions. On the other hand, *any* method of communicating securely requires some type of assumption, and the assumptions that we make in the case of IBE seem to be fairly reasonable compared to the assumptions required for other ways of communicating securely.

One way to communicate securely is to exchange messages in some secure fashion, perhaps by trusted couriers. This method cannot be defeated by computing power, but can be defeated through other means. If an adversary can intercept a courier carrying a message then they can certainly read it, for example. Or, the courier may decide to give the message to the adversary instead of to the intended recipient. So, an assumption that we need to make to trust such a system is that the couriers are trustworthy and will not be intercepted by an adversary.

A one-time pad offers another way to communicate securely. In this case, we generate a random key that is at least as big as the message that we want to encrypt and then securely distribute the random keys to the users with whom we want to communicate. This can be done in advance of the communication of the actual secure messages, so we can assume that users have their one-time pad handy when the need to communicate securely arises. They can then encrypt their messages using the one-time pad and send the encrypted message over an untrusted channel. In this case we have assumed that the one-time pad is truly random and that it was distributed in a secure fashion. If either of these two assumptions fails, then such a system can easily be defeated.

With symmetric encryption algorithms like Triple-DES or AES, we reduce the number of keys that need to be securely distributed. In this case, we only need to distribute the key that is used in the symmetric algorithm instead of a key that is as long as the messages that we want to encrypt. So in addition to the same assumptions that we make in the case of a one-time pad system, we need to make an additional assumption if we use a symmetric encryption algorithm: that it is infeasible for an adversary to recover the original message from the encrypted message. This can be a significant assumption. There are typically no proofs that decrypting a message that has been encrypted with a symmetric algorithm is difficult, and we need to rely on the judgment of experts who have demonstrated an aptitude for finding weaknesses in symmetric algorithms in the past. If these experts cannot find any weaknesses, then we can assume that the symmetric algorithm is reasonably secure. This is an additional assumption that we need to accept if we are going to trust the security of using a symmetric algorithm. The tools available to an adversary will also determine how well we can trust a system that uses a symmetric algorithm. If an adversary can build a large-scale quantum computer, for example, then they will be able to perform computations that might be infeasible without such a device.

Public-key algorithms allow us to communicate securely with others with whom we have not previously exchanged cryptographic keys, so it reduces the difficulty and expense of managing keys. This increase in convenience and decrease in cost comes with an additional assumption. In the case of traditional public-key algorithms, where we use a digital certificate to manage a user's public key, we need to assume that the TTP who created the certificate is trustworthy. If the TTP makes an error and associates an incorrect name of a user with a public key, we can easily be fooled into encrypting a message with the incorrect key. And since most uses of traditional public-key technologies also archive copies of users' private keys, we also need to trust that the TTP that stores these keys does not provide them to unauthorized users.

In the case of IBE, we have assumptions that are different than those that we make for traditional public-key technologies. Anyone can calculate an IBE private key from a user's identity with the correct IBE public parameters, but we need to assume that users receive the correct set of IBE public parameters. If we can trick a user into using the incorrect public parameters, we can trick them into sending messages that can easily be decrypted. We also need to assume that the IBE PKG is authenticating users appropriately before granting IBE private keys to them. If we can trick the PKG into giving us an IBE private key that is meant for a different user then we will be able to decrypt messages then are encrypted with that user's IBE public key.

In the case of both traditional public-key technologies and IBE, we also make an assumption about the intractability of certain number-theoretical calculations. If these calculations are sufficiently difficult for an adversary to perform, then we can reasonably assume that they cannot perform the calculations, and that our system is reasonably secure. On the other hand, this is also a significant assumption, because it is based on the best-known algorithm for performing certain calculations. If a new algorithm is discovered that can factor large integers efficiently, for example, then the assumptions behind some public-key technologies will need to be reexamined. Similarly, if large-scale quantum computers ever become available, then the assumptions behind many public-key technologies will need to be rethought because the existence of quantum computers will make implementing efficient algorithms for factoring integers [1] and calculating discrete logarithms [1, 2] possible.

5.1 Cryptography

5.1.1 Definitions

The following interrelated definitions define the concepts from cryptography that we will refer to in later sections.

Definition 5.1

A *negligible* function is one that is asymptotically smaller that the reciprocal of any polynomial. More precisely, a function $\epsilon : \mathbb{N} \rightarrow \mathbb{R}$ is negligible if for any $c \in \mathbb{N}$ there is an $n_0 \in \mathbb{N}$ such that we have $\epsilon(n) < 1/n^c$ for all $n > n_0$.

Definition 5.2

A probabilistic algorithm whose running time is polynomial in $\log n$ is said to be *efficient*. The use of $\log n$ instead of n is due to the fact that the parameters and keys that determine the operation of cryptographic functions are traditionally measured in the number of bits comprising a parameter instead of in the size of the parameters themselves.

Definition 5.3

A calculation for which any efficient algorithm succeeds on random input with only negligible probability is said to be *hard*. A calculation that is not hard is *easy*. So a calculation for which there exists an efficient algorithm that succeeds on random input with a nonnegligible probability is easy. A useful encryption algorithm has the property that both encrypting and decrypting data is easy with the right key, but decrypting data without the right key is hard.

Definition 5.4

Plaintext is the information for which encryption provides privacy. An encryption algorithm takes plaintext and a key as inputs and produces ciphertext as an output.

Definition 5.5

Ciphertext is the output of an encryption algorithm.

Definition 5.6

An *encryption* algorithm takes plaintext and a key as inputs and produces ciphertext as an output.

Definition 5.7

A *decryption* algorithm takes ciphertext and a key as inputs and produces plaintext as an output.

Definition 5.8

A cryptographic *key* is a value that defines the operation of an encryption or decryption algorithm. Values that are used for all users of a system are called *parameters* instead. While traditional public-key algorithms have only public and private keys, IBE algorithms typically have a set of public parameters.

Definition 5.9

An *asymmetric* or *public-key* encryption algorithm is an encryption algorithm that uses two related keys: a public key and a private key, which have the property that given the public key it is hard to find the private key.

Definition 5.10

A *randomized* encryption algorithm is one that requires a random number as an input in addition to plaintext and a key.

Definition 5.11

Let H be a hash function with inputs x_1 and x_2 and outputs y_1 and y_2. Then H is a *cryptographic hash function* if it is efficient to compute and has the following three properties. Note that the word "difficult" is intentionally left ambiguous in this context because the security of most commonly used cryptographic hash functions is not based on computational problems for which it is easy to get accurate estimates of running times.

1. *Collision resistance.* It is difficult to find x_1 and x_2 with $x_1 \neq x_2$ and $H(x_1) = H(x_2)$.
2. *Preimage resistance.* Given any y_1 it is difficult to find an x_1 with $y_1 = H(x_1)$.

3. *Second preimage resistance.* Given an x_1 with $y_1 = H(x_1)$ it is difficult to find an x_2 with $x_1 \neq x_2$ and $y_1 = H(x_2)$.

5.1.2 Protection Provided by Encryption

There are six general categories of attacks that the use of encryption can protect against. In each of these cases, an attacker attempts to either determine a key needed to decrypt a message or the plaintext message that was encrypted.

1. *Ciphertext-only attack.* A ciphertext-only attack is carried out by an adversary who has access to only ciphertext. This is the most difficult attack for an adversary to carry out, and any cryptographic system needs to be resistant to such an attack to provide any level of security at all.
2. *Known-plaintext attack.* A known-plaintext attack is carried out by an adversary who has access to both plaintext and corresponding ciphertext. The matching plaintext and ciphertext need not comprise all of an encrypted message. This type of attack is very easy for an adversary to carry out, and protection against known-plaintext attacks is essential for any useful cryptographic system. Almost any type of information that is transmitted electronically has enough structure to guarantee some level of matching plaintext and ciphertext. The structure required by document or spreadsheet file formats can provide this, for example, as can the format of e-mail or other message formats. The structure of data can also provide the basis for a known-plaintext attack. Bytes representing ASCII text have some fixed bits while others can be guessed with a high probability, for example.
3. *Chosen-plaintext attack.* A chosen-plaintext attack is carried out by an adversary who can select the plaintext and then be given the corresponding ciphertext. Such an adversary could use this capability, for example, to create a list of all possible plaintext-ciphertext pairs and then decrypt any other encrypted messages that he observes by looking up the correct plaintext in this table. One way to counter such a capability in an adversary is to include random information with the plaintext that gets encrypted, so that a single plaintext message will typically get encrypted to a different ciphertext each time that it is encrypted.
4. *Adaptive chosen-plaintext attack.* In an adaptive chosen-plaintext attack, an adversary selects an initial plaintext message to encrypt and then selects the next plaintext messages that he encrypts based on the ciphertext that he receives from the previous encryption. He can repeat this process as often as needed to gather more information about the

key being used. Otherwise, this attack has the same properties as a chosen-plaintext attack.

5. *Chosen-ciphertext attack.* In a chosen-ciphertext attack, an adversary selects a ciphertext and is able to obtain the corresponding plaintext. If an algorithm encrypts a particular plaintext to the same ciphertext every time it is encrypted then it is vulnerable to a chosen-ciphertext attack, so many encryption algorithms add a random input to the plaintext to make such an attack infeasible. Portable devices like smartcards may be susceptible to chosen-ciphertext attacks, because they can often be obtained by an adversary. Being secure against chosen-ciphertext attacks is the standard level of security that is currently expected of public-key systems.
6. *Adaptive chosen-ciphertext attack.* In an adaptive chosen-ciphertext attack, an adversary selects an initial ciphertext message to decrypt and then selects the next ciphertext messages that he decrypts based on the plaintext that he receives from the previous decryption.

In the case of IBE, there are additional opportunities for attackers. In particular, when an attacker tries to recover the private key for a particular identity or recover a plaintext encrypted to a particular identity, he may also have the private keys that correspond to other identities. This leads to the following two additional cases that apply only to IBE schemes.

1. *Chosen-identity attack.* In a chosen-identity attack, also called a *selective-identity attack*, an adversary attempting to attack a particular private key or a ciphertext encrypted to a particular identity can choose any other identity and then use the private key for this identity to help him in his attack.
2. *Adaptive chosen-identity attack.* In an adaptive chosen-identity attack, an adversary can carry out a chosen-identity attack, and can then perform additional chosen-identity attacks based on the results of the first attack. He can then repeat this as often as he likes in an attempt to recover an IBE private key, master secret, or plaintext.

Not all encryption schemes protect against all categories of attacks. In particular, the IBE algorithms described in this book are susceptible to chosen-ciphertext attacks, so that an additional step of processing needs to be added past the application of the encryption algorithm to get a system that will resist such attacks. This can be accomplished through using the Fujisaki-Okamoto transform.

5.1.3 The Fujisaki-Okamoto Transform

A technique due to Fujisaki and Okamoto [3] transforms a public-key encryption algorithm with fairly weak properties into one which is secure against chosen-ciphertext attacks. Some public-key algorithms are vulnerable to chosen-ciphertext attacks, and this transformation can be used to create a more secure scheme from a less secure algorithm.

In particular, let $E(P, X, R)$ be a randomized public-key encryption algorithm that encrypts the plaintext X using the random input r and the public key P; let D be the decryption function that corresponds to E; and let H_1 and H_2 be cryptographic hash functions. Then for a plaintext message M, the encryption algorithm E' is resistant to chosen-ciphertext attacks, where

$$E'(P, M, r) = (C_1, C_2) = C$$

where

$$C_1 = E(P, r, H_1(r, M))$$

and

$$C_2 = H_2(r) \oplus M$$

To decrypt a message that is encrypted with this hybrid scheme, the recipient performs the following steps:

1. Calculate $D(C_1) = s$.
2. Calculate $H_2(s) \oplus C_2 = M$.
3. Set $r = H_1(s, M)$ and check that $E(P, s, r) = C_1$. If this is not true, raise an error condition and exit.
4. Output M as the decryption of C.

5.2 Running Times of Useful Algorithms

One goal of the theory of computation is to provide the framework needed to classify computational problems according to the resources needed to solve them. In particular, the resources needed for an adversary to defeat the protection provided by encryption is of interest here, and we will use this framework to justify why certain IBE algorithms are reasonably secure when their parameters are chosen appropriately. The main focus here is the running time required to solve certain computational problems, which is the way that the most widely accepted standard [4] defines cryptographic strength.

While many discussions of the running times of algorithms focus on the size of an input n, in the case of cryptography, a more useful measure is in terms of the number of bits that it takes to represent an input. Thus we are more interested in running times that are expressed in terms of log n instead of in terms of n. So, an algorithm that would often be through of as having running time $O(\sqrt{n})$ is more usefully thought of as having the equivalent running time

$$O\left(e^{\frac{1}{2}\log n}\right)$$

which makes it clearer that while an algorithm with such a running time might be considered relatively fast as a function of n, it might be considered relatively slow as a function of log n.

5.2.1 Finding Collisions for a Hash Function

For most hash functions, finding a collision is easier than finding a preimage or a second preimage, so the strength of a cryptographic hash function is usually measured by the expected number of outputs that need to be computed to make the probability of finding a collision equal to 1/2.

Finding the probability of a collision in a hash function is much like the so-called birthday problem, in which we want to find the probability that two people in a group of k people share the same birthday. In this case, we can think of the birthday as being the output of a hash function that maps people to the day on which they were born. To find this probability, it is easier to find the probability that all k people have different birthdays. This is given by

$$\begin{aligned} p &= \frac{364}{365}\frac{363}{365}\cdots\frac{365-k+1}{365} \\ &= \prod_{i=1}^{k-1}\left(\frac{365-i}{365}\right) \end{aligned}$$

So we want the largest k for which $p < 1/2$, or

$$\prod_{i=1}^{k-1}\left(\frac{365-i}{365}\right) < \frac{1}{2}$$

Now we have

$$\prod_{i=1}^{k-1}\left(\frac{365-i}{365}\right) < \left(\frac{1}{k-1}\sum_{i=1}^{k-1}\left(\frac{365-i}{365}\right)\right)^{k-1} \tag{5.1}$$

$$= \left(\frac{1}{k-1}(k-1)365)\sum_{i=1}^{k-1} i\right)^{k-1}$$

$$= \left(\frac{1}{k-1}(k-1)365)\left(\frac{k(k-1)}{2}\right)\right)^{k-1}$$

$$= \left(1-\frac{k}{2\cdot 365}\right)^{k-1} < \left(e^{-\frac{k}{2\cdot 365}}\right)^{k-1} \tag{5.2}$$

$$= e^{-\frac{k^2-k}{2\cdot 365}} \tag{5.3}$$

where the inequality in (5.1) follows from the properties of the arithmetic-geometric mean, and the inequality in (5.2) follows from the property that $1 - x < e^{-x}$. Solving for k in

$$e^{-\frac{k^2-k}{2\cdot 365}} = \frac{1}{2} \tag{5.4}$$

we get that $k \approx 23$, which is the familiar solution to this problem.

We can further simplify (5.3) by noting that for large values of k we have that

$$e^{-\frac{k^2-k}{2\cdot 365}} \approx e^{-\frac{k^2}{2\cdot 365}} \tag{5.5}$$

We can easily generalize (5.5) to any hash function that takes an input that is one of n elements to estimate that we get a probability of 1/2 a collision when

$$e^{-\frac{k^2}{2n}} = \frac{1}{2}$$

or that

$$k = \sqrt{2\log 2}\sqrt{n} \approx 1.17741\sqrt{n} \tag{5.6}$$

The constant in (5.6) is often ignored to give $k \approx \sqrt{n}$, so that we expect to have a collision after calculating approximately $\sqrt{n}$ hashes. For a cryptographic hash function that creates an output of n bits, or 2^n possible outputs, this will require the calculation and comparison of approximately $2^{n/2}$ hashes, so that we think of such a hash function as providing $n/2$ bits of cryptographic strength because finding a collision takes approximately the same level of effort as testing all $2^{n/2}$ possible keys of length $n/2$ bits. The SHA-512 algorithm, a cryptographic hash algorithm that produces a 512-bit output is considered to provide 256 bits of cryptographic strength, for example. On the other hand, collisions are typically not as useful to an adversary as preimages or second preimages are, so defining the strength of a cryptographic hash function by its collision resistance may not be the most useful metric in some cases.

5.2.2 Pollard's Rho Algorithm

Pollard's rho algorithm [5] is an application of Floyd's cycle-finding algorithm [6] for calculating discrete logarithms in a cyclic group of order n, and is currently the best-known algorithm for calculating discrete logarithms in elliptic curve groups. Its name comes from the fact that the shape of the Greek letter ρ is reminiscent of a random walk through a sequence of group elements that eventually hits a cycle, after which the sequence will repeat; the tail of the ρ represents the random walk before a cycle is found and the loop of the ρ represents the resulting cycle. This algorithm creates two approximately random sequences of group elements $\{x_i\}$ and $\{x_{2i}\}$ and looks for two group elements where $x_i = x_{2i}$, and finding such a collision provides a way to calculate a discrete logarithm. Because it needs to find a collision in an approximately random sequence, its expected running time is $O(\sqrt{n})$, which is exponential in log n. Thus a cryptanalytic attack based on calculating a discrete logarithm with this algorithm is hard, and is reasonably difficult for an attacker to carry out.

Suppose that we want to use Pollard's rho algorithm to calculate the discrete logarithm $x = \log_\alpha \beta$ where α is a generator of a cyclic group G of prime order n and β is an arbitrary element of G. To implement this algorithm we partition G into three sets S_1, S_2, and S_3 of roughly equal size with $1 \neq S_2$. If the group G is $\mathbb{Z}_n$, for example, we might pick $S_1 = \{x : x \equiv 0 (\text{mod } n)\}$, $S_2 = \{x : x \equiv 2 (\text{mod } n)\}$, and $S_3 = \{x : x \equiv 1 (\text{mod } n)\}$. We then create a sequence of group elements $\{x_i\}$ where $x_0 = 1$ and for $i > 0$ we have

$$x_{i+1} = \begin{cases} \beta \cdot x_i, \text{ if } x_i \in S_1 \\ x_i^2, \text{ if } x_i \in S_2 \\ \alpha \cdot x_i, \text{ if } x_i \in S_3 \end{cases}$$

We can think of the sequence $\{x_i\}$ as defining two sequences $\{a_i\}$ and $\{b_i\}$ where $x_i = \alpha^{a_i}\beta^{b_i}$ where

$$a_{i+1} = \begin{cases} a_i, \text{ if } x_i \in S_1 \\ 2a_i \bmod n, \text{ if } x_i \in S_2 \\ a_i + 1 \bmod n, \text{ if } x_i \in S_3 \end{cases}$$

and

$$b_{i+1} = \begin{cases} b_i + 1 \bmod n, \text{ if } x_i \in S_1 \\ 2b_i \bmod n, \text{ if } x_i \in S_2 \\ b_i, \text{ if } x_i \in S_3 \end{cases}$$

Then if we find x_i and x_{2i} with $x_i = x_{2i}$ then we have found a case where

$$\alpha^{a_i}\beta^{b_i} = \alpha^{a_{2i}}\beta^{b_{2i}}$$

or that

$$\beta^{b_i - b_{2i}} = \alpha^{a_{2i} - a_i} \tag{5.7}$$

Taking the logarithm of (5.7) to the base α we get that

$$(b_i - b_{2i}) \log_\alpha \beta \equiv (a_{2i} - a_i) \pmod{n}$$

or

$$\log_\alpha \beta = \frac{a_{2i} - a_i}{b_i - b_{2i}} \pmod{n}$$

There are a few cases where this algorithm will fail, like when $b_i \equiv b_{2i} \pmod{n}$, which happen with a very small probability. If this happens, it is possible to repeat the algorithm with a different starting value until the failure is avoided, using an initial state of $x_0 = \alpha^{a_0}\beta^{b_0}$ where a_0 and b_0 are random elements of G.

5.2.3 The General Number Field Sieve

The general number field sieve (GNFS) [7] is currently the best-known algorithm for factoring large integers. The GNFS is one a family of factoring algorithms that are based on the "difference of squares" technique, which uses the observation that if we have

$$(x - y)(x + y) \equiv 0(\text{mod } n)$$

or

$$x^2 \equiv y^2(\text{mod } n)$$

then $\gcd(x - y, n)$ and $\gcd(x + y, n)$ are factors of n, although they may be either 1 or n. If n is the product of two primes p and q, then Table 5.1 lists the possible cases that may occur. Most, but not all, of these cases result in either $\gcd(x - y, n)$ or $\gcd(x + y, n)$ giving a nontrivial factor of n.

The GNFS extends Dixon's algorithm [8] to number fields, extensions of the field of rational numbers, and picks parameters cleverly to get improved performance. The first step in Dixon's algorithm is to fix a set of factors $F = \{p_1, p_2, \ldots, p_m\}$ and to randomly generate integers r_i such that r_i^2 is F-smooth. So we can think of such integers r_i as vectors $(e_{i,1}, e_{i,2}, \ldots, e_{i,m})$, the components of which indicate the powers of the elements of F in the factorization of r_i, so that

$$r_i = \prod_{j=1}^{m} p_j^{e_{i,j}}$$

Once we find a suitable r_i we calculate a corresponding vector v_i that represents the parity of each of the exponents of the primes in the factorization of r_i, so that $v_{i,j} = e_{i,j} \bmod 2$. If we can find $m + 1$ such vectors v_i then we

Table 5.1
Possible Cases for $x^2 \equiv y^2 \pmod{n}$

$p \mid (x+y)$	$p \mid (x-y)$	$q \mid (x+y)$	$q \mid (x-y)$	$\gcd(x+y, n)$	$\gcd(x-y, n)$
Yes	Yes	Yes	Yes	n	n
Yes	Yes	Yes	No	n	p
Yes	Yes	No	Yes	p	n
Yes	No	Yes	Yes	n	q
Yes	No	Yes	Yes	n	1
Yes	No	No	Yes	p	q
No	Yes	Yes	Yes	q	n
No	Yes	Yes	No	q	p
No	Yes	No	Yes	1	n

have $m + 1$ vectors, each of dimension m, so they must be linearly dependent. Thus there is a nonempty subset $U \subseteq \{1, 2, \ldots, t + 1\}$ so that

$$\sum_{i \in U} v_i \equiv 0 (\text{mod } 2)$$

Thus the parity of each of the exponents in

$$\prod_{i \in U} r_i^2$$

is even, so that if we write

$$x = \prod_{i \in U} r_i$$

and

$$y = \prod_{i=1}^{m} p_i^{e_i}$$

then we have that

$$x^2 = \prod_{i \in U} r_i^2 \equiv y^2 \ (\text{mod } n)$$

Once we have found suitable x and y in this way, we then calculate $\gcd(x - y, n)$ or $\gcd(x + y, n)$, hoping to get a nontrivial factor of n. If we get either 1 or n for both of these results, we start over and calculate new random values for r_i.

The GNFS increases the performance of this technique through a clever selection of parameters and by generalizing the set of factors, but the algorithm still has steps that are similar to the steps described earlier: pick a set of random values that are smooth relative to some set, after enough such values are generated, solve a system of equations to find a dependency that can be manipulated to get a difference of squares, and then calculate a greatest common divisor to get a nontrivial factor.

The GNFS has an expected running time of

$$O(\exp((64/9)^{1/3} (\log n)^{1/3} (\log \log n)^{2/3}))$$

Thus a cryptanalytic attack based on using the GNFS is reasonably difficult for an attacker to carry out.

5.2.4 The Index Calculus Algorithm

The index calculus algorithm is currently the best-known algorithm for calculating discrete logarithms in the multiplicative group of a finite field. It uses ideas that are very similar to those used in the GNFS, and can be traced back to the work of Kraitchik in 1922 [9]. In particular, let g be a primitive element of $\mathbb{F}_p^*$ and $F = \{p_1, p_2, \ldots, p_m\}$ be a set of primes. We then pick random $z \in \mathbb{Z}_p^*$ and calculate g^z. If g^z is F-smooth then we can we can write

$$g^z = \prod_{i=1}^{m} p_i^{\alpha_i}$$

or that

$$z = \sum_{i=1}^{m} \alpha_i \cdot \log_g p_i$$

where we know the value of z and all of the values of α_i. We continue this process until we find $m + 1$ such values of z for which g^z is F-smooth. Once we have $m + 1$ such values, we solve the resulting system of equations to find a unique solution for $\log_g p_i$. This will then let us find the discrete logarithm of any $y \in \mathbb{F}_p^*$. To do this we again generate random values of z until we find a value of z such that $y \cdot g^z$ is F-smooth. Using this value of z we find that

$$\log_g y \equiv -z + \sum_{i=1}^{m} \alpha_i \cdot \log_g p_i \tag{5.8}$$

We know all of the values appearing on the right-hand side of (5.8), so that we can thus calculate any such discrete logarithm. The index calculus algorithm has an expected running time of

$$O(\exp((64/9)^{1/3} (\log n)^{1/3} (\log \log n)^{2/3}))$$

where $n = p - 1$ is the order of the group $\mathbb{Z}_p^*$. Thus a cryptanalytic attack based on using the index calculus algorithm is reasonably difficult for an attacker to carry out. Although this discussion is specific to calculating discrete logarithms in $\mathbb{F}_p^*$, it is also possible to extend this technique to $\mathbb{F}_{p^n}^*$ [10].

5.2.5 Relative Strength of Algorithms

The traditional metric for comparing the relative strength of cryptographic algorithms is an ideal symmetric algorithm for which there is no way that an attacker can recover a secret key of n bits that is easier than trying all 2^n possible n-bit keys to find the one that produces a known plaintext-ciphertext pair. Equating the running time of this computation to the time required by either Pollard's rho algorithm, the GNFS, or the index calculus algorithm, we can get an estimate for the bit strength or "computational entropy" of public-key algorithms. There have been many attempts [4, 11–13] at creating such estimates, all of which have produced slightly different results, but the estimates of [4] have been used in the most important cryptographic standards [14, 15]. These estimates seem to assume that an adversary will create a special-purpose machine to perform the calculations instead of using widely available computing resources like commodity desktop computers, so that practical difficulties, like the storage space required to solve the very large system of equations that the GNFS and index calculus algorithms require, are not considered.

The estimates provided by this approach are summarized in Table 5.2. So, according to this approach, calculating a discrete logarithm in a group with a size of 256 bits by Pollard's rho algorithm takes roughly the same time as trying all possible 128-bit symmetric keys, which also takes roughly the same time as factoring a 3,072-bit integer or calculating a discrete logarithm in a finite field which has a size of 3,072 bits.

In 1998, the Electronic Frontier Foundation sponsored the construction of the DES Cracker [16], a special-purpose computer that used massively parallel computation on 36,864 custom processing units to test over 92 billion DES keys per second, which let it test all possible 56-bit DES keys in about 9 days. If we could build a machine that can test keys 1 million times faster than this, perhaps through a combination of more processing units and faster clock speeds, we would find that it will take over 117 trillion years to test all 2^{128} possible 128-bit keys. Table 5.3 lists various events in the future [17] and how many bits out of the 128 possible bits will have been tested as the events take place. This seems to indicate that 128 bits of strength is probably adequate for the foreseeable future.

Table 5.2
Equivalent Cryptographic Strength Provided by Different Algorithms [4]

Bit Strength	Size of Group	Size of Integer or Finite Field
80	160	1,024
112	224	2,048
128	256	3,072
192	384	7,168
256	512	15,360

Table 5.3
Progress Towards Testing All 128-Bit Keys on Hypothetical Machine

Event	Years in the Future	Bits of Key Tested
Earth's continents collide	250 million	110
Milky Way collides with the Andromeda galaxy	3 billion	114
Sun becomes a white dwarf	8 billion	115

Fundamental limits on computation tell us that a 256-bit key is even more secure, because computation is not just logical, but also physical. Consider an AND gate: two bits go in but only one bit comes out. If we represent each bit by only a single electron, we can have two electrons entering the gate but only one leaving. The energy carried by this extra electron has to go somewhere, so we see that erasing a bit actually requires energy. This is summarized in Landauer's principle [18], a corollary of the second law of thermodynamics that tells us that erasing a bit costs at least $kT \log 2$ in energy, where $k = 1.38 \times 10^{-23} m^2 kg/s^2 K$ is Boltzmann's constant and T is the temperature at which the operation takes place. Existing technologies are far from being limited by Landauer's principle, but it is a fundamental limit to computation that we cannot overcome if we need to erase bits to perform calculations, like all modern computers do.

On the other hand, if we want to build a bigger and faster computer much like the DES Cracker, but one that tries all possible 256-bit AES keys, we find that Landauer's principle actually limits us, and that there is actually not enough energy in the visible universe to try all of these keys. So although 256 is a fairly small number, the number of possible 256-bit keys is a huge number, and this number is so large that we can never hope to try them all—fundamental limits on computation tell us that we can never do it, at least not with technology which requires bits to be erased when it operates.

5.3 Useful Computational Problems

Some computational problems have the property that they are suitably hard, yet can be stated in terms of quantities that can be used to create public-key algorithms that get their cryptographic strength from the difficulty of the hard problem. In particular, computational problems whose best-known solution is calculated by Pollard's rho algorithm, the GNFS, or the index calculus algorithm are suitably difficult. The Diffie-Hellman key exchange [19], the first practical public-key algorithm, provides the motivation for many of the computational problems.

In the Diffie-Hellman key exchange, we have a cyclic group G of prime order p with generator g. The private key of a user is an element $\alpha \in \mathbb{Z}_p^*$ and the corresponding public key is g^α. Suppose that we have two users, Alice and Bob, who want to agree upon a shared secret, and that Alice's private key is a and Bob's private key is b, so that Alice's public key is g^a and Bob's public key is g^b. Alice can obtain Bob's public key g^b and then calculate $(g^b)^a = g^{ba} = g^{ab}$ from it, while Bob can obtain Alice's public key g^a and then calculate $(g^a)^b = g^{ab}$ from it. By doing this, they both end up with the common value g^{ab} which they can then use as a shared secret. The values g, g^a, and g^b are public, but without the private values a and b, it is believed to be hard for an adversary to calculate g^{ab}. In the discussion below, this general framework is used to describe problems related to the Diffie-Hellman key exchange. So that g will represent a generator of a multiplicative cyclic group, and a, b, and c are elements of $\mathbb{Z}_p^*$. In cases where the group is an additive group, P will represent a generator of the group. Where a pairing is needed, we will assume that we have $e : G_1 \times G_1 \to G_T$. Cases where $e : G_1 \times G_2 \to G_T$ can be similarly described.

In many cases there are two related problems: a *computational* problem and a *decision* problem. Solving a computational problem is roughly equivalent to calculating a correct answer, and if the relevant computational problem is hard then calculating a correct answer is hard. In some cases, this may not be good enough. In particular, we also want it to be difficult to guess a correct answer or to determine part of the correct answer. If the relevant decision problem is hard then guessing a correct answer or determining part of the correct answer is also hard.

5.3.1 The Computational Diffie-Hellman Problem

The computational Diffie-Hellman problem (CDHP) [20] models the situation in a Diffie-Hellman key exchange: given g, .g^a and g^b, calculate g^{ab}. Multiplicative notation is used because the multiplicative group of a finite field is the usual setting for implementing the Diffie-Hellman key exchange. The CDHP can also be written in additive notation as: given P, aP, bP, calculate abP.

One obvious way to solve this problem is to determine b by calculating the discrete logarithm of g^b and then to use that value of b along with g^a to calculate $(g^a)^b = g^{ab}$, so that solving the CDHP is no more difficult than calculating discrete logarithms. On the other hand, there is no guarantee that an adversary cannot determine *some* information about the shared secret from g, g^a and g^b, perhaps being able to determine several of the bits of g^{ab} but not all of them. To avoid such a possibility, another problem needs to be hard: the decision Diffie-Hellman problem.

5.3.2 The Decision Diffie-Hellman Problem

The decision Diffie-Hellman problem (DDHP) [21] is: given g, g^a, g^b, and x, determine whether or not $x = g^{ab}$. One obvious way to solve this problem is to determine b solving the CDHP and then to calculate $(g^a)^b = g^{ab}$, and to then compare this value of g^{ab} to the given value of x. Thus solving the DDHP is no more difficult than the CDHP. If the DDHP is hard then it is hard to distinguish between g^{ab} and any other element of G, so that g^{ab} looks like a random element of G.

In some cases, the DDHP is much easier, particularly when a pairing is available. If we have a pairing, then we can then calculate $e(g^a, g^b) = e(g, g)^{ab}$. If $x = g^{ab}$ then we will also have that $e(g, x) = e(g, g^{ab}) = e(g, g)^{ab}$, so that we can easily solve the DDHP problem by comparing $e(g^a, g^b)$ to $e(g, x)$.

Being able to calculate Legendre symbols in $\mathbb{F}_p^*$ also makes solving the DDHP easy in $\mathbb{F}_p^*$. The value g^{ab} will be a square modulo p exactly when the product $a \cdot b$ is even, which happens when either a or b is even, which will happen with probability 3/4 for random a and b. On the other hand, for a random c, c is a square with probability 1/2. So the probability of (g^{ab}/p) and (c/p) being different is

$$\Pr((g^{ab}/p) = +1 \wedge (c/p) = -1) + \Pr((g^{ab}/p) = -1 \wedge (c/p) = +1)$$
$$= (3/4)(1/2) + (1/4)(1/2) = 1/2$$

So comparing the Legendre symbols (g^{ab}/p) and (c/p) has a 1/4 probability of distinguishing between g^{ab} and a random c, which is a nonnegligible probability of success, and so the DDHP is easy in $\mathbb{F}_p^*$ if p is a prime, where we can calculate Legendre symbols. Although the DDHP is easy in $\mathbb{F}_p^*$, it is conjectured to be difficult in $\mathbb{F}_{p^n}^*$. for $n > 1$.

Groups in which the DDHP is easy and the CDHP is believed to be hard are sometimes called *gap Diffie-Hellman groups.* Figure 5.1 shows the relationships between the various Diffie-Hellman problems, where the notation "Problem 1 → Problem 2" indicates that a solution to Problem 1 makes finding a solution to Problem 2 easy.

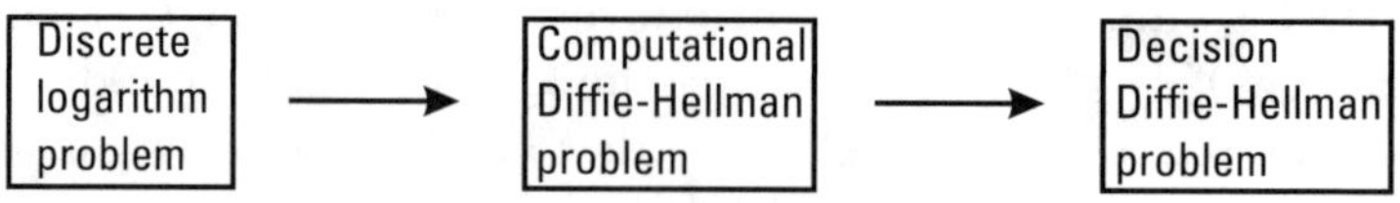

Figure 5.1 Relationship between the various Diffie-Hellman problems.

5.3.3 The Bilinear Diffie-Hellman Problem

The bilinear Diffie-Hellman problem (BDHP) [22] generalizes the CDHP to groups with a pairing. The BDHP is: given P, aP, bP, cP, calculate $e(P, P)^{abc}$. Additive notation is used because the setting for the BDHP is typically an elliptic curve group, where additive notation is traditional. The BDHP can also be written in multiplicative notation as: given g, g^a, g^b, g^c, calculate $e(g, g)^{abc}$.

Solving the BDHP is no more difficult than calculating discrete logarithms in either G_1 or G_T.If we can find the value of c by calculating the discrete logarithm of cP in G_1, then we can calculate $e(aP, bP)^c = (e(P, P)^{ab})^c = e(P, P)^{abc}$ or, if we can find the value of c by calculating the discrete logarithm of $e(P, cP) = e(P, P)^c$ in G_2 then we also calculate $e(P, P)^{abc}$ in a similar way.

Note that $f_P : G_1 \rightarrow G_T$ defined by $f_P(Q) = e(P, Q)$ is an isomorphism of groups. If f_P is easy to invert, that is we can easily calculate $f_P^{-1}(e(P, Q)) = Q$ then the BDHP is also easy. We can first calculate $g = e(aP, bP) = e(P, abP)$, and then $f_P^{-1}(g) = abP$, and finally $e(abP, cP) = e(P, P)^{abc}$, solving the BDHP.

On the other hand, if f_P is easy to invert, we can also easily solve the DDHP in G_T. Suppose that we have g, g^a, g^b, and x, in G_T. If $f_P^{-1}(g) = Q$ then we have $f_P^{-1}(g^a) = aQ$ and $f_P^{-1}(g^b) = bQ$. Suppose that $f_P^{-1}(x) = X$. If $x = g^{ab}$ then we will have $f_P^{-1}(x) = abQ$, so that $e(Q, X) = e(Q, abQ) = e(Q, Q)^{ab}$ while $e(aQ, bQ) = e(Q, Q)^{ab}$, so that if $e(Q, X) = e(aQ, bQ)$ then $x = g^{ab}$.

Even if it is hard for an adversary to calculate $e(P, P)^{abc}$ from P, aP, bP, and cP, here is no guarantee that an adversary cannot determine *some* information about $e(P, P)^{abc}$ from P, aP, bP, and cP, perhaps being able to determine several of the bits of $e(P, P)^{abc}$ but not all of them. To avoid such a possibility, another problem needs to be hard: the decision bilinear Diffie-Hellman problem.

5.3.4 The Decision Bilinear Diffie-Hellman Problem

The decision bilinear Diffie-Hellman problem (DBDHP) [22] generalizes the DDHP. The DBDHP is: given P, aP, bP, cP, and x, determine whether or not $x = e(P, P)^{abc}$. Solving the DBDHP is no more difficult that calculating discrete logarithms in either G_1 or G_T. If we can find the value of c by calculating the discrete logarithm of cP in G_1, then we can calculate

$$e(aP, bP)^c = (e(P, P)^{ab})^c = e(P, P)^{abc}$$

or, if we can find the value of c by calculating the discrete logarithm of $e(P, cP) = e(P, P)^c$ in G_T then we also calculate $e(P, P)^{abc}$ in a similar way. If the DBDHP is hard then it is hard to distinguish between $e(P, P)^{abc}$ and any other element of G_T, so that $e(P, P)^{abc}$ looks like a random element of G_T. Figure 5.2 shows the relationship between the various Diffie-Hellman problems and their bilinear variants, where the notation "Problem 1 → Problem 2" indicates that a solution to Problem 1 makes finding a solution to Problem 2 easy.

5.3.5 *q*-Bilinear Diffie-Hellman Inversion

The q-bilinear Diffie-Hellman inversion problem (q-BDHIP) [23] is: given P, aP, a^2P, . . . , a^qP, calculate $e(P, P)^{1/a}$. Solving the q-BDHIP is no more difficult than calculating discrete logarithms in either G_1 or G_2. If we can find the value of a by calculating the discrete logarithm of aP in G_1, then we can calculate $1/a$ and then calculate $e(P, P)^{1/a}$. Or if we can find the value of a by calculating the discrete logarithm of $e(P, aP) = e(P, P)^a$ in G_T then we also calculate $e(P, P)^{1/a}$ in a similar way.

Even if it is hard for an adversary to calculate $e(P, P)^{1/a}$ from P, aP, a^2P, . . . , a^qP cP, here is no guarantee that an adversary cannot determine *some* information about $e(P, P)^{1/a}$ from P, aP, a^2P, . . . , a^qP cP, perhaps being able to determine several of the bits of $e(P, P)^{1/a}$ but not all of them. To avoid such a possibility, another problem needs to be hard: the q-decision bilinear Diffie-Hellman inversion problem.

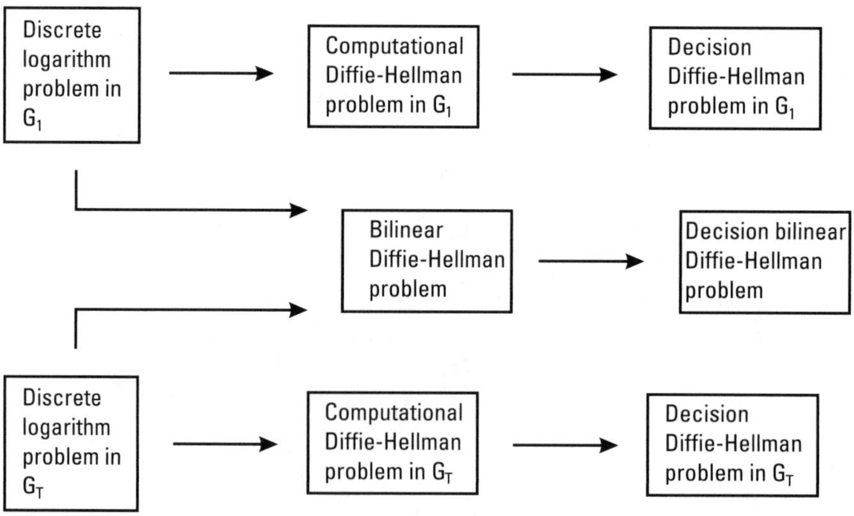

Figure 5.2 Relationship between the various Diffie-Hellman problems and their bilinear variants.

5.3.6 q-Decision Bilinear Diffie-Hellman Inversion

The q-decision bilinear Diffie-Hellman inversion problem (q-DBDHIP) is: given $P, aP, a^2P, \ldots, a^qP$ and x, decide whether or not $x = e(P, P)^{1/a}$. Solving the q-DBDHIP is no more difficult than the q-BDHP. If we can calculate $e(P, P)^{1/a}$ from $P, aP, a^2P, \ldots, a^qP$ we do so and compare it to x. If the q-DBDHP is hard then it is hard to distinguish between $e(P, P)^{1/a}$ and any other element of G_T, so that $e(P, P)^{1/a}$ looks like a random element of G_T.

5.3.7 Cobilinear Diffie-Hellman Problems

In the case where we have a pairing $e : G_1 \times G_2 \rightarrow G_T$ with $G_1 \neq G_2$, it is necessary to modify the framework of all of the problems that use a pairing. This gives the cobilinear Diffie-Hellman problem (co-BDHP), which is: given $P, aP, bP \in G_1$ and $Q \in G_2$, calculate $e(P, Q)^{ab}$. The other problems involving a pairing $e : G_1 \times G_2 \rightarrow G_T$ can be generalized to related coproblems in a similar way.

It is no more difficult to solve the co-BDHP than it is to calculate discrete logarithms in either G_T or in G_1, which is the same bound that occurs with the BDHP. The more general framework of the cobilinear Diffie-Hellman problems is more useful for describing general results, and some research publications use the term "BDHP" to describe what we call the "co-BDHP" to keep the familiar terminology in the more general setting. In the following we will often state simpler results in terms of the BDHP that can easily be generalized to the co-BDHP.

5.3.8 Integer Factorization

If n is a composite integer with prime factorization $n = \prod_{i=1}^{k} p_i^{\alpha_i}$ then the integer factorization problem is to determine one of the factors of n. If we can do this, we can divide n by this factor and repeat the process until we find all of the factors of n. For a given integer m, determining whether or not n has a factor less than m for some integer m is probably the most relevant related decision problem. The problem of determining whether or not n is composite can be efficiently determined by the AKS primality test [24].

5.3.9 Quadratic Residuosity

If n is a composite integer, then the quadratic residuosity problem is: given x modulo n, determine whether or not x is a quadratic residue modulo n. The quadratic residuosity problem has been studied for many years, dating at least to 1801, when Gauss discussed the problem in his *Disquisitiones Arithmeticae*

[25], and it is believed to be as difficult as integer factorization. Suppose that we can factor n into the product of two distinct odd primes p and q. In this case, x is a quadratic residue modulo n exactly when it is a square modulo p and a square modulo q. This can be generalized to integers with more general factorizations, so that solving the quadratic residuosity problem is no more difficult that integer factorization.

5.4 Selecting Parameter Sizes

5.4.1 Security Based on Integer Factorization and Quadratic Residuosity

If the difficulty of attacking a cryptographic algorithm is based on the difficulty of either the integer factorization problem or the quadratic residuosity problem, then we assume that an adversary attacking such systems will need to factor a large composite integer to defeat the protection provided by such algorithms. Table 5.2 gives the sizes of the composite integer that needs to be factored to attain standard levels of security against such an attack.

Example 5.1

(i) Suppose that we want a composite modulus for which solving the integer factorization problem is as difficult as attacking a 128-bit symmetric key. A 3,072-bit composite integer will accomplish this.

(ii) Suppose that we want a composite modulus for which solving the quadratic residuosity problem is as difficult as attacking an 80-bit symmetric key. A 1,024-bit composite integer will accomplish this.

5.4.2 Security Based on Discrete Logarithms

If the difficulty of attacking a cryptographic algorithm is based on the difficulty of any of the Diffie-Hellman problems, then we assume that an adversary attacking such systems will need to calculate a discrete logarithm to defeat the protection provided by such algorithms. There may be more than one way to calculate such discrete logarithms, and the parameters of a system using such algorithms need to reflect this. Suppose that calculations are done in a group $G = \langle g \rangle$.

An adversary can always use Pollard's rho algorithm to calculate the necessary discrete logarithms, so to be sufficiently secure, all calculations should be done in a group in which all subgroups are at least as big as the sizes shown in Table 5.2. Using a subgroup of prime order is an easy way to accomplish this. If calculations are done in a subgroup of the multiplicative group of a finite field, then the index calculus algorithm can also be used to calculate discrete logarithms, so if this is the case, then the size of the finite field also needs to be at least as big as the sizes shown in Table 5.2.

Finally, if the adversary can calculate a pairing $e : G \times G \to \mathbb{F}_{q^k}^*$, he can also use the MOV reduction to map calculating discrete logarithms in G to calculating discrete logarithms in the group generated by $e(g, g)$, so similar concerns about the subgroup size and finite field size need to also be addressed in $\langle e(g, g)\rangle \subseteq \mathbb{F}_{q^k}^*$. Table 5.2 gives the sizes of the subgroups and finite fields that need to be used to attain standard levels of security against such attacks.

Example 5.2

(i) Suppose that we want an elliptic curve group in which solving the CDHP is as difficult as attacking an 80-bit symmetric key. In an elliptic curve group in which calculating a pairing is infeasible, requiring a 160-bit order of a group makes calculating discrete logarithms as difficult as attacking an 80-bit symmetric key and will accomplish this.

(ii) Suppose that we want a subgroup G of $\mathbb{F}_p^*$ in which solving the CDHP is as difficult as attacking an 80-bit symmetric key. If p is a prime and G is of prime order, then requiring the order of G be at least 160 bits and that p has at least 1,024 bits will makes calculating discrete logarithms as difficult as attacking an 80-bit symmetric key and will accomplish this.

(iii) Suppose that we want groups $G_1 \subseteq E(\mathbb{F}_q)$ for some elliptic curve $E/\mathbb{F}_q$, $G_T \subseteq \mathbb{F}_{q^k}^*$ and a pairing $e : G_1 \times G_1 \to G_T$, and want solving the BDHP to be as difficult as attacking an 80-bit symmetric key. Requiring G_1 to be of prime order of at least 160 bits and having that q^k has at least 1,024 bits will make calculating discrete logarithms in both G_1 and G_T as difficult as attacking an 80-bit symmetric key and will accomplish this.

5.5 Important Special Cases

The estimates of the difficulty in factoring an integer or in calculating a discrete logarithm assume that there is no additional structure that can be used to make the calculation even faster. This is not true in a few cases, and in these cases it is possible to either factor an integer or calculate a discrete logarithm much faster than in the average case. There are three particular cases that apply to calculating discrete logarithms in an elliptic curve group and additional cases that apply to factoring integers.

5.5.1 Anomalous Curves

Anomalous curves are elliptic curves for which $\#E(\mathbb{F}_p) = p$. The description of the algorithm used to efficiently calculate discrete logarithms on anomalous curves is beyond the scope of this book. Details are given in [26, 27]. This algorithm runs in linear time, making such curves unsuitable for use in most cryptographic applications.

5.5.2 Supersingular Elliptic Curves

Supersingular elliptic curves, as well as any other elliptic curves with a low embedding degree, are susceptible to an MOV reduction [28], in which it is possible to reduce the problem of calculating a discrete logarithm in an elliptic curve group to calculating the discrete logarithm in a finite field. This can be done as follows. Let G_1 be an elliptic curve group, G_T be a multiplicative group of a finite field, and $e : G_1 \times G_1 \rightarrow G_T$ a pairing. Suppose that we have $P \in G_1$ and want to calculate the discrete logarithm of aP. If $e(P, P) = g$ then $e(P, aP) = e(P, P)^a = g^a$, so by calculating the discrete logarithm of $g^a \in G_T$ we find the value of a. If G_1 is an elliptic curve group with an order of n bits, for example, calculating a discrete logarithm in G_1 by Pollard's rho algorithm requires $O(\sqrt{n})$ time, while calculating a discrete logarithm in G_T using the index calculus algorithm requires

$$O(\exp((64/9)^{1/3} (\log n)^{1/3} (\log \log n)^{2/3}))$$

time, which may be much less than the time to calculate a discrete logarithm in G_1.

To get 80 bits of strength with ordinary elliptic curve, a subgroup G of $E(\mathbb{F}_q)$ with an order of 160 bits is adequate. This is based on the running time of Pollard's rho algorithm, which is roughly the same for a 160-bit group order, which is also roughly the same as the running time for the index calculus algorithm for a 1,024-bit finite field order. If we have that $E/\mathbb{F}_q$ is supersingular with an embedding degree of $k = 2$, for example, then we can also calculate a discrete logarithm in G by calculating a discrete logarithm in $\mathbb{F}_{q^2}^*$ by using the index calculus algorithm. In typical applications, the size of q is roughly the same size as $\#E(\mathbb{F}_q)$, being no more than one or two bits larger, so we might have a 162-bit q in this case. With such a q we could use the MOV reduction to calculate discrete logarithms in G by calculating discrete logarithms in a finite field with an order of only $2 \times 162 = 324$ bits, a calculation that is much easier than calculating a discrete logarithm in a finite field with an order of 1,024 bits. It is, however, possible to attain the same levels of bit security with supersingular curves as with ordinary curves by using larger group orders. Increasing the size of this q to be 512 bits, for example, will increase q^2 to approximately

1,024 bits, making calculating discrete logarithms in $\mathbb{F}_{q^k}^*$ as difficult as attacking an 80-bit symmetric key.

Note that there is nothing about supersingular curves aside from their low embedding degree that allows the MOV reduction to be carried out; even an ordinary curve with a low embedding degree is vulnerable to the MOV reduction. Because the calculation of parings requires a curve with low embedding degree to make the pairing calculation feasible, all such curves need to have their parameters chosen so that they are secure even if an MOV reduction is possible.

5.5.3 Singular Elliptic Curves

Singular elliptic curves have discriminant $\Delta = 0$. Let $E/\mathbb{F}_q$ be a singular elliptic curve with singular point P. Then discrete logarithms in $E(\mathbb{F}_q)\backslash\{P\}$ can be calculated as discrete logarithms in a finite field as follows [29]:

1. If P is a node, then discrete logarithms in $E(\mathbb{F}_q)\backslash\{P\}$ can be calculated as discrete logarithms in either $\mathbb{F}_q^*$ or $\mathbb{F}_{q^2}^*$, depending on the structure of the elliptic curve.
2. If P is a cusp, then discrete logarithms in $E(\mathbb{F}_q)\backslash\{P\}$ can be reduced to discrete logarithms in $\mathbb{F}_q^+$, the additive group of the finite field $\mathbb{F}_q$.

Much like in the case of supersingular elliptic curves, it is possible to increase the size of the group to compensate for the reduced security that singular curves with a node have. On the other hand, the case with a singular curve with a cusp makes it easy to calculate discrete logarithms in $E(\mathbb{F}_q)\backslash\{P\}$, making them essentially useless for cryptographic applications. Because the structure of the group of points on a singular elliptic curve behaves more like a finite field than an elliptic curve group, the definition of an elliptic curve sometimes explicitly excludes singular curves.

5.5.4 Weak Primes

There are also cases where integer factorization is much easier than the general case due to either the structure of prime factors or the relationship between prime factors. One of these cases happens when one of the prime factors p of an integer n has the property that $p - 1$ is smooth relative to some set of prime powers $F = \left\{p_1^{\alpha_1}, p_2^{\alpha_2}, \ldots, p_l^{\alpha_l}\right\}$. The algorithm that can use this information is Pollard's $p - 1$ algorithm [30]. This algorithm works in the following way. Let

$$m = \prod_{i=1}^{l} p_i^{\alpha_i}$$

and suppose that $(p - 1) \mid m$, so that we can write $m = d(p - 1)$. Then for any value of a with $\gcd(a, p) = 1$ we have

$$a^M = a^{(p-1)d} = (a^{p-1})^d \equiv 1 (\text{mod } p)$$

so that we can write $a^M - 1 = pk$ for some k. And since p is a factor of n we can also write $n = pq$. Thus $\gcd(a^M - 1, n) = \gcd(pk, pq)$ is a divisor of n that is strictly greater than 1, at least having p as a factor, possibly being n itself. So if we can find a value of m such that $(p - 1) \mid m$ we find a factor of n by calculating $\gcd(a^M - 1, n)$. Some values of a will not provide any useful information on this, resulting in $\gcd(a^M - 1, n) = n$. In this case, we can pick another random a with $\gcd(a, p) = 1$ and try again.

Other techniques can take advantage of other structures of prime factors or the relationship between prime factors. Because of these techniques, some standards require the use of "strong primes" to create keys for algorithms that rely on integer factorization. In particular, [31] requires the following conditions to be met for such primes where two primes p and q are needed to calculate a composite n which must be difficult to factor:

1. All of $p \pm 1$ and $q \pm 1$ must contain a prime factor greater than 2^{100}.
2. $\gcd(p - 1, q - 1)$ must be small.
3. If $p \cdot q$ has $1{,}024 + 256s$ bits, then p/q must not be close to a small integer and $|p - q| > 2^{412 + 128s}$.
4. $p - q$ must contain a prime factor greater than 2^{100}.

Requiring such strong primes is very conservative. Weak primes are fairly rare, so attempts to factor an integer that try to take advantage of the use of weak primes are very unlikely to succeed with most randomly generated primes. Despite this, some users of public-key cryptography feel that requiring the use of strong primes is necessary for their particular uses. When implementing cryptography, it is important to understand what assumptions the users of the resulting system are willing to make because they are the ones who will trust the system to protect their data.

5.6 Proving Security of Public-Key Algorithms

In some cases it is easy to see the correspondence between being able to one of the computational problems and the ability of an adversary to attack a public-key system. The CDHP, for example, is modeled after what an adversary observes in a Diffie-Hellman key exchange and what the adversary wants to obtain in order to defeat the system. In other cases, however, the correspondence is not as clear. The fact that the strength of some of the IBE algorithms that will be discussed in the following chapters is at least as strong as certain computational problems may be unclear due to the complexity of the algorithms, for example, and it is good to know that there are proofs that defeating them is at least as hard as computational problems that are believed to be hard.

To prove that a cryptographic algorithm is at least as strong as a certain computational problem, the typical technique is to assume that an adversary who has an algorithm capable of defeating the cryptographic algorithm of interest and to show that he can then use his attack algorithm to construct an algorithm that will solve the computational problem of interest. Thus if we believe that the computational problem is hard to solve, it is also hard to defeat the cryptographic algorithm. Note that this does not show that the cryptographic algorithm is actually secure; if we can solve the related computational problem then we can defeat the cryptographic algorithms.

So to show that the Diffie-Hellman key exchange is at least as strong as the CDHP, we could show that an attacker capable of defeating the Diffie-Hellman key exchange can use his algorithm for doing this to solve the CDHP. This would not show that the Diffie-Hellman key exchange is secure, but instead shows that if an attacker can defeat the Diffie-Hellman key exchange then he could also accomplish something that is believed to be hard to do. If we believe that the CDHP is indeed hard to solve, then such a proof would also convince us that defeating the Diffie-Hellman key exchange is also hard.

There are two general classes of proofs that cryptographic algorithms are at least as difficult to defeat as they are to solve the related computational problem. One type of proof models parts of the algorithm as oracles whose outputs are truly random. True random oracles are impossible to implement, so once a proof is obtained in this model, the random oracles are replaced by functions whose behavior is similar enough that the security of the system still seems plausible. Cryptographic hash functions are typically used for this. There are pathological cases [32] where such practical implementations are always insecure despite the proof of security using random oracles, but such behavior seems to appear in only the most contrived of cases.

We say that such a proof is obtained using the *random oracle model* [33]. A proof that does not use such random oracles is said to use the *standard model.* In the discussions of IBE schemes, their proofs of security will be summarized by listing a computational problem and a proof technique. An example of this is that, "defeating the ABC scheme has been proven in the random oracle model to be at least as difficult as solving the XYZ problem." By this we mean that a proof has shown that an adversary capable of constructing an algorithm that lets him defeat the ABC scheme can use this algorithm to efficiently solve the XYZ problem. So that if we believe that the XYZ problem is appropriately hard then it must also be hard to defeat the ABC scheme.

5.7 Quantum Computing

All of the run times mentioned earlier assume that the algorithms are implemented on a computer that can be implemented using existing technology. This technology is implemented using devices that have the internal states that are either a logical "0" or a logical "1" that are commonly called "bits." The framework of quantum mechanics assumes that a quantum device exists in multiple states at once, with a device having probabilities of being in each of its states. With such a device a single state is not decided upon until the state is measured, at which time the result of the measurement is determined by the probabilities of being in each of the possible states. This allows for the creation of quantum bits, or qubits, that are both a logical "0" and a logical "1" at the same time, and allows for the creation of computers that can calculate all 2^n values of a function on n qubits in a single operation.

A computer built of qubits instead of classical bits allows for the implementation of algorithms that run much more quickly than the best-known algorithms on classical computers. In particular, Grover's algorithm can be used to defeat symmetric algorithms and Shor's algorithm can be used to defeat many symmetric algorithms. Each of these algorithms are random, reflecting the probabilistic nature of the underlying qubits, so the best that they can do is to return the correct result with a high probability, after which the result can easily be verified by additional testing.

5.7.1 Grover's Algorithm

Let $f\colon \{0, 1\}^n \rightarrow \{0, 1\}$ be an efficiently computable function. Then Grover's algorithm [34] finds a string $a \in \{0, 1\}^n$ such that $f(a) = 1$, if such a string exists, in $O(2^{n/2})$ time. So, if we have a symmetric encryption algorithm that uses n bits of key and we have a matched plaintext-ciphertext pair, we can use the function

$$f(a) = \begin{cases} 1, & a \text{ produces the given plaintext-ciphertext pair} \\ 0, & \text{otherwise} \end{cases}$$

in Grover's algorithm so that finding $f(a) = 1$ corresponds to finding the desired symmetric key. So being able to implement such an attack reduces the level of security provided this symmetric algorithm to no more than $n/2$ bits. Although this is a significant increase in performance over classical computers, being able to use Grover's algorithm does not make it easy to defeat symmetric algorithms; such a reduction is easy to deal with, and we can attain a goal of n bits of strength by using a symmetric algorithm with $2n$ bits of strength against an adversary equipped with nonquantum computers.

5.7.2 Shor's Algorithm

Shor's algorithm [1] uses a fast implementation of a Fourier transform using qubits to factor an integer, and similar algorithms are known that can be used to calculate discrete logarithms in a finite field [1] or in an elliptic curve group [2]. Suppose that we want to factor the integer n. Shor's algorithm first uses the Fourier transform to find the period of an integer a modulo n where $\gcd(a, n) = 1$, or the smallest integer r such that $a^r \equiv 1 \pmod{n}$, or that $n \mid (a^r - 1)$. If r is even then we can use it to write

$$a^r - 1 = (a^{r/2} - 1)(a^{r/2} + 1)$$

so that

$$n \mid (a^{r/2} - 1)(a^{r/2} + 1)$$

Because r is the smallest integer such that $n \mid (a^r - 1)$, we cannot have either $n \mid (a^{r/2} - 1)$ or $n \mid (a^{r/2} + 1)$, so as long as $a^{r/2} \neq -1$, n must share a nontrivial factor with each of $a^{r/2} - 1$ and $a^{r/2} + 1$, and calculating $\gcd(n, a^{r/2} - 1)$ and $\gcd(n, a^{r/2} + 1)$ will find these factors.

Shor's algorithm has an expected running time of

$$O((\log n)^2 (\log \log n)(\log \log \log n))$$

which makes an attack based on it easy for an attacker to carry out. Thus the security of an algorithm which relies on integer factorization being hard is no longer reasonably secure if an adversary can use a quantum computer. And, unlike the case of using Grover's algorithm to attack a symmetric algorithm, it would not be possible to simply increase the size of a key to compensate for this attack: it would now be no more difficult to factor an integer than it is to multiply integers.

On the other hand, implementing Shor's requires a quantum computer with $2n$ qubits to factor an n-bit integer. Constructing quantum computers currently seems a daunting engineering task because of the extremely precise control that is required of the qubits during quantum calculations. If the qubits interact with each other or with the world outside the quantum computer, the effect is just like measuring the state of a qubit, causing some the quantum information that it carries to be lost when the qubit collapses to a single state. Because of this, the difficulty of constructing quantum computers with large numbers of qubits seems to increase rapidly as the number of qubits increases. This will make it extremely difficult, if not impossible, to build a quantum computer that is capable of factoring integers of the sizes that are typically used in public-key cryptography. So even if it was possible to build a quantum computer capable of factoring a 1,024-bit integer, it might be the case that adding just a few additional bits to the size of the integer would be enough to make factoring the slightly larger integer impractical until quantum computing technology advances enough.

References

[1] Shor, P., "Polynomial-Time Algorithms for Prime Factorization and Discrete Logarithms on a Quantum Computer," *SIAM Journal of Computing*, Vol. 26, No. 5, 1997, pp. 1484–1509.

[2] Garcia, J., and R. Menchaca, "Quantum Cryptoanalysis of Elliptic Curve Systems," *Computación y Sistemas*, Vol. 4, No. 3, 2001, pp. 242–248.

[3] Fujisaki, E., and T. Okamoto, "Secure Integration of Asymmetric and Symmetric Encryption Schemes," *Proceedings of CRYPTO '99*, Santa Barbara, CA, August 20–24, 1999, pp. 537–554.

[4] Barker, E., et al., *Recommendation for Key Management—Part 1: General (Revised)*, Washington, NIST Special Publication 800-57, Part 1, Washington, D.C.: U.S. Government Printing Office, 2007.

[5] Pollard, J., "Monte Carlo Methods for Index Computation (mod p)," *Mathematics of Computation*, Vol. 32, No. 143, 1978, pp. 918–924.

[6] Floyd, J., "Non-Deterministic Algorithms," *Journal of the ACM*, Vol. 14, No. 4, 1967, pp. 636–644.

[7] Buhler, J., H. Lenstra, and C. Pomerance, "Factoring Integers with the Number Field Sieve," in *The Development of the Number Field Sieve*, H. Lenstra, (ed.), Heidelberg, Germany: Springer-Verlag, 1993, pp. 50–94.

[8] Dixon, J., "Asymptotically Fast Factorization of Integers," *Mathmatics of Computing*, Vol. 36, No. 153, 1981, pp. 255–260.

[9] Kraitchick, M., *Théorie des Nombres*, Vol. 1, Paris: Gauthier-Villars, 1922.

[10] Hellman, M., and J. Reyneri, "Fast Computation of Discrete Logarithms in GF(q)," *Proceedings of CRYPTO '82*, Santa Barbara, CA, August 23–25, 1982, pp. 3–13.

[11] Lenstra, A., and E. Verheul, "Selecting Cryptographic Key Sizes," *Journal of Cryptology*, Vol. 14, No. 4, 2001, pp. 255–293.

[12] Gehrmann, C., and M. Näslund, *ECRYPT Yearly Report on Algorithms and Keysizes (2006)*, European Network of Excellence for Cryptology Report D.SPA.21, 2007.

[13] Orman, H., and P. Hoffman, "Determining Strengths for Public Keys Used for Exchanging Symmetric Keys," RFC 3766, 2004.

[14] National Institute of Standards and Technology, *Security Requirements for Cryptographic Modules*, Federal Information Processing Standard 140–2, Washington, D.C.: U.S. Government Printing Office, 2001.

[15] American National Standards Institute, *Public Key Cryptography for the Financial Services Industry: Agreement of Symmetric Keys Using Discrete Logarithm Cryptography*, American National Standard for Financial Services X9.42-2003, Annapolis, MD: American National Standards Institute, 2003.

[16] Electronic Freedom Foundation, *Cracking DES: Secrets of Encryption Research, Wiretap Politics & Chip Design*, Sebastapol, CA: O'Reilly, 1998.

[17] Barrow, J., and F. Tipler, *The Anthropic Cosmological Principle*, Oxford, U.K.: Oxford University Press, 1988.

[18] Landauer, R.,"Irreversibility and Heat Generation in the Computing Process," *IBM Journal of Research and Development*, Vol. 5, No. 3, 1961, pp. 183–191.

[19] Diffie, W., and M. Hellman, "New Directions in Cryptography," *IEEE Transactions on Information Theory*, IT-22, No. 6, 1976, pp. 644–654.

[20] Joux, A., and K. Nguyen, "Separating Decision Diffie-Hellman from Diffie-Hellman in Cryptographic Groups," *Journal of Cryptology*, Vol. 16, No. 4, 2003, pp. 239–247.

[21] Boneh, D., "The Decision Diffie-Hellman Problem," *Algorithmic Number Theory Third International Symposium*, Portland, OR, June 21–25, 1998, pp. 48–63.

[22] Boneh, D., and M. Franklin, "Identity Based Encryption from the Weil Pairing," *SIAM Journal of Computing*, Vol. 32, No. 3, pp. 586–615.

[23] Boneh, D., and X. Boyen, "Efficient Selective-ID Secure Identity-Based Encryption without Random Oracles," *Proceedings of EUROCRYPT 2004*, Interlaken, Switzerland, May 2–6, 2004, pp. 223–238.

[24] Agrawal, M., N. Kayal, and N. Saxena, "PRIMES Is in P," *Annals of Mathematics*, Vol. 160, No. 2, 2004, pp. 781–793.

[25] Gauss, K., *Disquisitiones Arithmeticae*, Fleisher: Leipzig, 1801.

[26] Blake, I., G. Seroussi, and N. Smart, *Advances in Elliptic Curve Cryptography*, Cambridge, U.K.: Cambridge University Press, 2005.

[27] Silverman, J., *The Arithmetic of Elliptic Curves*, New York: Springer-Verlag, 1985.

[28] Menezes, A., T. Okamoto, and S. Vanstone, "Reducing Elliptic Curve Logarithms to Logarithms in a Finite Field," *IEEE Transactions on Information Theory*, Vol. 39, No. 5, 1993, pp. 1639–1646.

[29] Menezes, A., and S. Vanstone, "A Note on Cyclic Groups, Finite Fields, and the Discrete Logarithm Problem," *Applicable Algebra in Engineering, Communication and Computing*, Vol. 3, No. 1, 1992, pp. 67–74.

[30] Pollard, J., "Theorems on Factorization and Primality Testing," *Proceedings of the Cambridge Philosophical. Society*, Vol. 76, 1974, pp 521–528.

[31] American National Standards Institute, *Digital Signatures Using Reversible Public Key Cryptography for the Financial Services Industry (rDSA)*, American National Standard for Financial Services X9.31-1998, Annapolis, MD: American National Standards Institute, 1998.

[32] Canetti, R., O. Goldreich, and S. Halevi, "The Random Oracle Methodology, Revisited," *Proceedings of the ACM Symposium on Theory of Computing*, Dallas, TX, May 23–26, 1998, pp. 209–218.

[33] Bellare, M., and P. Rogaway, "Random Oracles Are Practical: A Paradigm for Designing Efficient Protocols," *Proceedings of the ACM Conference on Computer and Communications Security*, Fairfax, VA, November 3–5, 1993, pp. 62–73.

[34] Grover, L., "From Schrödinger's Equation to Quantum Search Algorithm," *American Journal of Physics*, Vol. 69, No. 7, 2001, pp. 769–777.

6

Related Cryptographic Algorithms

IBE algorithms are very similar to other public-key algorithms, and understanding these other algorithms may provide some insight into the nature of the IBE algorithms. In particular, Goldwasser-Michali encryption uses Jacobi symbols to encrypt information on a bit-by-bit basis, and provides the framework for understanding the Cocks IBE algorithm that is discussed in Chapter 7. The Diffie-Hellman key exchange and its elliptic curve variant provide the basic framework for using the difficulty of calculating discrete logarithms to create a public-key encryption scheme. Joux's generalization of these schemes uses a pairing to allow three users to securely agree upon a common shared secret. The combination of the Diffie-Hellman scheme and Joux's scheme provides some insight into operation of the Boneh-Frankin IBE scheme that is discussed in Chapter 8, and provides some insight into the operation of Sakai-Kasahara IBE scheme that is discussed in Chapter 10. ElGamal encryption provides some insight into the operation of the Boneh-Boyen IBE scheme that is discussed in Chapter 9.

All of the following descriptions of algorithms assume that two participants, traditionally called Alice and Bob, want to communicate securely, while an eavesdropper named Eve does her best to determine the content of the secret messages that Alice and Bob exchange. In the case where a third legitimate participant is needed, Charlie is assumed to have joined Alice and Bob.

6.1 Goldwasser-Michali Encryption

Goldwasser-Michali encryption [1] uses the quadratic residuosity problem to create a public-key scheme. It works in the following way. Bob starts by generating a pair of random primes p and q and calculating $n = p \cdot q$. He then picks a random $y \in \mathbb{Z}_n^*$ and so that y is a quadratic nonresidue modulo n, but the Jacobi symbol $(y/n) = +1$. To do this, Bob can first find one quadratic nonresidue a modulo p and another quadratic nonresidue b modulo q and then calculate y by solving the system of congruences

$$y \equiv a (\text{mod } p)$$

$$y \equiv b (\text{mod } q)$$

by Gauss' algorithm to find y. This y will then have the property that

$$(y/n) = (y/p)(y/q) = (-1)(-1) = +1$$

as desired. Once y is computed, Bob's public key is the pair (y, n) and his private key is the pair (p, q).

Alice then encrypts her message a bit at a time to Bob, who then decrypts the received message a bit at a time. To encrypt a message bit m to Bob, Alice performs the following steps:

1. Alice picks a random $x \in \mathbb{Z}_n^*$.
2. If $m = 1$, then Alice sets $c = y \cdot x^2$, otherwise she sets $c = x^2 (\text{mod } n)$.
3. Alice sends the ciphertext c to Bob.

To decrypt the ciphertext c, Bob performs the following steps:

1. Bob calculates the Legendre symbol $e = (c/p)$.
2. If $e = 1$, then Bob decrypts c to 0, otherwise he decrypts c to 1.

If the message bit sent by Alice is $m = 0$, then $c = x^2 (\text{mod } n)$ is a quadratic residue modulo n. By Property 2.8 we have that c is a quadratic residue modulo p if and only if c is a quadratic residue modulo n, so that Bob will calculate

$$e = (c/p) = (x^2/p) = (x^2/n) = +1$$

and decrypt c to 0 correctly.

If the message bit sent by Alice is $m = 1$, then $c = y \cdot x^2 (\text{mod } n)$ is a quadratic nonresidue modulo n, so that Bob will calculate

$$e = (c/p) = (y \cdot x^2/p) = (y \cdot x^2/n) = (y/n)(x^2/n) = (-1)(+1) = -1$$

and decrypt c to 1 correctly.

On the other hand, if Eve observes the ciphertext c, she needs to determine whether or not c is a quadratic residue modulo n or not, which is exactly the quadratic residuosity problem.

Because it encrypts a single bit at a time, the Goldwasser-Micali encryption scheme is vulnerable to an adaptive chosen-ciphertext attack. Suppose that Eve has the plaintext $(m_1, m_2, \ldots, m_k)$ and corresponding ciphertext $(c_1, c_2, \ldots, c_k)$ that is encrypted to Bob, and that she wants to obtain the plaintext corresponding to the ciphertext $(c_1', c_2', \ldots, c_k')$. She can then send the message $(c_1', c_2, \ldots, c_k)$ to Bob and observe his reaction. If Bob uses the ciphertext as a shared secret that he uses to derive a session key, for example, Eve can check to see if Bob creates the same session key from $(c_1', c_2, \ldots, c_k)$ that he does from $(c_1, c_2, \ldots, c_k)$ to determine whether the decryption of c_1 and c_1' are the same or different. Eve can then repeat this process to recover the additional bits of the decryption of $(c_1', c_2', \ldots, c_k')$, recovering a single bit every time she repeats this process.

Example 6.1

Suppose that Bob wants to generate a Goldwasser-Micali public and private key. First Bob picks two primes p and q. Suppose that he picks $p = 7$ and $q = 11$, so that $n = p \cdot q = 77$. He then picks a quadratic nonresidue modulo p and another quadratic nonresidue modulo q and uses the Chinese remainder theorem to find the value of y. Suppose that he picks the quadratic nonresidues 3 modulo 7 and 2 modulo 11. In this case he solves the congruences

$$y \equiv 3 (\text{mod } 7)$$

$$y \equiv 2 (\text{mod } 11)$$

to get $y \equiv 24 (\text{mod } 77)$. Thus Bob's public key is $(y, n) = (24, 77)$ and his private key is $(p, q) = (7, 11)$.

Suppose that Alice wants to encrypt the bit "1" to Bob. She obtains Bob's public key $(y, n) = (24, 77)$ and picks a random $y \in \mathbb{Z}_{77}^*$. In this case, suppose that she picks $x = 17$. Then to encrypt the bit "1" to Bob she calculates the ciphertext $c = y \cdot x^2 (\text{mod } n) = 24 \cdot 17^2 (\text{mod } 77) \equiv 6 (\text{mod } 77)$. She then sends the ciphertext 6 to Bob.

Upon receiving the ciphertext 6, Bob calculates the Jacobi symbol

$$e = (c/p) = (6/7) = -1$$

which he then decrypts to "1."

6.2 The Diffie-Hellman Key Exchange

The Diffie-Hellman key exchange [2] was the first practical public-key algorithm. The Diffie-Hellman key exchange produces a secret that is shared between Alice and Bob that is difficult for Eve to determine from what she observes by watching the communications between Alice and Bob. Its security is based on the difficulty of calculating discrete logarithms in a prime-order subgroup G of the multiplicative group $\mathbb{F}_q^*$. Let g be a generator of G and G be of order p. Then the Diffie-Hellman key exchange has the following four steps:

1. Alice chooses a random $a \in \mathbb{Z}_{p-1}^*$, calculates g^a, which she sends to Bob.
2. Bob chooses a random $b \in \mathbb{Z}_{p-1}^*$, calculates g^b, which he sends to Alice.
3. Alice receives g^b and calculates the shared secret $K = (g^b)^a$.
4. Bob receives g^a and calculates the shared secret $K = (g^a)^b$.

Note that the range allowed for the integers a and b is from 1 to $p - 2$. If a was allowed to be $p - 1$, for example, then by Euler's theorem we would have that $g^a \equiv 1 \pmod{p}$, so that the shared secret K ends up being 1, and an adversary observing the transmission of g^a will then be able to easily recover K.

At the end of these steps, Alice and Bob both have the shared secret $K = g^{ab}$. Eve's task is to recover $K = g^{ab}$ given g, g^a and g^b, which is exactly the CDHP, which is assumed to be as hard as calculating discrete logarithms in either G. On the other hand, because there is absolutely no authentication for either Alice or Bob in the steps listed above, it is easy for Eve to mount a man-in-the-middle attack against Alice and Bob. She does this by positioning herself between Alice and Bob and carrying out a legitimate Diffie-Hellman key exchange with each of Alice and Bob, after which she uses the shared secrets constructed in this way to securely communicate with each the unsuspecting pair. Eve's man-in-the-middle attack is carried out in the following steps:

1. Alice chooses a random $a \in \mathbb{Z}_{p-1}^*$, calculates $g^a \bmod p$, which she unknowingly sends to Eve.
2. Eve chooses a random $e \in \mathbb{Z}_{p-1}^*$, calculates $g^e \bmod p$, which she sends to Alice.
3. Alice receives $g^e \bmod p$ from Eve and calculates the shared secret $K_1 = (g^e)^a \bmod p$.
4. Eve receives $g^a \bmod p$ from Alice and calculates the shared secret $K_1 = (g^a)^e \bmod p$.

5. Eve sends $g^e \bmod p$ to Bob.
6. Bob chooses a random $b \in \mathbb{Z}_{p-1}^*$, calculates g^b, which he sends to Eve, believing her to be Alice.
7. Eve receives g^b from Bob and calculates the shared secret $K_2 = (g^b)^e$.
8. Bob receives g^e from Eve and calculates the shared secret $K_2 = (g^e)^b$.

At this point Eve has established two shared secrets: K_1, which is shared with Alice and K_2, which is shared with Bob. Suppose that Alice sends a message to Bob that is encrypted using the shared secret K_1. Eve can then intercept this message and then use the shared secret K_1 to decrypt messages from Alice that are encrypted using the shared secret K_1, then reencrypt the message using the shared secret K_2 which she shares with Bob. Bob will then be able to decrypt the message using the shared secret K_2, which he believes is only in the possession of him and Alice.

Example 6.2

Suppose that Alice and Bob want to use the Diffie-Hellman key exchange to create a shared secret. Suppose that all calculations are done in the subgroup of $\mathbb{F}_{59}^*$ of order 29, which has generator $g = 2$. They can do this in the following steps.

1. Alice chooses a random $a \in \mathbb{Z}_{28}^*$, say $a = 7$, and calculates $g^a = 2^7 \equiv 10 \pmod{59}$, which she sends to Bob.
2. Bob chooses a random $b \in \mathbb{Z}_{28}^*$, say $b = 23$, and calculates $g^b = 2^{23} \equiv 47 \pmod{59}$, which he sends to Alice.
3. Alice receives the value 47 from Bob and calculates the shared secret $K = 47^b = 47^7 \equiv 13 \pmod{59}$.
4. Bob receives the value 10 from Alice and calculates the shared secret $K = 10^b = 10^{23} \equiv 13 \pmod{59}$.

6.3 Elliptic Curve Diffie-Hellman

There is nothing special about the group $\mathbb{F}_q^*$ that is used in the Diffie-Hellman key exchange, and any other group in which it is hard to calculate discrete logarithms can be used in its place. In particular, an elliptic curve group $E(\mathbb{F}_q)$ can be used in this way. The security of the resulting algorithm is then based on the difficulty of calculating discrete logarithms in the group $E(\mathbb{F}_q)$. Let G be a subgroup of $E(\mathbb{F}_q)$ of prime order p generated by P. Then the elliptic curve Diffie-Hellman key exchange [3] has the following five steps:

1. Alice chooses a random $a \in \mathbb{Z}_p^*$ and calculates aP, which she sends to Bob.
2. Bob chooses a random $b \in \mathbb{Z}_p^*$ and calculates bP, which he sends to Alice.
3. Alice receives bP and calculates the shared secret $K = a(bP)$.
4. Bob receives aP and calculates the shared secret $K = b(aP)$.
5. If $K = O$ then raise an error condition and restart at step 1.

At the end of these steps, Alice and Bob both have the shared secret $K = b(aP)$. Eve's task is to recover $K = a(bP)$ given P, aP, and bP, which is exactly the CDHP, which is assumed to be as hard as calculating discrete logarithms in G. The elliptic curve Diffie-Hellman key exchange is vulnerable to a man-in-the-middle attack just like the Diffie-Hellman key exchange is.

Example 6.3

Suppose that Alice and Bob want to use the elliptic curve Diffie-Hellman key exchange to create a shared secret. Suppose that E is the elliptic curve $E: y^2 = x^3 + 1$, and G be the subgroup of order 11 of $E(\mathbb{F}_{131})$ generated by $P = (98, 58)$. They can do this in the following steps.

1. Alice chooses a random $a \in \mathbb{Z}_{11}^*$, say $a = 7$, and calculates $aP = 7 \cdot (98, 58) = (33, 100)$, which she sends to Bob.
2. Bob chooses a random integer b with $b \in \mathbb{Z}_{11}^*$, say $b = 5$, and calculates $bP = 5 \cdot (98, 58) = (34, 23)$, which he sends to Alice.
3. Alice receives (34, 23) from Bob and calculates the shared secret $K = a \cdot (34, 23) = 7 \cdot (34, 23) = (128, 57)$.
4. Bob receives (33, 100) from Alice and calculates $K = b \cdot (33, 100) = 5 \cdot (33, 100) = (128, 57)$.
5. $K \neq O$ so that no error condition is raised.

6.4 Joux's Three-Way Key Exchange

Another generalization of the Diffie-Hellman key exchange is due to Joux [4], who noticed that a clever use of a pairing allows for the creation of a way to allow three participants to agree upon a shared secret in a secure way. To do this, let G_1 and G_T be groups of prime order $p = |G_1| = |G_T|$ and $\hat{e} : G_1 \times G_1 \to G_T$ be a pairing, and let P be a generator of G_1. Then Joux's three-way key exchange has the following seven steps:

1. Alice chooses a random $a \in \mathbb{Z}_p^*$, calculates aP, which she sends to Bob and Charlie.
2. Bob chooses a random $b \in \mathbb{Z}_p^*$, calculates bP, which he sends to Alice and Charlie.
3. Charlie chooses a random $c \in \mathbb{Z}_p^*$, calculates bP, which he sends to Alice and Charlie.
4. Alice receives bP and cP and calculates the shared secret $K = \hat{e}(bP, cP)^a = \hat{e}(P, P)^{abc}$.
5. Bob receives aP and cP and calculates the shared secret $K = \hat{e}(aP, cP)^b = \hat{e}(P, P)^{abc}$.
6. Charlie receives aP and bP and calculates the shared secret $K = \hat{e}(aP, bP)^c = \hat{e}(P, P)^{abc}$.
7. If $K = O$, raise an error condition and restart at step 1.

At the end of these steps, each of Alice, Bob, and Charlie have the shared secret $\hat{e}(P, P)^{abc}$. Eve's task is to recover $K = \hat{e}(P, P)^{abc}$ given P, aP, bP, and cP which is exactly the BDHP, which is assumed to be as hard as calculating discrete logarithms in either G_1 or G_T. Joux's three-way key exchange is vulnerable to a man-in-the-middle attack just like the Diffie-Hellman key exchange is.

Example 6.4

Suppose that Alice, Bob, and Charlie want to use Joux's three-way key exchange to create a shared secret. Suppose that E is the elliptic curve $E/\mathbb{F}_{131} : y^2 = x^3 + 1$. Let G_1 be the subgroup of order 11 of $E(\mathbb{F}_{131})$ with generator $P = (98, 58)$ and let G_T be the subgroup of $(\mathbb{F}_{11^2})^*$ generated by $\hat{e}(P, P) = 28 + 93i$, where $\mathbb{F}_{11^2}$ is represented by $\mathbb{F}_{11}[x]/(x^2 + 1)$. Let $\hat{e} : G_1 \times G_1 \to G_T$ be the reduced modified Tate pairing, where $\hat{e} : G_1 \times G_1 \to G_T$ is the Tate pairing, and $\hat{e}(P, Q) = e(P, \phi(Q))^{1560}$ where ϕ is the distortion map given by $\phi(x, y) = (\xi x, y)$, where $\xi = 65 + 112i$. Then Alice, Bob, and Charlie can carry out Joux's three-way key exchange as follows.

1. Alice picks the random $a \in \mathbb{Z}_{11}^*$, say $a = 3$, and calculates $aP = (113, 8)$, which she sends to Bob and Charlie.
2. Bob picks the random $b \in \mathbb{Z}_{11}^*$, say $b = 5$, and calculates $bP = (34, 23)$, which he sends to Alice and Charlie.
3. Charlie picks the random $c \in \mathbb{Z}_{11}^*$, say $c = 7$, and calculates $cP = (33, 100)$, which he sends to Alice and Bob.
4. Alice receives $bP = (34, 23)$ and $cP = (33, 100)$ and calculates $K = \hat{e}(bP, cP)^a = 39 + 107i$.

5. Bob receives $aP = (113, 8)$ and $cP = (33, 100)$ and calculates $K = \hat{e}(aP, cP)^b = 39 + 107i$.
6. Charlie receives $aP = (113, 8)$ and $bP = (34, 23)$ and calculates $K = \hat{e}(aP, bP)^c = 39 + 107i$.
7. $K \neq O$ so no error condition is raised.

6.5 ElGamal Encryption

ElGamal encryption [5] creates an encryption algorithm from the Diffie-Hellman key exchange, essentially using a Diffie-Hellman shared secret to encrypt a block of plaintext by multiplying the plaintext by the Diffie-Hellman shared secret. To decrypt the resulting ciphertext, the intended recipient then divides by the Diffie-Hellman shared secret to recover the plaintext. More precisely, the ElGamal encryption works as follows. Let Bob have the public key (p, g, g^b), where p is a prime, G a prime-order subgroup of $\mathbb{Z}_p^*$, and $b \in \mathbb{Z}_{p-1}^*$. Bob's corresponding private key is b. To encrypt a message $M \in \mathbb{F}_p^*$ to Bob, Alice performs the following steps:

1. Alice obtains Bob's public key (p, g, g^b), picks a $a \in \mathbb{Z}_{p-1}^*$ and then calculates $(g^b)^a = g^{ab}$.
2. Alice calculates Mg^{ab} and then sends ciphertext $C = (Mg^{ab}, g^a)$ to Bob. The value of g^a that Alice sends in this ciphertext is sometimes called a "hint."

To decrypt the ciphertext $C = (Mg^{ab}, g^a)$ Bob performs the following steps:

1. Bob calculates $(g^a)^b = g^{ab}$.
2. Bob calculates

$$\frac{Mg^{ab}}{g^{ab}} = M$$

to recover the message M.

Note that ElGamal encryption is subject to a chosen-ciphertext attack. If an adversary knows that the ciphertext $C = (Mg^{ab}, g^a)$ corresponds to the plaintext M encrypted with the random value g^a, then he can easily decrypt any other ciphertext $C' = ((kM)g^{ab}, g^a)$ by calculating

$$\frac{Mg^{ab}}{M} = g^{ab}$$

from the ciphertext C and then

$$\frac{(kM)g^{ab}}{g^{ab}} = kM$$

from the ciphertext C'.

It is no more difficult to recover the plaintext M from the ciphertext $C = (Mg^{ab}, g^a)$ than it is to calculate discrete logarithms in G: if an adversary can determine b from Bob's public key g^b he can then decrypt the ciphertext as easily as Bob can.

Example 6.5

Suppose that Bob's public key is $(p, g, g^b) = (59, 2, 47)$, and his private key is $b = 23$, and that Alice wants to encrypt the message $M = 17$ to Bob. She can do this in the following steps.

1. Alice obtains Bob's public key $(p, g, g^b) = (59, 2, 47)$. Alice then chooses a random a, say $a = 7$, and calculates $(g^b)^a = 47^7 \equiv 13 \pmod{37}$.
2. Alice calculates $Mg^{ab} = 17 \cdot 13 \equiv 44 \pmod{59}$ and $g^a = 2^7 \equiv 10 \pmod{59}$ and then sends the ciphertext $C = (Mg^{ab}, g^a) = (44, 10)$.

When Bob receives the ciphertext $C = (44, 10)$ he performs the following steps.

1. Bob calculates $(g^a)^b = 10^b = 10^{23} \equiv 13 \pmod{59}$.
2. Bob calculates

$$M = \frac{Mg^{ab}}{g^{ab}} = \frac{44}{13} = 44 \cdot 9^{-1} = 44 \cdot 50 \equiv 17 \pmod{59}$$

to recover the message M.

References

[1] Goldwasser, S., and S. Micali, "Probabilistic Encryption," *Journal of Computer and System Sciences*, Vol. 28, No. 2, 1984, pp. 270–299.

[2] Diffie, W., and M. Hellman, "New Directions in Cryptography," *IEEE Transactions on Information Theory*, Vol. IT-22, No. 6, 1976, pp. 644–654.

[3] American National Standards Institute, *Key Agreement and Key Transport using Elliptic Curve Cryptography*, American National Standard for Financial Services X9.63-2001, Annapolis, MD: American National Standards Institute, 2001.

[4] Joux, A., "A One-Round Protocol for Tripartite Diffie-Hellman," *Proceedings of the 4th International Algorihtmic Number Theory Symposium*, Leider, the Netherlands, July 2–7, 2000, pp. 385–394.

[5] ElGamal, T., "A Public-Key Cryptosystem and a Signature Scheme Based on Discrete Logarithms," *IEEE Transactions on Information Theory*, Vol. IT-31, No. 4, 1985, pp. 469–472.

7

The Cocks IBE Scheme

The Cocks IBE scheme was invented by Clifford Cocks of the Communications-Electronics Security Group (CESG) of the United Kingdom government, the same gentleman who has a fairly strong claim to having invented the first public-key algorithm in 1973, when he published a classified (now declassified) CESG report [1], which described a scheme roughly comparable to the RSA scheme. The security of the Cocks IBE scheme is based on both the computational difficulty of integer factorization and on the quadratic residuosity problem. The Cocks IBE scheme was first described in [2].

The Cocks IBE scheme encrypts each bit of the plaintext as a pair of integers modulo a composite number, each as large as an integer which is suitably difficult to factor. For example, to encrypt a 128-bit symmetric key, per Table 5.2, each of these integers must be 3,072 bits in length to provide the same bit strength as a 128-bit symmetric key. The Cocks IBE scheme uses many of the same ideas as the Goldwasser-Micali scheme, and is notable for being an IBE scheme that does not use a pairing in its operation, as well as the IBE scheme most likely to get you fired for searching the Internet for it while at work.

7.1 Setup of Parameters

The Cocks scheme requires a public value n which is the product of two primes p and q, each of which are congruent to 3 modulo 4. While the value n is public, its factors p and q are known only to the PKG. It also requires a well-known cryptographic hash function $H_1 : \{0, 1\}^* \rightarrow \mathbb{Z}_n$. We also require that for an identity ID, if $H_1(ID) = a$, then we have the Jacobi symbol $(a/n) = +1$, which will guarantee that either a or $-a$ is a square modulo n. This can easily be done, for example, by using a cryptographic hash function H hash an identity to an integer a modulo n and then incrementing a until $(a/n) = +1$.

Because we have that

$$\left(\frac{a}{n}\right) = \left(\frac{a}{p}\right)\left(\frac{a}{q}\right) \tag{7.1}$$

we must have that either both Jacobi symbols have the value +1 or both have the value −1 in (7.1). When both have the value +1 we have

$$\left(\frac{a}{n}\right) = \left(\frac{a}{p}\right)\left(\frac{a}{q}\right) = (+1)(+1) = +1$$

so that a is a square modulo n because it is a square modulo both p and q.

In the other case we have

$$\left(\frac{a}{n}\right) = \left(\frac{a}{p}\right)\left(\frac{a}{q}\right) = (-1)(-1) = +1$$

If this happens, then it turns out that $-a$ must be a square modulo n. Because we have that p and q are congruent to 3 modulo 4, we have

$$\left(\frac{-1}{p}\right) = \left(\frac{-1}{q}\right) = -1$$

so that

$$\left(\frac{-a}{n}\right) = \left(\frac{-a}{p}\right)\left(\frac{-a}{q}\right) = \left(\frac{a}{p}\right)\left(\frac{-1}{p}\right)\left(\frac{a}{q}\right)\left(\frac{-1}{q}\right)$$
$$= \left(\frac{a}{p}\right)(-1)\left(\frac{a}{q}\right)(-1) = \left(\frac{a}{p}\right)\left(\frac{a}{q}\right) = (+1)(+1) = +1$$

So that $-a$ is a square because it is the product of two numbers that are squares.

The ambiguity introduced by not knowing whether a or $-a$ is a square causes some inefficiency when Cocks IBE is used to encrypt, and results in doubling the size of the ciphertext to account for each of the two cases. In either case, the value a then is the public key corresponding to the identity ID. Note that using Algorithm 2.2, it is possible to calculate the Jacobi symbol

$$\left(\frac{a}{n}\right)$$

without knowing the factors of n.

7.2 Extraction of the Private Key

The PKG then calculates the private key corresponding to the public key a by calculating the square root of either a or $-a$ modulo n. Because p and q are both congruent to 3 modulo 4, $p-1$ and $q-1$ are both congruent to 2 modulo 4 so that we can write $p = 4k_1 + 2$ and $q = 4k_2 + 2$. Because we have $n = p \cdot q$, we have that $\phi(n) = (p-1)(q-1)$, so that

$$\begin{aligned}\phi(n) + 4 &= (p-1)(q-1) + 4 \\ &= (4k_1 + 2)(4k_2 + 2) + 4 = (2k_1k_2 + k_1 + k_2 + 1)8\end{aligned}$$

so that 8 divides $\phi(n)$.

We can use this fact to calculate a square root modulo n as

$$r = a^{(\phi(N)+4)/8} \bmod n \tag{7.2}$$

This gives a square root of a modulo n because

$$r^2 = a^{2(\phi(N)+4)/8} = a^{\phi(N)+4)/4} = (a^{\phi(n)})^{1/4} a \equiv \pm a (\text{mod } n)$$

by Euler's theorem. If a is a square root modulo n, then r will satisfy $r^2 \equiv a(\text{mod } n)$ and if $-a$ is a square root modulo n, then r will satisfy $r^2 \equiv -a(\text{mod } n)$. In either case, the value r acts as the private key corresponding to the public key a.

The parameters of the Cocks IBE scheme are summarized in Table 7.1.

7.3 Encrypting with Cocks IBE

The Cocks IBE scheme encrypts a single bit at a time as a pair of integers. Both of the pair are needed because we do not know which of a or $-a$ is a square root modulo n. On the other hand, the recipient can easily check whether $r^2 \equiv a(\text{mod } n)$ or $r^2 \equiv -a(\text{mod } n)$, so he knows which of the two choices to decrypt. For a message bit m we first encode the bit as $x = (-1)^m$, which encodes

Table 7.1
Summary of Cocks IBE Parameters

Type of Parameter	Parameter	Properties
Private global parameters	p, q	primes $\equiv 3 \pmod 4$
Public global parameter	n	$n = p \cdot q$
Public hash function	H_1	$H_1 : \{0, 1\}^* \to \mathbb{Z}_n$, $(H_1(ID)/n) = +1$
Per-user public key	a	$(a/n) = +1$
Per-user private key	r	$r^2 \equiv +a \pmod n$

the bit "0" as +1 and the bit "1" as −1. We then pick random t_1 and t_2 with both

$$\left(\frac{t_1}{n}\right) = x$$

and

$$\left(\frac{t_2}{n}\right) = x$$

and then send the ciphertext (s_1, s_2) to the recipient, where

$$s_1 = \left(t_1 + \frac{a}{t_1}\right) \bmod n$$

and

$$s_2 = \left(t_2 - \frac{a}{t_2}\right) \bmod N$$

The recipient will then either decrypt s_1 or s_2, choosing s_1 if a is a square root modulo n and s_2 if $-a$ is a square root modulo n.

Note that two different random values t_1 and t_2 are needed. If the same value t is used to calculate both

$$s_1 = \left(t + \frac{a}{t}\right) \bmod n$$

and

$$s_2 = \left(t - \frac{a}{t}\right) \bmod n$$

then an adversary could calculate

$$\frac{s_1 + s_2}{2} = \frac{1}{2}\left(t + \frac{a}{t}\right) + \left(t - \frac{a}{t}\right) \bmod n = t \bmod n$$

and then calculate

$$\left(\frac{t}{n}\right) = x$$

to decrypt the ciphertext.

7.4 Decrypting with Cocks IBE

After receiving the pair s_1 and s_2, the recipient decides which of the two choices he needs to decrypt, letting $s = s_1$ if $r^2 \equiv a (\bmod\ n)$ and $s = s_2$ if $r^2 \equiv -a (\bmod\ n)$. If $r^2 \equiv a (\bmod\ n)$ he calculates

$$x = \left(\frac{s + 2r}{n}\right) \tag{7.3}$$

In the case that $r^2 \equiv a (\bmod\ n)$, we note that

$$\begin{aligned} s + 2r &= \left(t_1 - \frac{a}{t_1}\right) + 2r = t_1 + 2r - \frac{a}{t_1} \\ &= t_1 \left(1 + \frac{2r}{t_1} - \frac{a}{t_1^2}\right) \equiv t_1 \left(1 + \frac{2r}{t_1} + \frac{r^2}{t_1^2}\right) (\bmod\ n) \\ &\equiv t_1 \left(1 + \frac{r}{t_1}\right)^2 (\bmod\ n) \end{aligned}$$

so that $s + 2r$ is a square modulo n exactly when t_1 is, so that we have

$$\left(\frac{s + 2r}{n}\right) = \left(\frac{t_1}{n}\right) = x$$

so that (7.3) recovers the plaintext bit x.

In the case that $r^2 \equiv -a \pmod{n}$, we note that

$$\begin{aligned} s + 2r &= \left(t_2 + \frac{a}{t_2}\right) + 2r = t_2 + 2r + \frac{a}{t_2} \\ &= t_2\left(1 + \frac{2r}{t_2} + \frac{a}{t_2^2}\right) = t_2\left(1 + \frac{2r}{t_2} + \frac{r^2}{t_2^2}\right) \pmod{n} \\ &= t_1\left(1 + \frac{r}{t_1}\right)^2 \pmod{n} \end{aligned}$$

so that we still have that $s + 2r$ is a square modulo n exactly when t_2 is, so that

$$\left(\frac{s + 2r}{n}\right) = \left(\frac{t_2}{n}\right) = x$$

so that (7.3) will correctly decrypt an encrypted bit in both possible cases.

7.5 Examples

(i) Let $p = 7$ and $q = 11$, so that $n = 77$. If we have $a = 9$ for the public key, we find that (7.2) gives us $r = 25$ for the corresponding private key, and that in this case $r^2 \equiv a \pmod{n}$.

To encrypt the bit "0" with this public key the sender first encodes the bit "0" as +1 and picks a random t that satisfies

$$\left(\frac{t}{n}\right) = +1$$

In this case, we randomly pick $t_1 = 4$ and $t_2 = 6$ note that

$$\left(\frac{4}{77}\right) = \left(\frac{6}{77}\right) = +1$$

The sender then calculates the two values

$$s_1 = \left(t_1 + \frac{a}{t_1}\right) \bmod n = \left(4 + \frac{9}{4}\right) \bmod 77 = 64$$

and

$$s_2 = \left(t_2 - \frac{a}{t_2}\right) \bmod n = \left(6 - \frac{9}{6}\right) \bmod 77 = 43$$

and then sends the ciphertext pair $(s_1, s_2) = (64, 43)$ to the recipient.

The recipient knows that his private key satisfies $r^2 \equiv a \pmod{n}$, so he picks s_1 to decrypt. He then calculates

$$\left(\frac{s_1 + 2r}{N}\right) = \left(\frac{64 + 50}{77}\right) = \left(\frac{114}{77}\right) = +1$$

which he then decodes to the bit "0" as his plaintext.

(ii) Let $p = 7$ and $q = 11$, so that $n = 77$. If we have $a = 10$ for the public key, we find that (7.2) gives us $r = 23$ for the corresponding private key, and that in this case $r^2 \equiv -a \pmod{n}$.

To encrypt the bit "1" with this public key the sender first encodes the bit "1" as -1 and picks a random t that satisfies

$$\left(\frac{t}{n}\right) = -1$$

In this case, we randomly pick $t_1 = 8$ and $t_2 = 2$ and note that

$$\left(\frac{8}{77}\right) = \left(\frac{2}{77}\right) = -1$$

The sender then calculates the two values

$$s_1 = \left(t_1 + \frac{a}{t_1}\right) \bmod n = \left(8 + \frac{10}{8}\right) \bmod 77 = 67$$

and

$$s_2 = \left(t_2 - \frac{a}{t_2}\right) \bmod n = \left(2 - \frac{10}{2}\right) \bmod 77 = 74$$

and then sends the ciphertext pair $(s_1, s_2) = (67, 74)$ to the recipient.

The recipient knows that his private key satisfies $r^2 \equiv -a \pmod{n}$, so he picks s_2 to decrypt. He then calculates

$$\left(\frac{s_2 + 2r}{n}\right) = \left(\frac{74 + 46}{77}\right) = \left(\frac{120}{77}\right) = -1$$

which he then decodes to the bit "1" as his plaintext.

(iii) Let $p = 7$ and $q = 11$, so that $n = 77$. If we have $a = 10$ for the public key, we find that (7.2) gives us $r = 23$ for the corresponding private key, and that in this case $r^2 \equiv -a (\text{mod } n)$.

To encrypt the bit "1" with this public key the sender first encodes the bit "1" as -1 and picks a random t that satisfies

$$\left(\frac{t}{n}\right) = -1$$

In this case, we randomly pick $t_1 = 12$ and $t_2 = 5$ and note that

$$\left(\frac{12}{77}\right) = \left(\frac{5}{77}\right) = -1$$

The sender then calculates the two values

$$s_1 = \left(t_1 + \frac{a}{t_1}\right) \text{ mod } n = \left(12 + \frac{10}{12}\right) \text{ mod } 77 = 0$$

and

$$s_2 = \left(t - \frac{a}{t}\right) \text{ mod } n = \left(5 - \frac{10}{5}\right) \text{ mod } 77 = 3$$

and then sends the ciphertext pair $(s_1, s_2) = (0, 3)$ to the recipient.

The recipient knows that his private key satisfies $r^2 \equiv -a (\text{mod } n)$, so he picks s_2 to decrypt. He then calculates

$$\left(\frac{s_2 + 2r}{n}\right) = \left(\frac{3 + 46}{77}\right) = \left(\frac{49}{77}\right) = 0$$

In this case the decryption fails, because $\gcd(s_2 + 2r, n) \neq 1$. This will happen whenever either p or q divides $s_1 + 2r$ (or $s_2 + 2r$, if it is calculated instead). There are $q - 1$ multiples of p for which this can happen and $p - 1$ multiples of q for which this can happen. Note that this counts 0 twice, once as a multiple of p and again as a multiple of q, so there are a total of $(p - 1) + (q - 1) - 1$ ways for this to happen. If we assume that is uniformly distributed in $\{0, 1, \ldots, n - 1\}$, this gives a probability of

$$Pr(\text{decryption failure}) = \frac{(p-1) + (q-1) - 1}{n}$$

of this happening. For a typical use, say with a 1,024-bit n and 512-bit values for p and q, this probability is extremely small. So, although this may happen, it happens so rarely that it is probably not worth handling as a special case in an implementation of the Cocks IBE scheme, although it may occur in examples with artificially small parameters.

7.6 Security of the Cocks IBE Scheme

7.6.1 Relationship to the Quadratic Residuosity Problem

An adversary can defeat the Cocks IBE system if he can factor the modulus n. If he can do this, he can calculate arbitrary private keys by (7.2) and then decrypt any messages that he intercepts. As discussed in Chapter 5, the best-known algorithm for factoring integers is sufficiently difficult to provide the security levels listed in Table 5.2. The fact that the security of the Cocks IBE scheme relates to the quadratic residuosity problem, however, is not immediately obvious. The fact that it does relates to the fact that the ability to decrypt a message encrypted with Cocks IBE requires deciding whether or not the per-user public key a is a square modulo n.

Note that

$$\left(\frac{1}{n}\right) = \left(\frac{t}{n}\right)\left(\frac{1/t}{n}\right) = +1$$

so that

$$\left(\frac{t}{n}\right) = \left(\frac{1/t}{n}\right)$$

and thus

$$\left(\frac{a/t}{n}\right) = \left(\frac{a}{n}\right)\left(\frac{1/t}{n}\right) = \left(\frac{a}{n}\right)\left(\frac{t}{n}\right)$$

Now consider the following four systems of congruences:

$$\begin{cases} t_1 = t \bmod p \\ t_1 = t \bmod q \end{cases} \tag{7.4}$$

$$\begin{cases} t_2 = t \bmod p \\ t_2 = (a/t) \bmod q \end{cases} \tag{7.5}$$

$$\begin{cases} t_3 = (a/t) \bmod p \\ t_3 = t \bmod q \end{cases} \tag{7.6}$$

$$\begin{cases} t_4 = (a/t) \bmod p \\ t_4 = (a/t) \bmod q \end{cases} \tag{7.7}$$

By the Chinese remainder theorem, these have the following solutions:

$$\begin{aligned} t_1 &= t \cdot e_1 + t \cdot e_2 \\ t_2 &= t \cdot e_1 + (a/t) \cdot e_2 \\ t_3 &= (a/t) \cdot e_1 + t \cdot e_2 \\ t_4 &= (a/t) \cdot e_1 + (a/t) \cdot e_2 \end{aligned}$$

where e_1 and e_2 have the property that

$$e_1 \equiv \begin{cases} 1 (\bmod p) \\ 0 (\bmod q) \end{cases}$$

and

$$e_2 \equiv \begin{cases} 0 (\bmod p) \\ 1 (\bmod q) \end{cases}$$

The solutions to (7.4) through (7.7) also have the following properties:

$$\left(\frac{t_1}{n}\right) = \left(\frac{t}{p}\right)\left(\frac{t}{q}\right)$$

$$\left(\frac{t_2}{n}\right) = \left(\frac{t}{p}\right)\left(\frac{a/t}{q}\right) = \left(\frac{t}{p}\right)\left(\frac{a}{q}\right)\left(\frac{t}{q}\right)$$

$$\left(\frac{t_3}{n}\right) = \left(\frac{a/t}{p}\right)\left(\frac{t}{q}\right) = \left(\frac{a}{p}\right)\left(\frac{t}{p}\right)\left(\frac{t}{q}\right)$$

$$\left(\frac{t_4}{n}\right) = \left(\frac{a/t}{p}\right)\left(\frac{a/t}{q}\right) = \left(\frac{a}{p}\right)\left(\frac{t}{p}\right)\left(\frac{a}{q}\right)\left(\frac{t}{q}\right)$$

In the case where a is a square, we have

$$\left(\frac{a}{p}\right) = \left(\frac{a}{q}\right) = +1$$

so that

$$\left(\frac{t_1}{n}\right) = \left(\frac{t_2}{n}\right) = \left(\frac{t_3}{n}\right) = \left(\frac{t_4}{n}\right)$$

But in the case where a is not a square, we have

$$\left(\frac{a}{p}\right) = \left(\frac{a}{q}\right) = -1$$

so that

$$\left(\frac{t_1}{n}\right) = \left(\frac{t_4}{n}\right)$$

and

$$\left(\frac{t_2}{n}\right) = \left(\frac{t_3}{n}\right)$$

but

$$\left(\frac{t_1}{n}\right) = -\left(\frac{t_2}{n}\right)$$

Note that if any of t_1 through t_4 are used as the random input used in a Cocks IBE encryption, then the same ciphertext is created. For the random input t_1, for example, the sender will calculate

$$s = \left(t_1 + \frac{a}{t_1}\right) = \left(t \cdot e_1 + t \cdot e_2 + \frac{a}{t \cdot e_1 + t \cdot e_2}\right) = t + \frac{a}{t}$$

while for the random input t_2 the sender will calculate

$$s = \left(t_2 + \frac{a}{t_2}\right) = \left(t \cdot e_1 + \frac{a}{t} \cdot e_2 + \frac{a}{t \cdot e_1 + \frac{a}{t} \cdot e_2}\right) = t + \frac{a}{t}$$

Similarly, the random inputs t_3 and t_4, the sender will calculate the same value for s.

So in the case where a is not a square, we have cases where the same ciphertext can come from different plaintext values, and the only way to distinguish between these cases is to be able to determine whether or not a is a square modulo n, which is the quadratic residuosity problem.

7.6.2 Chosen Ciphertext Security

Because the Cocks IBE scheme encrypts a single bit at a time, it is vulnerable to an adaptive chosen ciphertext attack, for the same reason that the Goldwasser-Micali scheme is. Suppose that an attacker Eve has the plaintext $(m_1, m_2, \ldots, m_k)$ and corresponding ciphertext $(c_1, c_2, \ldots, c_k)$ that is encrypted to the user Bob, and that she wants to obtain the plaintext corresponding to the ciphertext $(c_1', c_2', \ldots, c_k')$. She can then send the message $(c_1', c_2, \ldots, c_k)$ to Bob and observe his reaction. If Bob uses the ciphertext as a shared secret that he uses to derive a session key, for example, Eve can check to see if Bob creates the same session key from $(c_1', c_2, \ldots, c_k)$ that he does from $(c_1, c_2, \ldots, c_k)$ to determine whether the decryption of c_1 and c_1' are the same or different. Eve can then repeat this process to recover the additional bits of the decryption of $(c_1', c_2', \ldots, c_k')$, recovering a single bit every time she repeats this process.

7.6.3 Proof of Security

Using the random oracle model, it is possible to prove that defeating the security of the Cocks IBE scheme is no more difficult that solving the quadratic residuosity problem, so that an adversary who can decrypt a message that is encrypted with the Cocks IBE scheme can use his decryption algorithm to solve the quadratic residuosity problem. So, if we believe that the quadratic residuosity problem is sufficiently intractable we should also believe that the Cocks IBE scheme is adequately secure.

7.6.4 Selecting Parameter Sizes

Suppose that we want to use the Cocks IBE scheme to transport a 128-bit symmetric key. Per Table 5.2, to get the same cryptographic strength as a 128-bit symmetric key, this modulus needs to be 3,072 bits. So for each of the 128 bits in the symmetric key we need to transmit $2 \times 3{,}072 = 6{,}144$ bits of ciphertext, for a total of 786,432 bits of ciphertext. To transport a 256-bit symmetric key, this modulus needs to be 15,360 bits. So for each of the 256 bits in the symmetric key we need to transmit $2 \times 15{,}360 = 30{,}720$ bits of ciphertext, for a total of 7,864,320 bits of ciphertext. This may make the use of the scheme impractical for many uses. The number of bits of ciphertext needed by the Cocks IBE scheme for transporting various lengths of symmetric keys is summarized in Table 7.2.

7.7 Summary

The following summarizes the algorithms comprising in the Cocks IBE scheme.

Algorithm 7.1: Cocks IBE Setup (global parameters)
INPUT: A security parameter κ
OUTPUT: p, q, n, H_1

1. Randomly pick a prime p with $p \equiv 3 \pmod 4$ large enough to satisfy the security parameter.

Table 7.2
Size of Cocks IBE Ciphertext for Selected Symmetric Key Lengths

Symmetric Key Length	Cocks IBE Ciphertext Size
80 bits	166,710 bits
112 bits	458,752 bits
128 bits	768,432 bits
256 bits	7,864,320 bits

2. Randomly pick a prime q with $q \equiv 3 \pmod 4$ large enough to satisfy the security parameter.
3. Let $n = p \cdot q$.
4. Select an appropriate hash function $H_1 : \{0, 1\}^* \rightarrow \mathbb{Z}_n$ such that $(H_1(ID)/n) = +1$ for any $ID \in \{0, 1\}^*$.

Algorithm 7.2: Cocks Public Key Calculation
INPUT: n, a string ID representing an identity, hash function H_1

1. Calculate $H_1(ID)$

Algorithm 7.3: Cocks IBE Private Key Extraction
INPUT: a, p, q
OUTPUT: r

1. Calculate r as:

$$r = a^{(\phi(n)+4)/8} \bmod n = a^{(pq-p-q+5)/8} \bmod n$$

Algorithm 7.4: Cocks IBE Encryption
INPUT: n, plaintext bit m
OUTPUT: Ciphertext (s_1, s_2), each component an integer modulo n

1. Encode m as $x = (-1)^m$.
2. Pick a random t_1 and t_2 with

$$\left(\frac{t_1}{n}\right) = \left(\frac{t_2}{n}\right) = x$$

3. Calculate s_1 by

$$s_1 = \left(t_1 + \frac{a}{t_1}\right) \bmod n$$

4. Calculate s_2 by

$$s_2 = \left(t_2 - \frac{a}{t_2}\right) \bmod n$$

Algorithm 7.5: Cocks IBE Decryption
INPUT: Private key r, ciphertext (s_1, s_2), n
OUTPUT: Plaintext bit m

1. If $r^2 \equiv a \pmod{n}$ then let $s = s_1$ else let $s = s_2$.
2. Calculate the encoded plaintext bit x by

$$x = \left(\frac{s + 2r}{n}\right)$$

3. If $x = -1$ then let $m = 0$ else let $m = 1$.

References

[1] Cocks, C., "A Note on Non-Secret Encryption," *CESG Report*, 1973.

[2] Cocks, C., "An Identity Based Encryption Scheme Based on Quadratic Residues," *Proceedings of the Eighth IMA International Conference on Cryptography and Coding*, Cirencester, U.K., December 17–19, 2001, pp. 360–363.

[3] Goldwasser, S., and S. Micali, "Probabilistic Encryption," *Journal of Computer and System Sciences*, Vol. 28, No. 2, 1984, pp. 270–299.

8

Boneh-Franklin IBE

This chapter discusses Boneh-Franklin IBE [1], the first practical and secure IBE scheme that was invented. Boneh-Franklin IBE is an example of the full-domain hash family of IBE schemes, schemes in which an identity *ID* is mapped to a point Q_{ID} on an elliptic curve that is then used in the encryption and decryption algorithms of the scheme. Mapping an identity to a point on an elliptic curve typically requires a modular exponentiation that is fairly expensive to calculate, so full-domain hash schemes often have a disadvantage in performance relative to some other types of IBE schemes. Because of this, current research seems to have abandoned full-domain hash schemes in favor of other techniques where it is only necessary to map an identity to an integer. Boneh-Franklin IBE also requires the calculation of a pairing, an expensive calculation that accounts for almost all of the computation required for a Boneh-Franklin decryption and most of the computation required for a Boneh-Franklin encryption.

The Boneh-Franklin IBE scheme has features of both Joux's three-way key exchange and ElGamal encryption. Joux's three-way key exchange generalized the Diffie-Hellman key exchange to three participants, each with their own secret integer values. In Boneh-Franklin IBE, there are also three secret integer values: one of them is the master secret of the IBE system, one is randomly generated by the sender, and the third is never known, but is the discrete logarithm of the identity of the recipient. Both use a public parameter P, which is a point on an elliptic curve, and a pairing $\hat{e}$. This comparison is shown in Table 8.1 and Table 8.2. In the case of Joux's three-way key exchange, the shared secret $\hat{e}(P, P)^{abc}$ is calculated from three points aP, bP and cP, while in the case of Boneh-Franklin IBE, the shared secret $\hat{e}(P, P)^{rst}$ is calculated from a similar set of three points rP, sP and tP. In the case of Boneh-Franklin IBE, the value of

Table 8.1
Summary of Public and Private Values in Joux's Three-Way Key Exchange

Source	Private Value	Public Value
Alice	a	aP
Bob	b	bP
Charlie	c	cP

Table 8.2
Summary of Public and Private Values in Boneh-Franklin IBE

Source	Private Value	Public Value
Alice	r	rP
System parameters	s	sP
Bob	$s \cdot tP = sQ_{ID}$	$tP = Q_{ID}$

t is never known; it only appears in the value $tP = Q_{ID}$ which is calculated from the recipient's identity.

Much like ElGamal encryption uses the shared secret from a Diffie-Hellman key exchange to encrypt a plaintext message, Boneh-Franklin IBE uses the shared secret from this variant of Joux's three-way key exchange to encrypt a plaintext message. So, after calculating the shared secret $\hat{e}(P, P)^{rst}$, Alice hashes the shared secret into a format compatible with the plaintext. The value of $\hat{e}(P, P)^{rst}$ is an element of some $\mathbb{F}_q$, for example, while a typical message is an element of $\{0, 1\}^*$, so that $\hat{e}(P, P)^{rst}$ needs to be mapped into $\{0, 1\}^*$ so that it can be combined with the plaintext to produce the ciphertext. So, Alice hashes the shared secret $\hat{e}(P, P)^{rst}$ to the message space and combines the resulting hash with the plaintext M to get the ciphertext $C = M \oplus Hash(\hat{e}(P, P)^{rst})$. Bob then calculates the shared secret $\hat{e}(P, P)^{rst}$, hashes it to the message space, and recovers $M = C \oplus Hash(\hat{e}(P, P)^{rst})$. The rest of this chapter defines these steps more carefully and adds refinements to make the resulting scheme more secure.

The original Boneh-Franklin paper [1] used a slightly different notation than the convention followed here. In particular, the roles of p and q were reversed. In the original paper, the value of p defined the order of the finite field $\mathbb{F}_p$ while q was a prime that defined the order of the group $E(\mathbb{F}_p)[q]$. Later publications switched these roles, using q to define the order of the finite field $\mathbb{F}_q$ and p to define the order of the group G_1, the convention that most pairing-based cryptography literature now follows. So when reading descriptions of the Bohen-Franklin IBE system, it may be necessary to carefully note the meaning of the system parameters.

8.1 Boneh-Franklin IBE (Basic Scheme)

The Boneh-Franklin basic scheme uses a shared secret that can be calculated by both the sender and receiver of a message to encrypt a plaintext message. While it is easier to understand than the full Boneh-Franklin IBE scheme, it also is not as secure. The fully secure and more complicated scheme is described in Section 8.2.

8.1.1 Setup of Parameters (Basic Scheme)

To implement Boneh-Franklin IBE we first need a security parameter that defines the level of bit strength that the encryption will provide. Then we need to define groups G_1 and G_T and a pairing $\hat{e} : G_1 \times G_1 \rightarrow G_T$. To do this we pick an elliptic curve $E/\mathbb{F}_q$ with embedding degree k, and a prime p such that $p \mid \#E(\mathbb{F}_q)$. We also require that $p^2 \nmid \#E(\mathbb{F}_q)$ to ensure that the subgroup of order p that we will hash identities into is unique. The parameter p is the order of the groups G_1 and G_T, and G_T is a subgroup of $\mathbb{F}_{q^k}^*$. To attain a particular level of security, these parameters need to be chosen as described in Section 5.4.

We then randomly pick a point $P \in E(\mathbb{F}_q)[p]$ and let $G_1 = \langle P \rangle$ and $G_T = \langle \hat{e}(P, P) \rangle$, which are cyclic groups of prime order p. Next, we pick a random integer $s \in \mathbb{Z}_p^*$ and use it to calculate sP. To map an identity ID to a point Q_{ID} we also need a cryptographic hash function $H_1 : \{0, 1\}^* \rightarrow G_1$. To encrypt a message of n bits using Boneh-Franklin IBE we also need another cryptographic hash function $H_2 : G_T \rightarrow \{0, 1\}^n$ that hashes elements of G_T into a form that we can combine with the plaintext message, which is a bit string of length n. These elements form the public parameters and master secret as shown in Table 8.3 and Table 8.4. The integer s is the master secret; all other values comprise the public parameters.

There are dependencies among the elements of Table 8.3. The values of p, q, and E, for example, are implicit in the definition of the group G_1. Because of this it is possible to reduce the number of required public parameters to a much shorter list, and we can define the public parameters of a Boneh-Franklin IBE system (basic scheme) to be *BFBasicParams* = $(G_1, G_T, \hat{e}, n, sP, H_1, H_2)$ without introducing any ambiguity.

Table 8.3
Public Parameters of Boneh-Franklin IBE System (Basic Scheme)

Element	Type	Comments
q	Prime power	Order of finite field $\mathbb{F}_q$
$E/\mathbb{F}_q$	Elliptic curve	$E(\mathbb{F}_q)$ has embedding degree k
p	Prime	$p \mid \#E(\mathbb{F}_q)$, $p^2 \nmid \#E(\mathbb{F}_q)$
G_1	Cyclic group	Subgroup of $E(\mathbb{F}_q)$, $G_1 = \langle P \rangle$
G_T	Cyclic group	Subgroup of $\mathbb{F}_{q^k}^*$, $G_T = \langle \hat{e}(P, P) \rangle$
$\hat{e}$	Pairing	$\hat{e} : G_1 \times G_1 \rightarrow G_T$
n	Integer	Length of plaintext (in bits)
P	Point on elliptic curve	$P \in G_1$
sP	Point on elliptic curve	$sP \in G_1$
H_1	Cryptographic hash function	$H_1 : \{0, 1\}^* \rightarrow G_1$
H_2	Cryptographic hash function	$H_2 : G_T \rightarrow \{0, 1\}^n$

Table 8.4
Master Secret for Boneh-Franklin IBE System (Basic Scheme)

Element	Type	Comments
s	Integer	$s \in \mathbb{Z}_p^*$

8.1.2 Extraction of the Private Key (Basic Scheme)

Once the public parameters listed in Table 8.3 and the master secret listed in Table 8.4 are determined, the private key associated with the identity ID is calculated by mapping the identity to a point on the curve E by calculating $Q_{ID} = H_1(ID)$ and then by multiplying this point Q_{ID} by the master secret s to get the private key sQ_{ID}. This is summarized in Table 8.5.

8.1.3 Encrypting with Boneh-Franklin IBE (Basic Scheme)

To encrypt the message $M \in \{0, 1\}^n$ to the recipient with identity ID, the sender follows the following steps.

Table 8.5
Private Key for Boneh-Franklin IBE System

Element	Type	Comments
sQ_{ID}	Point on elliptic curve	Private key corresponding to identity ID, $Q_{ID} = H_1(ID)$

1. Generates a random integer $r \in \mathbb{Z}_p^*$ and calculates rP.
2. Calculates $Q_{ID} = H_1(ID)$ from the recipient's identity ID and uses it to calculate

$$K = H_2(\hat{e}(rQ_{ID}, sP)) \tag{8.1}$$

3. Sets the ciphertext corresponding to the pair $C = (C_1, C_2)$ where $C_1 = rP$ and $C_2 = M \oplus K$.

8.1.4 Decrypting with Boneh-Franklin IBE (Basic Scheme)

When the recipient receives the ciphertext $C = (rP, M \oplus H_2(\hat{e}(rQ_{ID}, sP)) = (C_1, C_2)$ he performs the following steps.

1. Calculates $K = H_2(\hat{e}(sQ_{ID}, C_1))$ from the ciphertext component C_1 and his private key sQ_{ID}.
2. Calculates $M = C_2 \oplus K$.

This recovers the plaintext M because the sender calculates K as

$$K = H_2(\hat{e}(rQ_{ID}, sP)) = H_2(\hat{e}(Q_{ID}, sP)^{rs})$$

and the recipient calculates K as

$$K = H_2(\hat{e}(sQ_{ID}, C_1)) = H_2(\hat{e}(Q_{ID}, P)^{sr})$$

8.1.5 Examples (Basic Scheme)

(i) Suppose that E is the elliptic curve $E/\mathbb{F}_q : y^2 = x^3 + 1$, with q a prime and $q \equiv 11 \pmod{12}$, and G_1 a subgroup of order p of $E(\mathbb{F}_q)$. We can create a suitable hash function $H_1 : \{0, 1\}^* \rightarrow G_1$ from a cryptographic hash function H as follows. First, use H to map a string that represents an identity into the integers modulo q, perhaps by either iterating H until we get a result in the correct range or by interpreting the output of H as an integer and then reducing this integer modulo q. We can then use this result as the y-coordinate of a point $Q \in E(\mathbb{F}_q)$ and calculate the corresponding x-coordinate of a point on the curve from

$$x = (y^2 - 1)^{1/3}$$

From Euler's theorem, we have that

$$a^{q-1} \equiv 1(\text{mod } q)$$

so that

$$a^{2q-1} \equiv a(\text{mod } q)$$

and thus

$$a^{(2q-1)/3} \equiv a^{1/3}(\text{mod } q)$$

whenever we have that $3 \mid (2q - 1)$. This is the case when $q \equiv 11\,(\text{mod } 12)$, so we can calculate the x-coordinate of the point Q this way. One way to get $Q_{ID} \in E(\mathbb{F}_q)[p]$ from such a Q is to multiply it by an appropriate constant to get

$$Q_{ID} = \frac{\#E(\mathbb{F}_q)}{p} Q$$

With the curve $E/\mathbb{F}_q : y^2 = x^3 + 1$, we have that $\#E(\mathbb{F}_q) = q + 1$ when $q \equiv 11\,(\text{mod } 12)$, so we calculate $Q_{ID} \in E(\mathbb{F}_q)[p]$ as

$$Q_{ID} = \frac{q+1}{p} Q$$

Because we require that $p \mid \#E(\mathbb{F}_q)$ but $p^2 \nmid \#E(\mathbb{F}_q)$, we know that we have a unique subgroup of $E(\mathbb{F}_q)$ or order p, so this must result in $Q_{ID} \in G_1$ as needed.

(ii) Suppose that E is the elliptic curve $E/\mathbb{F}_q : y^2 = x^3 + x$, with q a prime and $q \equiv 11\,(\text{mod } 12)$, and G_1 a subgroup of order p of $E(\mathbb{F}_q)$. We can create a suitable hash function $H_1 : \{0, 1\}^* \rightarrow G_1$ from a cryptographic hash function H as follows. First, use H to map a string that represents an identity into the integers modulo q. We can then use this result as the x-coordinate of a point $Q \in E(\mathbb{F}_q)[p]$ and calculate the corresponding y-coordinate of Q from and then calculating the corresponding x-coordinate of a point on the curve from

$$y = (x^3 + x)^{1/2}$$

We can only do this if $x^3 + x$ is a quadratic residue modulo q, but because $q \equiv 3 \pmod 4$ we have that if $x^3 + x$ is a quadratic nonresidue modulo q then we have that $-(x^3 + x)$ is a quadratic residue modulo q. From Euler's theorem, we have that

$$a^{q-1} \equiv 1 \pmod q$$

so that

$$a^{q-1}a^2 = a^{q+1} \equiv a^2 \pmod q$$

and thus

$$a^{(q+1)/4} \equiv a^{1/2} \pmod q$$

whenever we have that $4 \mid (q + 1)$. This is the case when $q \equiv 11 \pmod{12}$, so we can calculate the y-coordinate of the point Q this way.

With the curve $E/\mathbb{F}_q : y^2 = x^3 + x$, we have that $\#E(\mathbb{F}_q) = q + 1$ when $q \equiv 11 \pmod{12}$, so we calculate $Q_{ID} \in E(\mathbb{F}_q)[p]$ as

$$Q_{ID} = \frac{q+1}{p} Q$$

(iii) Suppose that we want to avoid hashing an identity to a point on an elliptic curve, and try to avoid this by hashing the identity ID to an integer t and then using the point tP as the corresponding public key. This, however, will allow an adversary to calculate the shared secret $\hat{e}(P, P)^{rst}$ as $(\hat{e}(rP, sP))^t = \hat{e}(P, P)^{rst}$, which defeats the security provided by the Boneh-Franklin IBE scheme.

(iv) Elements of G_T are elements of the finite field $\mathbb{F}_{q^k}$, so we can write a typical element of G_T as $\alpha = (\alpha_1, \alpha_2, \ldots, \alpha_k)$ where each $\alpha_i \in \mathbb{F}_q$. So for a plaintext message $M \in \{0, 1\}^n$, one way to create a useful hash function $H_2 : \{0, 1\}^n \to G_T$ is to use the concatenation of the coordinates of α as the input to a cryptographic hash function H and then to reduce $H(\alpha_1 \mid \alpha_2 \mid \ldots \mid \alpha_k)$ to the range 0 to $2^n - 1$, perhaps by truncating $H(\alpha_1 \mid \alpha_2 \mid \ldots \mid \alpha_k)$ to n bits.

(v) Suppose that Alice wants to use Bohen-Franklin IBE to encrypt a message to Bob. Suppose that E is the elliptic curve $E/\mathbb{F}_{131} : y^2 = x^3 + 1$, and $P = (98, 58) \in E(\mathbb{F}_{131})[11]$, $G_1 = \langle P \rangle$, and $G_T = \langle \hat{e}(P, P) \rangle$, where $\hat{e} : G_1 \times G_1 \to G_T$ is the reduced modified Tate pairing where $\hat{e}(P, Q) = e(P, \phi(Q))^{1560}$, where ϕ is the distortion map given by $\phi(x, y) = (\xi x, y)$ for $\xi = 65 + 112i$. Let the master secret of this system be the integer $s = 7$, so that $sP = (33, 100)$, and suppose that Bob's identity gives us that $H_2(ID_{Bob}) = Q_{ID} = (128, 57)$, so that Bob's private key is $sQ_{ID} = (113, 8)$. The values used in this example are summarized in Table 8.6.

Alice can use these values to encrypt the message $s = 7$ to Bob. Suppose that she generates the random $r = 5 \in \mathbb{Z}_{11}^*$ to do this. Alice then calculates $rQ_{ID} = (5)(128, 57) = (98, 73)$ and uses it to calculate

$$rP = 5P = (34, 23)$$

and

$$\begin{aligned} K &= H_2(\hat{e}(rQ_{ID}, sP)) \\ &= H_2(\hat{e}(98, 73), (33, 100))) = H_2(49 + 58i) \end{aligned}$$

which she then uses to create the ciphertext (C_1, C_2) where $C_1 = rP$ and $C_2 = M \oplus K$.

When Bob receives this ciphertext, he then calculates

$$\begin{aligned} K &= H_2(\hat{e}(sQ_{ID}, C_1)) \\ &= H_2(\hat{e}(113, 8), (34, 23))) = H_2(49 + 58i) \end{aligned}$$

which he then uses to recover the plaintext M by calculating

$$\begin{aligned} M &= C_2 \oplus K \\ &= (M \oplus K) \oplus K = M \end{aligned}$$

Table 8.6
Summary of Values Used in Example 8.1.5(v)

Parameters	Type	Value	Comments
P	Point on elliptic curve	(98, 58)	$P \in E(\mathbb{F}_{131})$ [11]
sP	Point on elliptic curve	(33, 100)	
Q_{ID}	Point on elliptic curve	(128, 57)	$Q_{ID} \in E(\mathbb{F}_{131})$ [11]
sQ_{ID}	Point on elliptic curve	(113, 8)	Bob's private key
r	Integer	5	Generated randomly by Alice
s	Integer	7	Master secret

(vi) Suppose that E is the elliptic curve $E/\mathbb{F}_{131} : y^2 = x^3 + 1$, and we want to use the pairing $\hat{e} : G_1 \times G_2 \rightarrow G_T$ to implement the Boneh-Franklin scheme where G_1 is a subgroup of $E(\mathbb{F}_{131})$ and G_2 is a subgroup of $E'(\mathbb{F}_{131})$ where $E'/\mathbb{F}_{131} : y^2 = x^3 + 130$ is the quadratic twist of $E/\mathbb{F}_{131}$ constructed using the quadratic nonresidue $v = 130$. This will require the public parameters P and sP to be elements of $E'(\mathbb{F}_{131})$. We can use $P = (4, 71) \in E'(\mathbb{F}_{131})$ to generate G_2 for this, giving $sP = (56, 72)$ for $s = 7$. So we can use $G_1 = \langle Q \rangle = \langle (98, 58) \rangle$ and $G_2 = \langle P \rangle = \langle (4, 71) \rangle$. Let $\hat{e} : G_1 \times G_2 \rightarrow G_T$ be the reduced modified Tate pairing where $\hat{e}(P, Q) = e(P, \phi_2(Q))^{1560}$, where $\phi_2 : E' \rightarrow E$ is the mapping given by $\phi(x, y) = (130 \cdot x, i \cdot y)$. Let the master secret of this system be the integer $s = 7$, so that $sP = (56, 72)$, and suppose that Bob's identity gives us that $H_2(ID_{Bob}) = Q_{ID} = (128, 57)$, so that Bob's private key is $sQ_{ID} = (113, 8)$. The values used in this example are summarized in Table 8.7.

Alice can use these values to encrypt the message M to Bob. Suppose that she generates the random $r = 5 \in \mathbb{Z}_{11}^*$ to do this. Alice then calculates $rQ_{ID} = (5)(128, 57) = (98, 73)$ and uses it to calculate

$$rP = 5P = (54, 1)$$

and

$$\begin{aligned} K &= H_2(\hat{e}(rQ_{ID}, sP)) \\ &= H_2(\hat{e}((98, 73), (56, 72))) = H_2(39 + 107i) \end{aligned}$$

which she then uses to create the ciphertext (C_1, C_2) where $C_1 = rP$ and $C_2 = M \oplus K$.

When Bob receives this ciphertext, he then calculates

Table 8.7
Summary of Values Used in Example 8.1.5(vi)

Parameters	Type	Value	Comments
P	Point on elliptic curve	(4, 71)	$P \in E'(\mathbb{F}_{131})$ [11]
sP	Point on elliptic curve	(56, 72)	
Q_{ID}	Point on elliptic curve	(128, 57)	$Q_{ID} \in E(\mathbb{F}_{131})$ [11]
sQ_{ID}	Point on elliptic curve	(113, 8)	Bob's private key
r	Integer	5	Generated randomly by Alice
s	Integer	7	Master secret

$$K = H_2(\hat{e}(sQ_{ID}, C_1))$$
$$= H_2(\hat{e}((113, 8), (54, 1))) = H_2(39 + 107i)$$

which he then uses to recover the plaintext M by calculating

$$M = C_2 \oplus K$$
$$= (M \oplus K) \oplus K = M$$

8.2 Boneh-Franklin IBE (Full Scheme)

The basic scheme is also vulnerable to a chosen-ciphertext attack because the value of K calculated in (8.1) is not a function of the plaintext message M. So if an adversary wants to decrypt the ciphertext (C_1, C_2) which encrypts the message M he can do this by decrypting the ciphertext $(C_1, C_2 \oplus \epsilon)$ to get the plaintext message $M \oplus \epsilon$ and then recover M as $M = (M \oplus \epsilon) \oplus \epsilon$. The Fujisaki-Okamoto transform can easily eliminate this vulnerability; adding the additional level of hashing that the Fujisaki-Okamoto transform requires creates the more complex "full scheme" that is described below that is not vulnerable to such an attack. Adding the Fujisaki-Okamoto transform to create a scheme that is resistant to chosen-ciphertext attacks makes a more complex system. Two additional cryptographic hash functions are required, and both the encryption and decryption processes get more complex.

8.2.1 Setup of Parameters (Full Scheme)

In addition to the parameters listed in Table 8.3, we also need two additional hash functions to implement the Fujisaki-Okamoto transform. In particular, we need to hash functions $H_3 : \{0, 1\}^n \times \{0, 1\}^n \rightarrow \mathbb{Z}_p^*$ and $H_4 : \{0, 1\}^n \times \{0, 1\}^n \rightarrow \mathbb{Z}_p^*$. Adding these hash functions brings the list of public parameters for the full scheme to the public parameters that are listed in Table 8.8. The master secret is unchanged from the basic scheme, and is shown in Table 8.9.

There are dependencies among the elements of Table 8.8. The values of p, q, and E, for example, are implicit in the definition of the group G_1. Because of this it is possible to reduce the number of required public parameters to a much shorter list, and we can define the public parameters of a Boneh-Franklin IBE system to be $BFParams = (G_1, G_T, \hat{e}, n, P, sP, H_1, H_2, H_3, H_4)$ without introducing any ambiguity.

Table 8.8
Public Parameters of Boneh-Franklin IBE System (Full Scheme)

Element	Type	Comments
q	Prime power	Order of finite field $\mathbb{F}_q$
$E/\mathbb{F}_q$	Elliptic curve	$E(\mathbb{F}_q)$ has embedding degree k
p	Prime	$p \mid \#E(\mathbb{F}_q)$, $p^2 \nmid \#E(\mathbb{F}_q)$
G_1	Cyclic group	Subgroup of $E(\mathbb{F}_q)$, $G_1 = \langle P \rangle$
G_T	Cyclic group	Subgroup of $\mathbb{F}^*_{q^k}$, $G_T = \langle \hat{e}(P, P) \rangle$
$\hat{e}$	Pairing	$\hat{e} : G_1 \times G_1 \to G_T$
n	Integer	Length of plaintext
P	Point on elliptic curve	$P \in E(\mathbb{F}_q)\,[p]$
sP	Point on elliptic curve	$sP \in E(\mathbb{F}_q)\,[p]$
H_1	Cryptographic hash function	$H_1 : \{0, 1\}^* \to G_1$
H_2	Cryptographic hash function	$H_2 : G_T \to \{0, 1\}^n$
H_3	Cryptographic hash function	$H_3 : \{0, 1\}^n \times \{0, 1\}^n \to \mathbb{Z}^*_p$
H_4	Cryptographic hash function	$H_4 : \{0, 1\}^n \times \{0, 1\}^n \to \mathbb{Z}^*_p$

Table 8.9
Master Secret for Boneh-Franklin IBE System (Full Scheme)

Element	Type	Comments
s	Integer	$s \in \mathbb{Z}^*_p$

8.2.2 Extraction of the Private Key (Full Scheme)

The extraction of the private key for the full scheme is identical to the extraction of the private key in the basic scheme (Section 8.1.2). This is summarized in Table 8.10.

8.2.3 Encrypting with Boneh-Franklin IBE (Full Scheme)

To encrypt the message M to the recipient with identity ID, the sender performs the following steps:

Table 8.10
Private Key for Boneh-Franklin IBE System

Element	Type	Comments
sQ_{ID}	Point on elliptic curve	Private key corresponding to identity ID, $Q_{ID} = H_1(ID)$

1. Calculates $Q_{ID} = H_1(ID)$.
2. Picks a random $\sigma \in \{0, 1\}^n$.
3. Calculates $r = H_3(\sigma, M)$.
4. Calculates $C_1 = rP$.
5. Calculates $C_1 = \sigma \oplus H_2(\hat{e}(rQ_{ID}, sP))$.
6. Calculates $C_3 = M \oplus H_4(\sigma)$.
7. Sets the ciphertext to $C = (C_1, C_2, C_3)$.

8.2.4 Decrypting with Boneh-Franklin IBE (Full Scheme)

To decrypt the ciphertext $C = (C_1, C_2, C_3)$, the recipient performs the following steps:

1. Calculates $\sigma = C_2 \oplus H_2(\hat{e}(sQ_{ID}, C_1))$.
2. Calculates $M = C_3 \oplus H_4(\sigma)$, which is the plaintext message.
3. Calculates $r = H_3(\sigma, M)$.
4. Calculates rP. If $C_1 \neq rP$ then rejects the ciphertext as invalid.

8.3 Security of the Boneh-Franklin IBE Scheme

Note that we can write $Q_{ID} = tP$ for some (unknown) t, so we have $\hat{e}(rQ_{ID}, sP) = \hat{e}(rtP, sP) = \hat{e}(P, P)^{rst}$. So, we can also think of the ciphertext as being $C = (rP, M \oplus H_2(\hat{e}(P, P)^{rst}))$. An adversary can obtain P and sP from the public parameters, can calculate $Q_{ID} = tP$ from the recipient's identity, and observes rP in the ciphertext. If he can calculate $\hat{e}(P, P)^{rst}$ from P, rP, sP, and tP then he can recover the plaintext message M by calculating $(M \oplus H_2(\hat{e}(P, P)^{rst}) \oplus H_2(\hat{e}(P, P)^{rst} = M$, but calculating $\hat{e}(P, P)^{rst}$ in this way is exactly the BDHP. So, if the BDHP is sufficiently difficult then it will be difficult for an adversary to recover a plaintext message from a corresponding ciphertext. By choosing G_1 and G_T carefully this can easily be accomplished. The original Boneh-Franklin paper [1] used the random oracle model to prove that an adversary able to decrypt a message that has been encrypted with Boneh-Franklin IBE can use his decryption algorithm to solve the BDHP, so if we believe that the BDHP is sufficiently difficult to solve then Boneh-Franklin IBE must also be sufficiently difficult to decrypt. The basic Boneh-Franklin scheme is resistant to chosen-plaintext attacks and adaptive chosen-identity attacks; the full Boneh-Franklin scheme is resistant to chosen-ciphertext attacks and adaptive chosen-identity attacks.

8.4 Summary

The following summarizes the steps in the Boneh-Franklin IBE scheme (full scheme).

Algorithm 8.1: Boneh-Franklin IBE Setup
INPUT: a security parameter κ, an elliptic curve E, a plaintext bit length n
OUTPUT: $BFParams = (G_1, G_T, \hat{e}, n, P, sP, H_1, H_2, H_3, H_4)$ and master secret s

1. Select a prime p and prime power q with $p \mid \#E(\mathbb{F}_q)$ and $p^2 \nmid \#E(\mathbb{F}_q)$ and such that the bit security level provided by p and q meets the required security parameter κ. For best performance, p should be a Solinas prime.
2. Select a random $P \in E(\mathbb{F}_q)[p]$ and let $G_1 = \langle P \rangle$.
3. Let k be the embedding degree of $E/\mathbb{F}_q$; select a pairing $\hat{e} : G_1 \times G_1 \rightarrow \mathbb{F}_{q^k}^*$.
4. Let $G_T = \langle \hat{e}(P, P) \rangle$.
5. Select a random $s \in \mathbb{Z}_p^*$ and calculate sP.
6. Select appropriate cryptographic hash functions $H_1 : \{0, 1\}^* \rightarrow G_1$, $H_2 : G_T \rightarrow \{0, 1\}^n$, $H_3 : \{0, 1\}^n \times \{0, 1\}^n \rightarrow \mathbb{Z}_p^*$ and $H_4 : \{0, 1\}^n \times \{0, 1\}^n \rightarrow \mathbb{Z}_p^*$.
7. The master secret is the value s.
8. The public parameters are $BFParams = (G_1, G_T, \hat{e}, n, P, sP, H_1, H_2, H_3, H_4)$.

Algorithm 8.2: Boneh-Franklin IBE Private Key Extraction
INPUT: A string ID representing an identity and a set of public parameters $BFParams = (G_1, G_T, \hat{e}, n, P, sP, H_1, H_2, H_3, H_4)$.
OUTPUT: The private key sQ_{ID}

1. Calculate $sQ_{ID} = sH_1(ID)$.

Algorithm 8.3: Boneh-Franklin IBE Encryption
INPUT: A plaintext message M of length n bits, a string ID representing the identity of the recipient of the ciphertext, a set of public parameters $BFParams = (G_1, G_T, \hat{e}, n, P, sP, H_1, H_2, H_3, H_4)$.
OUTPUT: A ciphertext $C = (C_1, C_2, C_3)$

1. Calculate $Q_{ID} = H_1(ID)$.
2. Select a random $\sigma \in \{0, 1\}^n$.
3. Calculate $r = H_3(\sigma, M)$.
4. Calculate $C_1 = rP$.
5. Calculate $C_2 = \sigma \oplus H_2(\hat{e}(rQ_{ID}, sP))$.
6. Calculate $C_3 = M \oplus H_4(\sigma)$.

Algorithm 8.4: Boneh-Franklin IBE Decryption
INPUT: A ciphertext $C = (C_1, C_2, C_3)$, a set of public parameters *BFParams* $= (G_1, G_T, \hat{e}, n, P, sP, H_1, H_2, H_3, H_4)$, a private key sQ_{ID}.
OUTPUT: A plaintext message M or an error condition

1. Calculate $\sigma = C_2 \oplus H_2(\hat{e}(sQ_{ID}, C_1))$.
2. Calculate $M = C_3 \oplus H_4(\sigma)$.
3. Calculate $r = H_3(\sigma, M)$ and then calculate rP. If $C_1 \neq rP$ then raise an error condition that indicates an invalid ciphertext. Otherwise, return the plaintext M.

Reference

[1] Boneh, D., and M. Franklin, "Identity Based Encryption from the Weil Pairing," *SIAM Journal of Computing*, Vol. 32, No. 3, pp. 586–615.

9

Boneh-Boyen IBE

This chapter discusses Boneh-Boyen IBE [1], an example of the family of "commutative blinding" schemes. The name is due to the commuting of coefficients that occurs when computing the ratio of two pairings that is roughly of the form

$$\frac{e(aP, bQ)}{e(bP, aQ)}$$

A value that used to encrypt a plaintext message is calculated by the sender using public parameters of a Boneh-Boyen IBE scheme, and the recipient of the resulting ciphertext calculates the same value from the ciphertext and his private key by calculating such a ratio of pairings. Calculating the ratio of two pairings can be done more efficiently than calculating the two pairings separately and then calculating the ratio, an algorithm for which is discussed in Chapter 12.

In the Boneh-Boyen IBE scheme and other commutative blinding schemes, an identity *ID* is hashed to an integer that is then used in the encryption and decryption operations. This avoids a modular exponentiation, which generally makes such schemes faster then full-domain hash schemes, like the Boneh-Franklin scheme of Chapter 8, which require hashing an identity to a point on an elliptic curve.

Note that two IBE schemes were described in the same paper by Boneh and Boyen [1], so the name "Boneh-Boyen IBE scheme" can be ambiguous. The IBE scheme described here is the first of the two schemes that were described in this paper, and is often abbreviated BB_1 while the second scheme is often abbreviated BB_2. This chapter only discusses the BB_1 IBE scheme.

Two ways to describe the basic Boneh-Boyen scheme are given in the following sections. A simplified version of the scheme is described in Section 9.1 using the additive notation that is commonly used for operations in elliptic curve groups and is used in the many cryptographic standards. In Section 9.2 the same scheme is described using the multiplicative notation that is commonly used in more recent literature on pairing-based cryptography. The basic scheme is vulnerable to a chosen-ciphertext attack and a fully secure version of the scheme is described in Section 9.3.

9.1 Boneh-Boyen IBE (Basic Scheme—Additive Notation)

The Boneh-Boyen basic scheme uses a shared secret that can be calculated by both the sender and receiver of a message to encrypt a plaintext message; the sender of the message calculates the shared secret from public parameters and the recipient's identity, while the recipient calculates the shared secret from their private key and the ciphertext. While it is easier to understand than the full Boneh-Boyen IBE scheme, it also is not as secure. The fully secure and more complicated scheme is described in Section 9.3.

The following description of the Boneh-Boyen scheme uses the additive notation that is commonly used for operations in elliptic curve groups. So that if P and Q are elements of an elliptic curve group $E(\mathbb{F}_q)$ then we will write $P + Q$ to indicate the group operation of $E(\mathbb{F}_q)$ applied to the groups elements P and Q and aP to indicate the multiplication of the point P by the integer a. This notation is used by many cryptographic standards, but is rarely used in the literature of pairing-based cryptography, where the multiplicative notation that is used in Section 9.2 is more common.

9.1.1 Setup of Parameters (Basic Scheme—Additive Notation)

To implement Boneh-Boyen IBE we first need a security parameter that defines the level of bit strength that the encryption will provide. Then we need to define groups G_1 and G_T and a pairing $\hat{e} : G_1 \times G_1 \rightarrow G_T$. To do this we pick an elliptic curve $E/\mathbb{F}_q$ with embedding degree k, and a prime p such that $p \mid \#E(\mathbb{F}_q)$. The security parameter will define the size of the groups G_1 and G_T as described in Section 9.5.

We then randomly pick a point $P \in E(\mathbb{F}_q)[p]$ and let $G_1 = \langle P \rangle$ and $G_T = \langle \hat{e}(P, P) \rangle$, which are cyclic groups of order p. We need a cryptographic hash function $H_1 : \{0, 1\}^* \rightarrow \mathbb{Z}_p$ to map strings representing identities to integers. To encrypt a message of n bits using Boneh-Boyen IBE we also need another cryptographic hash function $H_2 : G_T \rightarrow \{0, 1\}^n$ that hashes elements of G_T into a form that we can combine with the plaintext message, which is a bit string of length n. Three integers α, β, $\gamma \in \mathbb{Z}_p$ are the master secret and are used to calculate the three additional public parameters αP, βP, and γP. There is also a constant $v = \hat{e}(P_1, P_2) = \hat{e}(\alpha P, \beta P) = \hat{e}(P, P)^{\alpha\beta}$ which is needed by the Boneh-Boyen scheme. This constant can either be distributed to users as part of the public parameters or can be precomputed by users before they perform a Boneh-Boyen encryption. We will assume that this constant v is part of the public parameters, in which case the parameter βP does not need to be listed in the public parameters because its only use outside a PKG is in calculating v. These elements form the public parameters and master secret as shown in Table 9.1 and Table 9.2.

There are dependencies among the elements of Table 9.1. The values of p, q, and E, for example, are implicit in the definition of the group G_1. Because of this it is possible to reduce the number of required public parameters to a

Table 9.1
Parameters of Boneh-Boyen IBE System (Basic Scheme—Additive Notation)

Element	Type	Comments
q	Prime power	Order of finite field $\mathbb{F}_q$
$E/\mathbb{F}_q$	Elliptic curve	$E(\mathbb{F}_q)$ has embedding degree k
p	Prime	$p \mid \#E(\mathbb{F}_q)$
G_1	Cyclic group	Subgroup of $E(\mathbb{F}_q)$, $G_1 = \langle P \rangle$
G_T	Cyclic group	Subgroup of $\mathbb{F}_{q^k}^*$, $G_T = \langle \hat{e}(P, P) \rangle$
$\hat{e}$	Pairing	$\hat{e} : G_1 \times G_1 \rightarrow G_T$
n	Positive integer	Length of plaintext (in bits)
P	Point on elliptic curve	$P \in G_1$
P_1	Point on elliptic curve	$P_1 = \alpha P$
P_2	Point on elliptic curve	$P_2 = \beta P$
P_3	Point on elliptic curve	$P_3 = \gamma P$
H_1	Cryptographic hash function	$H_1 : \{0, 1\}^* \rightarrow \mathbb{Z}_p$
H_2	Cryptographic hash function	$H_2 : G_T \rightarrow \{0, 1\}^n$
v	Element of $\mathbb{F}_{q^k}^*$	$v = \hat{e}(P_1, P_2) = \hat{e}(\alpha P, \beta P) = \hat{e}(P, P)^{\alpha\beta}$

Table 9.2
Master Secret for Boneh-Boyen IBE System (Basic Scheme—Additive Notation)

Element	Type	Comments
α, β, γ	Integers	$\alpha, \beta, \gamma \in \mathbb{Z}_p$

much shorter list, and we can define the public parameters of a Boneh-Boyen IBE system (basic scheme—additive notation) to be BB_1 *BasicParamsAdditive* = $(G_1, G_T, \hat{e}, n, P, P_1, P_3, H_1, H_2, v)$ without introducing any ambiguity.

9.1.2 Extraction of the Private Key (Basic Scheme—Additive Notation)

Once the public parameters listed in Table 9.1 and the master secret listed in Table 9.2 are determined, the private key associated with the identity ID is calculated by mapping the identity to an integer $q_{ID} \in \mathbb{Z}_p$ by calculating $q_{ID} = H_1(ID)$. A random per-user value $r \in \mathbb{Z}_p$ is then generated, which is then used to calculate the two components of the private key $D_{ID} = (q_{ID} \cdot rP_1 + \alpha P_2 + rP_3, rP) = (D_0, D_1)$. This is summarized in Table 9.3.

9.1.3 Encrypting with Boneh-Boyen IBE (Basic Scheme—Additive Notation)

To encrypt the message $M \in \{0, 1\}^n$ to the recipient with identity ID, the sender performs the following steps.

1. Calculate $q_{ID} = H_1(ID)$.
2. Pick random $s \in \mathbb{Z}_p$.
3. Calculate $k = v^s$.
4. Calculate $c = M \oplus H_2(k)$.
5. Calculate $C_0 = sP$.
6. Calculate $C_1 = q_{ID}(sP_1) + sP_3$.
7. Set ciphertext to $C = (c, C_0, C_1)$.

9.1.4 Decrypting with Boneh-Boyen IBE (Basic Scheme—Additive Notation)

When the recipient receives the ciphertext $C = (c, C_0, C_1)$ he performs the following steps.

Table 9.3
Private Key for Boneh-Boyen IBE System

Element	Comments
$D_{ID} = (q_{ID} \cdot rP_1 + \alpha P_2 + rP_3, rP) = (D_0, D_1)$	Private key corresponding to identity ID, $q_{ID} = H_1(ID)$

1. Calculate $k = \dfrac{\hat{e}(C_0, D_0)}{\hat{e}(C_1, D_1)}$.
2. Calculate $M = c \oplus H_2(k)$.

Note that

$$\begin{aligned}\hat{e}(C_0, D_0) &= \hat{e}(sP, q_{ID} \cdot rP_1 + \alpha P_2 + rP_3) \\ &= \hat{e}(sP, q_{ID} \cdot rP_1)\, \hat{e}(sP, \alpha P_2)\, \hat{e}(sP, rP_3) \\ &= \hat{e}(sP, \alpha q_{ID} \cdot rP)\, \hat{e}(sP, \alpha\beta P)\, \hat{e}(sP, \gamma rP) \\ &= \hat{e}(P, P)^{\alpha q_{ID} \cdot rs}\, \hat{e}(P, P)^{\alpha\beta s}\, \hat{e}(P, P)^{\gamma rs}\end{aligned}$$

and

$$\begin{aligned}\hat{e}(C_1, D_1) &= \hat{e}(q_{ID} \cdot sP_1 + sP_3, rP) \\ &= \hat{e}(\alpha q_{ID} \cdot sP + \gamma sP, rP) \\ &= \hat{e}(\alpha q_{ID} \cdot sP, rP)\, \hat{e}(\gamma sP, rP) \\ &= \hat{e}(P, P)^{\alpha q_{ID} \cdot rs}\, \hat{e}(P, P)^{\gamma rs}\end{aligned}$$

so that we have

$$\begin{aligned}\frac{\hat{e}(C_0, D_0)}{\hat{e}(C_1, D_1)} &= \frac{\hat{e}(P, P)^{\alpha q_{ID} \cdot rs}\, \hat{e}(P, P)^{\alpha\beta s}\, \hat{e}(P, P)^{\gamma rs}}{\hat{e}(P, P)^{\alpha q_{ID} \cdot rs}\, \hat{e}(P, P)^{\gamma rs}} \\ &= \hat{e}(P, P)^{\alpha\beta s} = v^s\end{aligned}$$

so that step 3 of Section 9.1.3 and step 1 of Section 9.1.4 calculate the same value of v^s, which allows the recipient to decrypt the ciphertext correctly.

Example 9.1 (Boneh-Boyen Basic Scheme—Additive Notation)

(i) To create a suitable hash function $H_1 : \{0, 1\}^* \rightarrow \mathbb{Z}_p$, suppose that we have a cryptographic hash function H that creates an output of at least $\lceil \log_2 p \rceil$ bits and want to calculate $H_1(ID)$. We can create a suitable H_1 from H by either repeatedly applying H to $H(ID)$ until we obtain a value in the correct range or by reducing $H(ID)$ modulo p.

(ii) To create a suitable hash function $H_2 : G_T \rightarrow \{0, 1\}^n$, suppose that we have a cryptographic hash function H that creates an output of at least n bits, and that G_T is a subgroup of $\mathbb{F}_{q^k}^*$, so that we can write a typical element of G_T as $\alpha = (x_1, x_2, \ldots, x_k)$, where $x_i \in \mathbb{F}_q^*$. We can create a suitable H_2 from H by calculating $H(x_1 \mid x_2 \mid \ldots x_k)$ and then truncating the result to n bits, for example.

(iii) Suppose that Alice wants to use Bohen-Boyen IBE to encrypt a message to Bob. Suppose that E is the elliptic curve $E : y^2 = x^3 + 1$, and G_1 be the subgroup of order 11 of $E(\mathbb{F}_{131})$ with generator $P = (98, 58)$. Let G_T be a subgroup of $\mathbb{F}_{131^2}^*$ generated by $\hat{e}(P, P) = 28 + 93i$, where $\mathbb{F}_{131^2}$ is represented by $\mathbb{F}_{131}[i]$ where $i^2 = -1 \equiv 130 \pmod{131}$. Let $\hat{e} : G_1 \times G_1 \rightarrow G_T$ be the reduced modified Tate pairing, where $e : G_1 \times G_1 \rightarrow G_T$ is the Tate pairing, and

$$\hat{e}(P, Q) \equiv e(P, \phi(Q))^{1560}$$

where ϕ is the distortion map given by $\phi(x, y) = (\xi x, y)$ where $\xi = 65 + 112i$. Let $\alpha = 3$, $\beta = 4$, and $\gamma = 5$ be the master secret, giving the additional parameters $P_1 = \alpha P = (113, 8)$, $P_2 = \beta P = (33, 31)$ and $P_3 = \gamma P = (34, 23)$, so that $v = \hat{e}(P_1, P_2) = \hat{e}(\alpha P, \beta P) = 28 + 93i$. Suppose that $q_{ID} = H_1(ID_{Bob}) = 6$.

For Bob's private key, suppose that the PKG picks the random $r = 8$ and then calculates

$$\begin{aligned} D_0 &= q_{ID} \cdot rP_1 + \alpha P_2 + rP_3 \\ &= (98, 58) + (98, 58) + (33, 100) = (128, 74) \end{aligned}$$

and

$$D_1 = rP = 8P = (113, 123)$$

Suppose that Alice wants to encrypt the short message M to Bob using this IBE system. To do this she picks a random s, say $s = 7$. She then calculates

$$C_0 = sP = 7P = (33, 100)$$

and

$$C_1 = q_{ID} \cdot sP_1 + sP_3 = (34, 23) + (128, 57) = (33, 100)$$

She then calculates $k = v^s = v^7 = 49 + 73i$. Then Alice calculates $k = H_2(49 + 73i)$ which she then XORs with the plaintext M to get the ciphertext component $c = M \oplus H_2(k)$.

Alice then sends ciphertext $C = (c, C_0, C_1) = (M \oplus H_2(k), (33, 100), (33, 100))$ to Bob.

Bob receives the ciphertext $C = (c, C_0, C_1) = (M \oplus H_2(k), (33, 100), (33, 100))$ and calculates

$$\hat{e}(C_0, D_0) = 85 + 51i$$

and

$$\hat{e}(C_1, D_1) = 28 + 93i$$

and then calculates the ratio of the two pairings

$$k = \frac{85 + 51i}{28 + 93i} = 49 + 73i$$

He then calculates $k = H_2(49 + 73i)$ which he then uses to recover the plaintext by calculating

$$c \oplus k = (M \oplus H_2(k)) \oplus H_2(k) = M$$

The values used in this example are summarized in Table 9.4.

(iv) Let $E/\mathbb{F}_q$ be an ordinary elliptic curve with $E'/\mathbb{F}_q$ a twist of order d of $E/\mathbb{F}_q$. We can then use a pairing $\hat{e} : G_1 \times G_2 \rightarrow G_T$ where we have $\phi_d : E' \rightarrow E$ and $\hat{e}(P, Q) = \hat{e}(P, \varphi_d(Q))^{(q^k - 1)/p}$ to implement the Boneh-Boyen scheme. We can then make G_1 a subgroup of $E(\mathbb{F}_q)$, G_2 a subgroup of $E'(\mathbb{F}_{q^{k/d}})$, and G_T a subgroup of $\mathbb{F}^*_{q^k}$. In this case, we will need four additional parameters, points Q, Q_1, Q_2,

Table 9.4
Summary of Parameters Used in Example 9.1(iii)

Parameters	Type	Value	Comments
$E/\mathbb{F}_{131}$	Elliptic curve	$y^2 = x^3 + 1$	
P	Point on elliptic curve	(98, 58)	Point of order 11
P_1	Point on elliptic curve	(113, 8)	
P_2	Point on elliptic curve	(33, 31)	
P_3	Point on elliptic curve	(34, 23)	
v	Element of $\mathbb{F}^*_{131^2}$	$28 + 93i$	$v = \hat{e}(P_1, P_2)$
q_{ID}	Integer	6	
(D_0, D_1)	Points on elliptic curve	((128, 74), (113, 123))	Bob's private key

and Q_3, all elements of $E'(\mathbb{F}_{q^{k/d}})$, and we will need to calculate D_0 as $D_0 = q_{ID} \cdot rQ_1 + \alpha Q_2 + rQ_3$ and D_1 as $D_1 = rQ$. Note that we need to have elements of $\mathbb{F}_{q^{k/d}}G_2$ because $\phi_d : E' \rightarrow E$ must map points on E' to points suitable for use in the pairing, so that they must end in a subgroup of $E(\mathbb{F}_{q^k})$. The mapping $\phi_d : E' \rightarrow E$ increases the dimension of the coordinates of its output by a factor of d, so to end up in $E(\mathbb{F}_{q^k})$ we need to start in $E(\mathbb{F}_{q^{k/d}})$.

9.2 Boneh-Boyen IBE (Basic Scheme—Multiplicative Notation)

The Boneh-Boyen basic scheme uses a shared secret that can be calculated by both the sender and receiver of a message to encrypt a plaintext message; the sender of the message calculates the shared secret from public parameters and the recipient's identity, while the recipient calculates the shared secret from their private key and the ciphertext. While it is easier to understand than the full Boneh-Boyen IBE scheme, it also is not as secure. The fully secure and more complicated scheme is described in Section 9.4.

The following description of the Boneh-Boyen scheme uses the multiplicative notation that is commonly used in the literature of pairing-based cryptography. So that if g_1 and g_2 are elements of an elliptic curve group $E(\mathbb{F}_q)$ then we will write g_1g_2 to indicate the group operation of $E(\mathbb{F}_q)$ applied to the group's elements g_1 and g_2 and g^a, to indicate multiplying the point g_1 by the integer a.

9.2.1 Setup of Parameters (Basic Scheme—Multiplicative Notation)

To implement Boneh-Boyen IBE we first need a security parameter that defines the level of bit strength that the encryption will provide. Then we need to define groups G_1 and G_T and a pairing $\hat{e} : G_1 \times G_1 \rightarrow G_T$ To do this we pick an elliptic curve $E/\mathbb{F}_q$ with embedding degree k, and a prime p such that $p \mid \#E(\mathbb{F}_q)$. The security parameter will define the size of the groups G_1 and G_T as described in Section 9.5.

We then randomly pick a point $P \in E(\mathbb{F}_q)[p]$ and let $G_1 = \langle P \rangle$ and $G_T = \langle \hat{e}(P, P) \rangle$, which are cyclic groups of order p. We need a cryptographic hash function $H_1 : \{0, 1\}^* \rightarrow \mathbb{Z}_p$ to map strings representing identities to integers. To encrypt a message of n bits using Boneh-Boyen IBE we also need another cryptographic hash function $H_2 : G_T \rightarrow \{0, 1\}^n$ that hashes elements of G_T into a form that we can combine with the plaintext message, which is a bit string of length n. Three integers α, β, $\gamma \in \mathbb{Z}_p$ are the master secret and are used to calculate the three additional public parameters αP, βP, and γP.

There is an additional constant $v = \hat{e}(g_1, g_2) = \hat{e}(g^\alpha, g^\beta) = \hat{e}(g, g)^{\alpha\beta}$ which is needed by the Boneh-Boyen scheme. This constant can either be distributed to users as part of the public parameters or can be precomputed by users before they perform a Boneh-Boyen encryption. We will assume that this constant v is part of the public parameters. We will assume that this constant v is part of the public parameters, in which the parameter g_2 does not need to be listed in the public parameters because its only use outside a PKG is in calculating v. These elements form the public parameters and master secret as shown in Table 9.5 and Table 9.6.

There are dependencies among the elements of Table 9.5. The values of p, q, and E, for example, are implicit in the definition of the group G_1. Because of this it is possible to reduce the number of required public parameters to a much shorter list, and we can define the public parameters of a Boneh-Boyen

Table 9.5
Parameters of Boneh-Boyen IBE System (Basic Scheme—Additive Notation)

Element	Type	Comments
q	Prime power	Order of finite field $\mathbb{F}_q$
$E/\mathbb{F}_q$	Elliptic curve	$E(\mathbb{F}_q)$ has embedding degree k
p	Prime	$p \mid \#E(\mathbb{F}_q)$
G_1	Cyclic group	Subgroup of $E(\mathbb{F}_q)$, $G_1 = \langle g \rangle$
G_T	Cyclic group	Subgroup of $\mathbb{F}_{q^k}^*$, $G_T = \langle \hat{e}(g, g) \rangle$
$\hat{e}$	Pairing	$\hat{e} : G_1 \times G_1 \rightarrow G_T$
n	Positive integer	Length of plaintext (in bits)
g	Point on elliptic curve	$g \in G_1$
g_1	Point on elliptic curve	$g_1 = g^\alpha$
g_2	Point on elliptic curve	$g_2 = g^\beta$
g_3	Point on elliptic curve	$g_3 = g^\gamma$
H_1	Cryptographic hash function	$H_1 : \{0, 1\}^* \rightarrow \mathbb{Z}_p$
H_2	Cryptographic hash function	$H_2 : G_T \rightarrow \{0, 1\}^n$
v	Element of $\mathbb{F}_{q^k}^*$	$v = \hat{e}(P_1, P_2) = \hat{e}(\alpha P, \beta P) = \hat{e}(P, P)^{\alpha\beta}$

Table 9.6
Master Secret for Boneh-Boyen IBE System (Basic Scheme—Multiplicative Notation)

Element	Type	Comments
α, β, γ	Integers	$\alpha, \beta, \gamma \in \mathbb{Z}_p$

IBE system (basic scheme—multiplicative notation) to be $BB_1 BasicParams Multiplicative = (G_1, G_T, \hat{e}, n, g, g_1, g_3, H_1, H_2, v)$ without introducing any ambiguity.

9.2.2 Extraction of the Private Key (Basic Scheme—Multiplicative Notation)

Once the public parameters listed in Table 9.5 and the master secret listed in Table 9.6 are determined, the private key associated with the identity ID is calculated by mapping the identity to an integer $q_{ID} \in \mathbb{Z}_p$ by calculating $q_{ID} = H_1(ID)$. A random per-user value $r \in \mathbb{Z}_p$ is then generated, which is then used to calculate the two components of the private key $d_{ID} = \left(g_1^{q_{ID} \cdot r} g_2^{\alpha} g_3^{r}, g^{r}\right) = (d_0, d_1)$. This is summarized in Table 9.7.

9.2.3 Encrypting with Boneh-Boyen IBE (Basic Scheme—Multiplicative Notation)

To encrypt the message $M \in \{0, 1\}^n$ to the recipient with identity ID, the sender performs the following steps.

1. Calculate $q_{ID} = H_1(ID)$.
2. Pick random $s \in \mathbb{Z}_p$.
3. Calculate $k = v^s$.
4. Calculate $c = M \oplus H_2(k)$.
5. Calculate $c_0 = g^s$.
6. Calculate $c_1 = g_1^{q_{ID} \cdot s} g_3^{s}$.
7. Set ciphertext to $C = (c, c_0, c_1)$.

9.2.4 Decrypting with Boneh-Boyen IBE (Basic Scheme—Multiplicative Notation)

When the recipient receives the ciphertext $C = (c, c_0, c_1)$ he performs the following steps.

Table 9.7
Private Key for Boneh-Boyen IBE System (Basic Scheme—Multiplicative Notation)

Element	Comments
$d_{ID} = (g_1^{q_{ID} \cdot r} g_2^{\alpha} g_3^{r}, g^{r}) = (d_0, d_1)$	Private key corresponding to identity ID, $q_{ID} = H_1(ID)$

1. Calculate $k = \dfrac{\hat{e}(c_0, d_0)}{\hat{e}(c_1, d_1)}$.
2. Calculate $M = c \oplus H_2(k)$.

Note that

$$\begin{aligned}
\hat{e}(c_0, d_0) &= \hat{e}(g^s, g_1^{q_{ID} \cdot r} g_2^{\alpha} g_3^{r}) \\
&= \hat{e}(g^s, g_1^{q_{ID} \cdot r})\, \hat{e}(g^s, g_2^{\alpha})\, \hat{e}(g^s, g_3^{r}) \\
&= \hat{e}(g^s, g_1^{q_{ID} \cdot r})\, \hat{e}(g^s, g^{\alpha\beta})\, \hat{e}(g^s, g^{\gamma r}) \\
&= \hat{e}(g, g)^{\alpha q_{ID} \cdot rs} \hat{e}(g, g)^{\alpha\beta s} \hat{e}(g, g)^{\gamma rs}
\end{aligned}$$

and

$$\begin{aligned}
\hat{e}(c_1, d_1) &= \hat{e}(g_1^{q_{ID} \cdot r} g_3^{s}, g^r) \\
&= \hat{e}(g^{\alpha q_{ID} \cdot s} g^{\gamma s}, g^r) \\
&= \hat{e}(g^{\alpha q_{ID} \cdot s}, g^r)\, \hat{e}(g^{\gamma s}, g^r) \\
&= \hat{e}(g, g)^{\alpha q_{ID} \cdot rs} \hat{e}(g, g)^{\gamma rs}
\end{aligned}$$

so that

$$\begin{aligned}
\frac{\hat{e}(c_0, d_0)}{\hat{e}(c_1, d_1)} &= \frac{\hat{e}(g, g)^{\alpha q_{ID} \cdot rs} \hat{e}(g, g)^{\alpha\beta s} \hat{e}(g, g)^{\gamma rs}}{\hat{e}(g, g)^{\alpha q_{ID} \cdot rs} \hat{e}(g, g)^{\gamma rs}} \\
&= \hat{e}(g, g)^{\alpha\beta s} = v^s
\end{aligned}$$

so that step 3 of Section 9.2.3 and step 1 of Section 9.2.4 calculate the same value of v^s, which allows the recipient to decrypt the ciphertext correctly.

9.3 Boneh-Boyen IBE (Full Scheme)

The basic Boneh-Boyen scheme is vulnerable to a chosen-ciphertext attack: if an adversary wants to decrypt the ciphertext (c, c_0, c_1) which corresponds to the plaintext message M he can do this by decrypting the ciphertext $(c + \epsilon, c_0, c_1)$ to get the plaintext message $M \oplus \epsilon$ and then recover M as $M = (M \oplus \epsilon) \oplus \epsilon$. The Fujisaki-Okamoto transform can easily eliminate this vulnerability.

The original specification of the Boneh-Boyen scheme defined a hashing scheme tailored to the scheme that accomplishes the same goal as the Fujisaki-Okamoto transform. This tailored scheme is used in the description of the full scheme that is described in Section 9.4.

The full Boneh-Boyen scheme is typically described using the multiplicative notation that was used in Section 9.2, a convention that we follow here. The full scheme is resistant to chosen-ciphertext attacks and adaptive chosen identity attacks.

9.3.1 Setup of Parameters (Full Scheme)

In addition to the parameters listed in Table 9.5, we also need an additional hash function to add chosen-ciphertext security. In particular, we need a hash function $H_3 : G_T \times \{0, 1\}^n \times G_1 \times G_1 \to \mathbb{Z}_p$. Adding this hash function brings the list of public parameters for the full scheme to the public parameters that are listed in Table 9.8. The master secret is unchanged from the basic scheme, and is shown in Table 9.9.

There are dependencies among the elements of Table 9.8. The values of p, q, and E, for example, are implicit in the definition of the group G_1. Because of this it is possible to reduce the number of required public parameters to a much shorter list, and we can define the public parameters of a Boneh-Boyen IBE system to be $BB_1params = (G_1, G_T, \hat{e}, n, g, g_1, g_3, H_1, H_2, H_3, v)$ without introducing any ambiguity.

Table 9.8
Parameters of Boneh-Boyen IBE System (Full Scheme)

Element	Type	Comments
q	Prime power	Order of finite field $\mathbb{F}_q$
$E/\mathbb{F}_q$	Elliptic curve	$E(\mathbb{F}_q)$ has embedding degree k
p	Prime	$p \mid \#E(\mathbb{F}_q)$
G_1	Cyclic group	Subgroup of $E(\mathbb{F}_q)$, $G_1 = \langle P \rangle$
G_T	Cyclic group	Subgroup of $\mathbb{F}_{q^k}^*$, $G_T = \langle \hat{e}(P, P) \rangle$
$\hat{e}$	Pairing	$\hat{e} : G_1 \times G_1 \to G_T$
n	Positive integer	Length of plaintext (in bits)
g	Point on elliptic curve	$g \in G_1$
g_1	Point on elliptic curve	$g_1 = g^{\alpha}$
g_2	Point on elliptic curve	$g_2 = g^{\beta}$
g_3	Point on elliptic curve	$g_3 = g^{\gamma}$
H_1	Cryptographic hash function	$H_1 : \{0, 1\}^* \to \mathbb{Z}_p$
H_2	Cryptographic hash function	$H_2 : G_T \to \{0, 1\}^n$
H_3	Cryptographic hash function	$H_3 : G_T \times \{0, 1\}^n \times G_1 \times G_1 \to \mathbb{Z}_p$
v	Element of $\mathbb{F}_{q^k}^*$	$v = \hat{e}(P_1, P_2) = \hat{e}(\alpha P, \beta P) = \hat{e}(P, P)^{\alpha\beta}$

Table 9.9
Master Secret for Boneh-Boyen IBE System (Full Scheme)

Element	Type	Comments
α, β, γ	Integers	$\alpha, \beta, \gamma \in \mathbb{Z}_p$

9.3.2 Extraction of the Private Key (Full Scheme)

The extraction of the private key for the full scheme is identical to the extraction of the private key in the basic scheme (Section 9.2.2). This is summarized in Table 9.10.

9.3.3 Encrypting with Boneh-Boyen IBE (Full Scheme)

To encrypt the message M to the recipient with identity ID, the sender performs the following steps:

1. Calculate $q_{ID} = H_1(ID)$.
2. Pick random $s \in \mathbb{Z}_p$.
3. Calculate $k = v^s$.
4. Calculate $c = M \oplus H_2(k)$.
5. Calculate $c_0 = g^s$.
6. Calculate $c_1 = g_1^{q_{ID} \cdot s} g_3^s$.
7. Calculate $t = s + H_3(k, c, c_0, c_1)$
8. Set ciphertext to $C = (c, c_0, c_1, t)$.

9.3.4 Decrypting with Boneh-Boyen IBE (Full Scheme)

To decrypt the ciphertext $C = (c, c_0, c_1, t)$, the recipient performs the following steps:

Table 9.10
Private Key for Boneh-Boyen IBE System

Element	Comments
$d_{ID} = (g_1^{q_{ID} \cdot r} g_2^{\alpha} g_3^{r}, g^r) = (d_0, d_1)$	Private key corresponding to identity ID, $q_{ID} = H_1(ID)$

1. Calculate $k = \dfrac{\hat{e}(c_0, d)}{\hat{e}(c_1, d_1)}$.
2. Calculate $s = t - H_3(k, c, c_0, c_1)$
3. Verify that $k = v^s$ and $c_0 = g^s$. If either condition fails, raise an error condition and exit.
4. Calculate $M = c \oplus H_2(k)$.

9.4 Security of the Boneh-Boyen IBE Scheme

An adversary observing a message that is encrypted with the Boneh-Boyen scheme has access to g, $g_1 = g^{\alpha}$, $g_3 = g^{\gamma}$, and $v = \hat{e}(g, g)^{\alpha\beta}$ from the public parameters of the system. He also observes g^s and $g_1^{q_{ID} \cdot s} g_3^s = g^{\alpha q_{ID} \cdot rs + \gamma s} = g^{s(\alpha q_{ID} + \gamma)}$ from the ciphertext. From these values he wants to recover $v^s = \hat{e}(g, g)^{\alpha\beta s}$. He can accomplish this in at least two ways. First, he can calculate s from g^s by calculating a discrete logarithm g^s in G_1, and then calculating v^s with this result. He can also calculate β as the discrete logarithm of $v = (\hat{e}(g, g)^{\alpha})^{\beta}$ in G_T and then calculate $v^s = (\hat{e}(g^{\alpha}, g^s))^{\beta} = \hat{e}(g, g)^{\alpha\beta s}$ with this value. So, an adversary who can calculate discrete logarithms in either G_1 or G_T can decrypt messages that are encrypted with the Boneh-Boyen scheme.

This is very close to solving the BDHP, and Boneh and Boyen have [1] proven two separate cases of this, depending on whether the random oracle or the standard model is used in the proof. In particular, they showed using the standard model that an adversary able to efficiently decrypt a message that has been encrypted with Boneh-Boyen IBE can use their decryption algorithm to solve the DBDHP, so if we believe that the DBDHP is sufficiently difficult to solve then Boneh-Boyen IBE must also be sufficiently difficult to decrypt. They also showed using the random oracle model that an adversary able to efficiently decrypt a message that has been encrypted with Boneh-Boyen IBE can use their decryption algorithm to solve the BDHP. So if we are willing to accept the stronger assumption of the DBDHP then a proof is possible using the standard model, but if the weaker BDHP assumption is adequate then a proof is possible using the random oracle model. The basic Boneh-Boyen scheme is resistant to chosen-plaintext attacks and adaptive chosen-identity attacks; the full Boneh-Boyen is resistant to chosen-ciphertext attacks and adaptive chosen identity attacks.

Note that in the extraction of a Boneh-Boyen private key a random value is used. Due to the way in which the two components of such a private key are used in decryption, a private key generated with any other random value will also work in the same decryption operation. This allows key recovery to be performed in a Boneh-Boyen system even though a random component is used in each private key. The security provided by the system, however, requires that the same random value is not reused to create private keys for different users.

9.5 Summary

The following summarizes the steps in the Boneh-Boyen IBE scheme (full scheme).

Algorithm 9.1: Boneh-Boyen IBE Setup
INPUT: a security parameter κ, an elliptic curve E, a plaintext length n
OUTPUT: $BB_1params = (G_1, G_T, \hat{e}, n, g, g_1, g_3, H_1, H_2, H_3, v)$ and master secret (α, β, γ)

1. Select a prime p and prime power q with $p \mid \#E(\mathbb{F}_q)$ and such that the bit security level provided by p and q meets the required security parameter κ (using Table 9.10, for example). For best performance, p should be a Solinas prime.
2. Select a random $g \in E(\mathbb{F}_q)[p]$ and let $G_1 = \langle g \rangle$.
3. Let k be the embedding degree of $E/\mathbb{F}_q$; select a pairing $\hat{e} : G_1 \times G_1 \rightarrow \mathbb{F}_{q^k}^*$.
4. Let $G_T = \langle \hat{e}(g, g) \rangle$.
5. Select random $\alpha, \beta, \gamma \in \mathbb{Z}_p$ and calculate $g^\alpha, g^\beta, g^\gamma$.
6. Select appropriate cryptographic hash functions $H_1 : \{0, 1\}^* \rightarrow G_1$, $H_2 : G_T \rightarrow \{0, 1\}^n$, and $H_3 : G_T \times \{0, 1\}^n \times G_1 \times G_1 \rightarrow \mathbb{Z}_p$.
7. The master secret is (α, β, γ).
8. The public parameters are $BB_1params = (G_1, G_T, \hat{e}, n, g, g_1, g_3, H_1, H_2, H_3, v)$.

Algorithm 9.2: Boneh-Boyen IBE Private Key Extraction
INPUT: A string ID representing an identity and a set of public parameters $BB_1params = (G_1, G_T, \hat{e}, n, g, g_1, g_3, H_1, H_2, H_3, v)$
OUTPUT: The private key $d_{ID} = (d_0, d_1)$

1. Calculate $q_{ID} = sH_1(ID)$.
2. Select a random $r \in \mathbb{Z}_p$.
3. Calculate $d_0 = g_1^{q_{ID} \cdot r} g_2^\alpha g_3^r$.
4. Calculate $d_1 = g^r$.
5. Set the private key to $d_{ID} = (d_0, d_1)$.

Algorithm 9.3: Boneh-Boyen IBE Encryption
INPUT: A plaintext message M of length n bits, a string ID representing the identity of the recipient of the ciphertext, a set of public parameters $BB_1 params = (G_1, G_T, \hat{e}, n, g, g_1, g_3, H_1, H_2, H_3, v)$
OUTPUT: A ciphertext $C = (c, c_0, c_1)$

1. Calculate $q_{ID} = H_1(ID)$.
2. Pick random $s \in \mathbb{Z}_p$.
3. Calculate $k = H_2(k)$.
4. Calculate $c = M \oplus H_2(k)$.
5. Calculate $c_0 = g^s$.
6. Calculate $c_1 = g_1^{q_{ID} \cdot s} g_3^s$.
7. Calculate $t = s + H_3(k, c, c_0, c_1)$.
8. Set ciphertext to $C = (c, c_0, c_1, t)$.

Algorithm 9.4: Boneh-Boyen IBE Decryption
INPUT: A ciphertext $C = (c, c_0, c_1, t)$, a set of public parameters $BB_1 params = (G_1, G_T, \hat{e}, n, g, g_1, g_3, H_1, H_2, H_3, v)$, a private key $d_{ID} = (d_0, d_1)$
OUTPUT: A plaintext message M or an error condition

1. Calculate $k = \dfrac{\hat{e}(c_0, d_0)}{\hat{e}(c_1, d_1)}$.
2. Calculate $s = t - H_3(k, c, c_0, c_1)$.
3. Verify that $k = v^s$ and $c_0 = g^s$. If either condition fails, raise an error condition and exit.
4. Calculate $M = c \oplus H_2(k)$.
5. Set plaintext to M.

Reference

[1] Boneh, D., and X. Boyen, "Efficient Selective-ID Secure Identity Based Encryption Without Random Oracles," *Proceedings of EUROCRYPT 2004*, Interlaken, Switzerland, May 2–6, 2004, pp. 223–238.

10

Sakai-Kasahara IBE

This chapter discusses Sakai-Kasahara IBE [1], an example of the family of "exponent inversion" schemes, in which a private key of the form $g^{1/a}$ is used to decrypt a ciphertext. In these schemes, a string representing an identity is hashed to an integer that is then used in the encryption and decryption operations. This avoids a modular exponentiation, which generally makes such schemes faster then full-domain hash schemes, like the Boneh-Franklin algorithm of Chapter 8, which require hashing an identity to a point on an elliptic curve. The name of the Sakai-Kasahara scheme is due to the way in which calculating keys is done, which is motivated by the work of Sakai and Kasahara, although the algorithms that comprise Sakai-Kasahara IBE scheme are quite different from those originally described by Sakai and Kasahara.

Two ways to describe the basic Sakai-Kasahara scheme are given in the following sections. A simplified version of the algorithm is described in Section 10.1 using the additive notation that is commonly used for operations in elliptic curve groups and is used in many cryptographic standards, and in Section 10.2 it is described using the multiplicative notation that is commonly used in more recent literature on pairing-based cryptography. The basic scheme is vulnerable to a chosen-ciphertext attack. A fully secure version of the algorithm is described in Section 10.3.

10.1 Sakai-Kasahara IBE (Basic Scheme—Additive Notation)

The Sakai-Kasahara basic scheme uses a shared secret that can be calculated by both the sender and receiver of a message to encrypt a plaintext message; the sender of the message calculates the shared secret from public parameters and the recipient's identity, while the recipient calculates the shared secret from their private key and the ciphertext. While it is easier to understand than the full Sakai-Kasahara IBE scheme, it also is not as secure. The fully secure and more complicated scheme is described in Section 10.3.

The following description of the Sakai-Kasahara scheme uses additive notation, so that if P_1 and P_2 are elements of an elliptic curve group $E(\mathbb{F}_q)$ then we will write $P_1 + P_2$ to indicate the group operation of $E(\mathbb{F}_q)$ applied to the group's elements P_1 and P_2, and aP to indicate multiplying the point P by the integer a.

10.1.1 Setup of Parameters (Basic Scheme—Additive Notation)

To implement Sakai-Kasahara IBE we first need a security parameter that defines the level of bit strength that the encryption will provide. Then we need to define groups G_1 and G_T and a pairing $\hat{e} : G_1 \times G_1 \rightarrow G_T$. To do this we pick an elliptic curve $E/\mathbb{F}_q$ with embedding degree k, and a prime p such that $p \mid \#E(\mathbb{F}_q)$. The security parameter will define the size of the groups G_1 and G_T as described in Section 5.4.

We then randomly pick a point $P \in E(\mathbb{F}_q)[p]$ and let $G_1 = \langle P \rangle$ and $G_T = \langle \hat{e}(P, P) \rangle$, which are cyclic groups of order p. We need a cryptographic hash function $H_1 : \{0, 1\}^* \rightarrow \mathbb{Z}_p$ to map strings representing identities to integers. To encrypt a message of n bits using Sakai-Kasahara IBE we also need another cryptographic hash function $H_2 : G_T \rightarrow \{0, 1\}^n$ that hashes elements of G_T into a form that we can combine with the plaintext message, which is a bit string of length n. An integer $s \in \mathbb{Z}_p$ is the master secret. These elements form the public parameters and master secret as shown in Table 10.1 and Table 10.2.

There are dependencies among the elements of Table 10.1. The values of p, q, and E, for example, are implicit in the definition of the group G_1. Because of this it is possible to reduce the number of required public parameters to a much shorter list, and we can define the public parameters of a Sakai-Kasahara IBE scheme (basic scheme) to be $BB_1 BasicParamsAdditive$ = $(G_1, G_T, \hat{e}, n, P, sP, H_1, H_2, v)$ without introducing any ambiguity.

10.1.2 Extraction of the Private Key (Basic Scheme—Additive Notation)

Once the public parameters listed in Table 10.1 and the master secret listed in Table 10.2 are determined, the private key associated with the identity ID is calculated by mapping the identity to an integer $q_{ID} \in \mathbb{Z}_p$ by calculating $q_{ID} = H_1(ID)$. The master secret s is then used to calculate the private key

Table 10.1
Parameters of Sakai-Kasahara IBE Scheme (Basic Scheme—Additive Notation)

Element	Type	Comments
q	Prime power	Order of finite field $\mathbb{F}_q$
$E/\mathbb{F}_q$	Elliptic curve	$E(\mathbb{F}_q)$ has embedding degree k
p	Prime	$p \mid \#E(\mathbb{F}_q)$
G_1	Cyclic group	Subgroup of $E(\mathbb{F}_q)$, $G_1 = \langle P \rangle$
G_T	Cyclic group	Subgroup of $\mathbb{F}_{q^k}^*$, $G_T = \langle \hat{e}(P, P) \rangle$
$\hat{e}$	Pairing	$\hat{e} : G_1 \times G_1 \rightarrow G_T$
n	Positive integer	Length of plaintext (in bits)
P	Point on elliptic curve	$P \in G_1$
sP	Point on elliptic curve	$sP \in G_1$
H_1	Cryptographic hash function	$H_1 : \{0, 1\}^* \rightarrow \mathbb{Z}_p$
H_2	Cryptographic hash function	$H_2 : G_T \rightarrow \{0, 1\}^n$
v	Element of $\mathbb{F}_{q^k}^*$	$v = \hat{e}(P, P)$

Table 10.2
Master Secret for Sakai-Kasahara IBE Scheme (Basic Scheme—Additive Notation)

Element	Type	Comments
s	Integer	$s \in \mathbb{Z}_p$

$$D_{ID} = \frac{1}{s + q_{ID}} P$$

where the value of $\frac{1}{s + q_{ID}}$ is calculated in $\mathbb{Z}_p^*$. This is summarized in Table 10.3.

Table 10.3
Private Key for Sakai-Kasahara IBE Scheme (Basic Scheme—Additive Notation)

Element	Comments
$D_{ID} = \frac{1}{s + q_{ID}} P$	Private key corresponding to identity ID, $q_{ID} = H_1(ID)$

10.1.3 Encrypting with Sakai-Kasahara IBE (Basic Scheme—Additive Notation)

To encrypt the message $M \in \{0, 1\}^n$ to the recipient with identity ID, the sender performs the following steps.

1. Calculate $q_{ID} = H_1(ID)$.
2. Select a random $r \in \mathbb{Z}_p$.
3. Calculate $U = r(sP + q_{ID}P) = r(s + q_{ID})P$.
4. Calculate $k = H_2(v^r)$.
5. Calculate $V = M \oplus k$.
6. Set the ciphertext to $C = (U, V)$.

10.1.4 Decrypting with Sakai-Kasahara IBE (Basic Scheme—Additive Notation)

When the recipient receives the ciphertext $C = (U, V)$ he performs the following steps.

1. Calculate $K = H_2(\hat{e}(U, D_{ID}))$
2. Calculate $M = V \oplus k$

Note that

$$\hat{e}(U, D_{ID}) = \hat{e}\left(r(s + q_{ID})P, \frac{1}{s + q_{ID}}P\right) = \hat{e}(g, g)^r$$

so that step 5 of Section 10.1.3 and step 1 of Section 10.1.4 calculate the same value of k, which allows the recipient to decrypt the ciphertext correctly.

Example 10.1

(i) The hash functions H_1 and H_2 can be constructed similarly to those described in Examples 9.1(i) and 9.1(ii).

(ii) Suppose that Alice wants to use Sakai-Kasahara IBE to encrypt a message to Bob. Suppose that E is the elliptic curve $E/\mathbb{F}_{131} : y^2 = x^3 + 1$, and G_1 be the subgroup of order 11 of $E(\mathbb{F}_{131})$ with generator $P = (98, 58)$. Let G_T be a subgroup of $\mathbb{F}^*_{131^2}$ generated by $v = \hat{e}(P, P) = 28 + 93i$, where $\mathbb{F}_{131^2}$ is represented by $\mathbb{F}_{131}[i]$ where $i^2 = -1 \equiv 130 \pmod{131}$. (See Table 10.4). Let $\hat{e} : G_1 \times G_1 \to G_T$ be the reduced modified Tate pairing, where $e : G_1 \times G_1 \to G_T$ is the Tate pairing, and

Table 10.4
Summary of Parameters Used in Example 10.1(ii)

Parameters	Type	Value	Comments
$E/\mathbb{F}_{131}$	Elliptic curve	$y^2 = x^3 + 1$	
P	Point on elliptic curve	(98, 58)	Point of order 11
sP	Point on elliptic curve	(33, 100)	Point of order 11
v	Element of $\mathbb{F}^*_{131^2}$	$28 + 93i$	$v = \hat{e}(P, P)$
q_{ID}	Integer	6	
s	Integer	7	
D_{ID}	Point on elliptic curve	(34, 108)	Bob's private key

$$\hat{e}(P, Q) = e(P, \phi(Q))^{1560}$$

where ϕ is the distortion map given by $\phi(x, y) = (\xi x, y)$ where $\xi = 65 + 112i$. Let $s = 7$ be the master secret, giving the additional parameters $sP = (33, 100)$.

Suppose that for Bob's identity we have that $q_{ID} = 6$. To calculate Bob's private key, the PKG calculates

$$D_{ID} = \frac{1}{s + q_{ID}} P = \frac{1}{13} P \equiv \frac{1}{2} P (\text{mod } 11)$$
$$= 2^{-1} (\text{mod } 11) P = 6P = (34, 108)$$

Suppose that Alice wants to encrypt the short message M to Bob using this IBE scheme. To do this she picks a random r, say $r = 5$. She first calculates

$$U = r(sP + q_{ID} P) = 5((33, 100) + 6(34, 108)) = (98, 73)$$

and $v^5 = (28 + 93i)^5 = 39 + 24i$, so that Alice finds that $k = H_2(39 + 24i)$ which she then uses to calculate the ciphertext component

$$V = M \oplus k = M \oplus H_2(39 + 24i)$$

Alice then sends the ciphertext (U, V) to Bob.

Bob receives the ciphertext $C = (U, V)$ and calculates

$$\hat{e}(U, D_{ID}) = \hat{e}((98, 73), (34, 108)) = 39 + 24i$$

from which he calculates $k = H_2(39 + 24i)$ which he then XORs with the ciphertext component V to recover the plaintext message, finding that

$$V \oplus k = (M \oplus k) \oplus k = M$$

(iii) If we want to use a pairing $\hat{e} : G_1 \times G_2 \to G_T$ then we will need to add an additional parameter Q where $G_2 = \langle Q \rangle$ and then calculate D_{ID} as $D_{ID} = \dfrac{1}{s + q_{ID}} Q$ and v as $v = \hat{e}(P, Q)$.

10.2 Sakai-Kasahara IBE (Basic Scheme—Multiplicative Notation)

The Sakai-Kasahara basic scheme uses a shared secret that can be calculated by both the sender and receiver of a message to encrypt a plaintext message; the sender of the message calculates the shared secret from public parameters and the recipient's identity, while the recipient calculates the shared secret from their private key and the ciphertext. While it is easier to understand than the full Sakai-Kasahara IBE scheme, it also is not as secure. The fully secure and more complicated scheme is described in Section 10.3.

The following description of the Sakai-Kasahara algorithm uses the multiplicative notation that is commonly used in the literature of pairing-based cryptography. So that if g_1 and g_2 are elements of an elliptic curve group $E(\mathbb{F}_q)$ then we will write $g_1 g_2$ to indicate the group operation of $E(\mathbb{F}_q)$ applied to the group's elements g_1 and g_2, and g^a to indicate multiplying the point g by the integer a.

10.2.1 Setup of Parameters (Basic Scheme—Multiplicative Notation)

To implement Sakai-Kasahara IBE we first need a security parameter that defines the level of bit strength that the encryption will provide. Then we need to define groups G_1 and G_T and a pairing $\hat{e} : G_1 \times G_1 \to G_T$. To do this we pick an elliptic curve $E/\mathbb{F}_q$ with embedding degree k, and a prime p such that $p \mid \#E(\mathbb{F}_q)$. The security parameter will define the size of the groups G_1 and G_T as described in Section 5.4.

We then randomly pick a point $g \in E(\mathbb{F}_q)[p]$ and let $G_1 = \langle g \rangle$ and $G_T = \langle \hat{e}(g, g) \rangle$, which are cyclic groups of order p. We need a cryptographic hash function $H_1 : \{0, 1\}^* \to \mathbb{Z}_p$ to map strings representing identities to integers. To encrypt a message of n bits using Sakai-Kasahara IBE we also need another cryptographic hash function $H_2 : G_T \rightarrow \{0, 1\}^n$ that hashes elements of G_T into a form that we can combine with the plaintext message, which is a bit string of length n. An integer $s \in \mathbb{Z}_p$ is the master secret. These elements form the public parameters and master secret as shown in Table 10.5 and Table 10.6.

There are dependencies among the elements of Table 10.1. The values of p, q, and E, for example, are implicit in the definition of the group G_1. Because of this it is possible to reduce the number of required public parameters to a much shorter list, and we can define the public parameters of a Sakai-Kasahara IBE scheme (basic scheme) to be *SKBasicParamsMultiplicative* = $(G_1, G_T, \hat{e}, n, g, g^s, H_1, H_2, v)$ without introducing any ambiguity.

10.2.2 Extraction of the Private Key (Basic Scheme—Multiplicative Notation)

Once the public parameters listed in Table 10.1 and the master secret listed in Table 10.2 are determined, the private key associated with the identity *ID* is

Table 10.5
Parameters of Sakai-Kasahara IBE Scheme (Basic Scheme—Multiplicative Notation)

Element	Type	Comments
q	Prime power	Order of finite field $\mathbb{F}_q$
$E/\mathbb{F}_q$	Elliptic curve	$E(\mathbb{F}_q)$ has embedding degree k
p	Prime	$p \mid \# E(\mathbb{F}_q)$
G_1	Cyclic group	Subgroup of $E(\mathbb{F}_q)$, $G_1 = \langle g \rangle$
G_T	Cyclic group	Subgroup of $\mathbb{F}_{q^k}^*$, $G_T = \langle \hat{e}(g, g) \rangle$
$\hat{e}$	Pairing	$\hat{e} : G_1 \times G_1 \rightarrow G_T$
n	Positive integer	Length of plaintext (in bits)
g	Point on elliptic curve	$g \in G_1$
g^s	Point on elliptic curve	$g^s \in G_1$
H_1	Cryptographic hash function	$H_1 : \{0, 1\}^* \rightarrow \mathbb{Z}_p$
H_2	Cryptographic hash function	$H_2 : G_T \rightarrow \{0, 1\}^n$
v	Element of $\mathbb{F}_{q^k}^*$	$v = \hat{e}(g, g)$

Table 10.6
Master Secret for Sakai-Kasahara IBE Scheme (Basic Scheme—Multiplicative Notation)

Element	Type	Comments
s	Integer	$s \in \mathbb{Z}_p$

calculated by mapping the identity to an integer $q_{ID} \in \mathbb{Z}_p$ by calculating $q_{ID} = H_1(ID)$. The master secret s is then used to calculate the private key

$$d_{ID} = g^{1/(s+q_{ID})}$$

This is summarized in Table 10.7.

10.2.3 Encrypting with Sakai-Kasahara IBE (Basic Scheme—Multiplicative Notation)

To encrypt the message $M \in \{0, 1\}^n$ to the recipient with identity ID, the sender performs the following steps.

1. Calculate $q_{ID} = H_1(ID)$.
2. Select a random $r \in \mathbb{Z}_p$.
3. Calculate $U = (g^s g^{q_{ID}})^r = g^{r(s+q_{ID})}$.
4. Calculate $K = H_2(v^r)$.
5. Calculate $V = M \oplus K$.
6. Set the ciphertext to $C = (U, V)$.

10.2.4 Decrypting with Sakai-Kasahara IBE (Basic Scheme—Multiplicative Notation)

When the recipient receives the ciphertext $C = (U, V)$, he performs the following step.

1. Calculate $K = H(\hat{e}(U, d_{ID}))$.
2. Calculate $M = V \oplus K$.

Note that

$$\hat{e}(U, d_{ID}) = \hat{e}(g^{r(s+q_{ID})}, g^{1/(s+q_{ID})}) = \hat{e}(g, g)^r$$

Table 10.7
Private Key for Sakai-Kasahara IBE Scheme
(Basic Scheme—Multiplicative Notation)

Element	Comments
$d_{ID} = g^{1/(s+q_{ID})}$	Private key corresponding to identity ID, $q_{ID} = H_1(ID)$

so that step 5 of Section 10.2.3 and step 1 of Section 10.2.4 calculate the same value of K, which allows the recipient to decrypt the ciphertext correctly.

10.3 Sakai-Kasahara IBE (Full Scheme)

The basic scheme is also vulnerable to a chosen-ciphertext attack: if an adversary wants to decrypt the ciphertext $C = (U, V)$ which corresponds to the plaintext message M he can do this by decrypting the ciphertext $C = (U, V \oplus \epsilon)$ to get the plaintext message $M \oplus \epsilon$ and then recover M as $M = (M \oplus \epsilon)$. The Fujisaki-Okamoto transform can easily eliminate this vulnerability. Adding the Fujisaki-Okamoto transform to the basic scheme gives the full scheme that is described next.

The full Sakai-Kasahara scheme is resistant to chosen-ciphertext attacks, and is typically described using the multiplicative notation that was used in Section 10.2, a convention that we follow here.

10.3.1 Setup of Parameters (Full Scheme)

In addition to the parameters listed in Table 10.1, we also need additional hash functions to add chosen-ciphertext security. In particular, we need two hash functions $H_3 : \{0, 1\}^n \to \mathbb{Z}_p$ and $H_4 : \{0, 1\}^n \to \{0, 1\}^n$. Adding these hash functions brings the list of public parameters for the full scheme to the public parameters that are listed in Table 10.8. The master secret is unchanged from the basic scheme, and is shown in Table 10.9.

There are dependencies among the elements of Table 10.8. The values of p, q, and E, for example, are implicit in the definition of the group G_1. Because of this it is possible to reduce the number of required public parameters to a much shorter list, and we can define the public parameters of a Sakai-Kasahara IBE scheme to be $SKParams = (G_1, G_T, \hat{e}, n, g, g^s, H_1, H_2, H_3, H_4, v)$ without introducing any ambiguity.

10.3.2 Extraction of the Private Key (Full Scheme)

The extraction of a private key for the full scheme is identical to the extraction of a private key for the basic scheme. This is summarized in Table 10.10.

10.3.3 Encrypting with Sakai-Kasahara IBE (Full Scheme)

To encrypt the message M to the recipient with identity ID, the sender performs the following steps:

Table 10.8
Parameters of Sakai-Kasahara IBE Scheme (Full Scheme)

Element	Type	Comments
q	Prime power	Order of finite field $\mathbb{F}_q$
$E/\mathbb{F}_q$	Elliptic curve	$E(\mathbb{F}_q)$ has embedding degree k
p	Prime	$p \mid \# E(\mathbb{F}_q)$
G_1	Cyclic group	Subgroup of $E(\mathbb{F}_q)$, $G_1 = \langle g \rangle$
G_T	Cyclic group	Subgroup of $\mathbb{F}_{q^k}^*$, $G_T = \langle \hat{e}(g, g) \rangle$
$\hat{e}$	Pairing	$\hat{e} : G_1 \times G_1 \rightarrow G_T$
n	Positive integer	Length of plaintext (in bits)
g	Point on elliptic curve	$g \in G_1$
g^s	Point on elliptic curve	$g^s \in G_1$
H_1	Cryptographic hash function	$H_1 : \{0, 1\}^* \rightarrow \mathbb{Z}_p$
H_2	Cryptographic hash function	$H_2 : G_T \rightarrow \{0, 1\}^n$
H_3	Cryptographic hash function	$H_3 : \{0, 1\}^n \rightarrow \mathbb{Z}_p^*$
H_4	Cryptographic hash function	$H_4 : \{0, 1\}^n \rightarrow \{0, 1\}^n$
v	Element of $\mathbb{F}_{q^k}^*$	$v = \hat{e}(g, g)$

Table 10.9
Master Secret for Sakai-Kasahara IBE Scheme (Full Scheme)

Element	Type	Comments
s	Integer	$s \in \mathbb{Z}_p$

Table 10.10
Private Key for Sakai-Kasahara IBE Scheme (Full Scheme)

Element	Comments
$d_{ID} = g^{1/(s+q_{ID})}$	Private key corresponding to identity ID, $q_{ID} = H_1(ID)$

1. Calculate $q_{ID} = H_1(ID)$.
2. Select a random $\sigma \in \{0, 1\}^n$.
3. Calculate $r = H_3(\sigma, M)$.
4. Calculate $U = (g^s g^{q_{ID}})^r = g^{r(s+q_{ID})}$.
5. Calculate $V = \sigma \oplus H_2(v^r)$.

6. Calculate $V = M \oplus H_4(\sigma)$.
7. Calculate $W = H_4(M)$.
8. Set ciphertext to $C = (U, V, W)$.

10.3.4 Decrypting with Sakai-Kasahara IBE (Full Scheme)

To decrypt the ciphertext $C = (U, V, W)$, the recipient performs the following steps:

1. Calculate $q_{ID} = H_1(ID)$.
2. Calculate $\alpha = \hat{e}(U, d_{ID})$.
3. Calculate $\sigma = V \oplus H_2(\alpha)$.
4. Calculate $M = W \oplus H_4(\sigma)$.
5. Calculate $r = H_3(\sigma, M)$.
6. If $U \neq (g^{q_{ID}} g^s)^r$ then raise an error condition and exit.
7. Otherwise set the plaintext to M.

10.4 Security of the Sakai-Kasahara IBE Scheme

Note that an adversary observing a message that is encrypted with the Sakai-Kasahara IBE has access to g, $g_1 = g^\alpha$, $g_3 = g^\gamma$, and $v = \hat{e}(g, g)^{\alpha\beta}$ from the public parameters of the scheme. He also observes g^s and $g_1^{q_{ID} \cdot s} g_3^s = g^{\alpha q_{ID} \cdot s + \gamma s} = g^{s(\alpha q_{ID} + \gamma)}$ from the ciphertext. From these values he wants to recover $v^s = \hat{e}(g, g)^{\alpha\beta s}$. He can accomplish this in at least two ways. First, he can calculate s from g^s by calculating a discrete logarithm g^s in G_1, and then calculating v^s with this result. He can also calculate β as the discrete logarithm of $v = (\hat{e}(g, g)^\alpha)^\beta$ in G_T and then calculate $v^s = (\hat{e}(g^\alpha, g^s))^\beta = \hat{e}(g, g)^{\alpha\beta s}$ with this value. So an adversary who can calculate discrete logarithms in either G_1 or G_T can decrypt messages that are encrypted with the Sakai-Kasahara algorithm. The q powers that are assumed in the q-BDHIP are not directly available to an adversary who intercepts an encrypted message, but are required in the proof of selective identity security, with the value of q indicating how many other private keys an attacker has access to.

The paper that describes the version of the Sakai-Kasahara IBE algorithm discussed in this chapter [1] proved that an adversary able to decrypt a message that has been encrypted with Sakai-Kasahara IBE can use their decryption algorithm to solve the q-BDHIP. So, if we believe that the q-BDHIP is sufficiently difficult to solve then Sakai-Kasahara IBE must also be sufficiently difficult to decrypt. The basic Sakai-Kasahara scheme is resistant to chosen-plaintext attacks and adaptive chosen-identity attacks; the full Sakai-Kasahara is resistant to chosen-ciphertext attacks and adaptive chosen-identity attacks.

10.5 Summary

The following summarizes the steps in the Sakai-Kasahara IBE algorithm (full scheme).

Algorithm 10.1: Sakai-Kasahara IBE Setup
INPUT: a security parameter κ, an elliptic curve E, a plaintext length n
OUTPUT: $SKParams = (G_1, G_T, \hat{e}, n, g, g^s, H_1, H_2, H_3, H_4, v)$ and master secret s

1. Select a prime p and prime power q with $p \mid \#E(\mathbb{F}_q)$ and such that the bit security level provided by p and q meets the required security parameter κ (using Table 5.2, for example). For best performance, p should be a Solinas prime.
2. Select a random $g \in E(\mathbb{F}_q)[p]$ and let $G_1 = \langle g \rangle$.
3. Let k be the embedding degree of $E/\mathbb{F}_q$; select a pairing $\hat{e} : G_1 \times G_1 \to \mathbb{F}_{q^k}^*$.
4. Let $G_T = \langle \hat{e}(g, g) \rangle$.
5. Select a random $s \in \mathbb{Z}_p^*$.
6. Select appropriate cryptographic hash functions $H_1 : \{0, 1\}^* \to G_1$, $G_T \to \{0, 1\}^n$, $H_3 : \{0, 1\}^n \to \mathbb{Z}_p^*$ and $H_4 : \{0, 1\}^n \to \{0, 1\}^n$.
7. The master secret is s.
8. The public parameters are $SKParams = (G_1, G_T, \hat{e}, n, g, g^s, H_1, H_2, H_3, H_4, v)$.

Algorithm 10.2: Sakai-Kasahara IBE Private Key Extraction
INPUT: A string ID representing an identity, a set of public parameters $SKParams = (G_1, G_T, \hat{e}, n, g, g^s, H_1, H_2, H_3, H_4, v)$ and a master secret s
OUTPUT: A private key d_{ID}

1. Calculate $d_{ID} = g^{1/(s + q_{ID})}$.

Algorithm 10.3: Sakai-Kasahara IBE Encryption
INPUT: A plaintext message $M \in \{0, 1\}^n$, a string ID representing the identity of the recipient of the ciphertext, a set of public parameters $SKParams = (G_1, G_T, \hat{e}, n, g, g^s, H_1, H_2, H_3, H_4, v)$

OUTPUT: A ciphertext $C = (U, V, W)$

1. Calculate $q_{ID} = H_1(ID)$.
2. Select a random $\sigma \in \{0, 1\}^n$.
3. Calculate $r = H_3(\sigma, M)$.
4. Calculate $U = (g^s g^{q_{ID}})^r = g^{r(s+q_{ID})}$.
5. Calculate $V = \sigma \oplus H_2(v^r)$.
6. Calculate $V = M \oplus H_4(\sigma)$.
7. Calculate $W = H_4(M)$.
8. Set ciphertext to $C = (U, V, W)$.

Algorithm 10.4: Sakai-Kasahara IBE Decryption
INPUT: A ciphertext $C = (U, V, W)$, a set of public parameters $SKParams = (G_1, G_T, \hat{e}, n, g, g^s, H_1, H_2, H_3, H_4, v)$, a private key d_{ID}
OUTPUT: A plaintext message M or an error condition

1. Calculate $q_{ID} = H_1(ID)$.
2. Calculate $\alpha = \hat{e}(U, d_{ID})$.
3. Calculate $\sigma = V \oplus H_2(\alpha)$.
4. Calculate $M = W \oplus H_4(\sigma)$.
5. Calculate $r = H_3(\sigma, M)$.
6. If $U \neq (g^{q_{ID}} g^s)^r$, then raise an error condition and exit.
7. Otherwise set the plaintext to M.

Reference

[1] Chen, L., et al., "An Efficient ID-KEM Based on the Sakai-Kasahara Key Construction," *IEE Proceedings Information Theory*, Vol. 153, No. 1, 2006, pp. 19–26.

11

Hierarchical IBE and Master Secret Sharing

The IBE schemes discussed in Chapters 7 through 10 share a common property: they use a single PKG to generate all private keys. This has some undesirable side effects. In particular, it is impossible to create hierarchies of PKGs, in which a higher-level PKG can control the keys granted to all PKGs subordinate to it. It also creates a single point where an attacker can subvert the security of an IBE system by compromising an IBE master secret. Hierarchical IBE (HIBE) can address the first of these concerns while sharing an IBE master secret among several different PKGs can address the second. The two concepts are very similar: in both cases all private keys are calculated using the master secret of more than one PKG.

The concept of an HIBE system was first described by Horwitz and Lynn [1]. HIBE allows for the creation of hierarchies of PKGs like the one shown in Figure 11.1, in which the operation of a PKG at a particular level depends on the operation of the PKGs above it in the hierarchy. This allows organizations to implement different security policies, while allowing upper levels of the hierarchy to enforce their security policy on all subordinate organizations. It can also enhance the security of a system using IBE because a compromise that affects part of a hierarchy will not necessarily affect other parts. Recovering from a compromise is also easier, because it is only necessary to recreate the affected parts of the hierarchy instead of the entire system.

An HIBE scheme is formally defined by five algorithms: root setup, lower-level setup, extract, encrypt, and decrypt. Root setup creates the parameters necessary for operation of the top level of the hierarchy while lower-level setup creates the additional parameters necessary for operation of each of the other

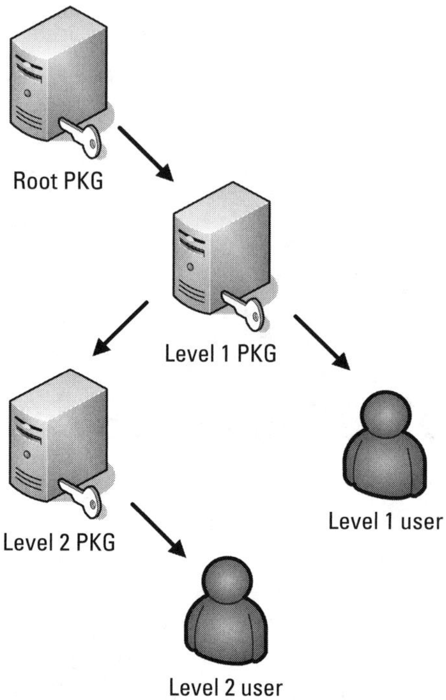

Figure 11.1 Hierarchical IBE system.

levels and may be needed to be executed once for each lower level. Extract, encrypt, and decrypt have the same functions that they do in a single-level IBE system, although their operation at a particular level in a hierarchy may require parameters that are created by levels above them. Not all HIBE systems will require different algorithms for root setup and lower-level setup, in which case a single setup algorithm will be sufficient.

In an HIBE scheme, a single user can have different identities for each level of the HIBE, so that for an HIBE scheme with a maximum of l levels, an identity can have the form $ID = (ID_1, ID_2, \ldots, ID_l)$. where each of the ID_i are potentially different.

The first HIBE scheme that was devised and proven to be secure was invented by Gentry and Silverberg [2], and extended the Boneh-Franklin IBE scheme to arbitrary hierarchies. The Boneh-Boyen IBE scheme was actually first described as an HIBE system, and the version of the Boneh-Boyen IBE scheme described in Chapter 9 is actually a case of limiting the HIBE construction to a single level. More recent work [3] has shown that extensions of exponent-inversion IBE algorithms to HIBE constructions are also possible.

In an IBE system that uses master secret sharing, a single master secret is distributed among n PKGs which each return a component of a user's private key called a *share*. A user can then calculate his private key from information that he receives from any t of the n possible shares, yet it is infeasible to calculate the same private key with any $t - 1$ shares. Master secret sharing also makes it infeasible for any $t - 1$ PKGs that might collude to reconstruct the master secret. This is illustrated below in Figure 11.2.

Use of master secret sharing makes the compromise of one or more of the n PKGs much less damaging than the compromise of a lone single-level PKG would be. With a single-level PKG, if an attacker compromises the single PKG then he gains the ability to create arbitrary private keys. If master secret sharing is used, an attacker will need to compromise any t of the n possible PKGs in order to gain this ability.

11.1 HIBE Based on Boneh-Franklin IBE

Suppose that we have a single-level Boneh-Franklin IBE scheme with parameters *BFBasicParams* $= (G_1, G_T, \hat{e}, n, P, s_0 P, H_1, H_2)$ as defined in Section 8.1, and with a master secret s_0 where we assume that $|G_1| = p$. The following sections describe how such a scheme can be extended to an l-level HIBE scheme using the technique described by Gentry and Silverberg (GS) [2]. Because such an HIBE scheme will be based on the basic Boneh-Franklin scheme, it will be vulnerable to chosen-ciphertext attacks, but the extension of what follows to a system with chosen-ciphertext security can easily be accomplished by using the Fujisaki-Okamoto transform. The security of the resulting HIBE system depends

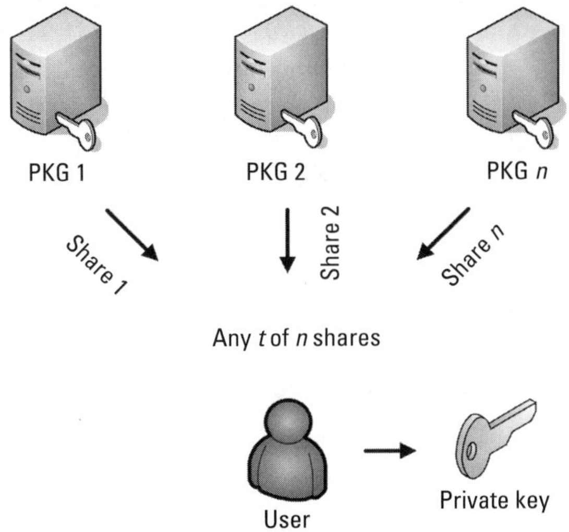

Figure 11.2 Use of master secret sharing in an IBE system.

on the difficulty of the BDHP. An adversary capable of decrypting such a system can also solve the BDHP; for a proof of this, see [2]. Assuming the BDHP is hard, the basic GS scheme is resistant to chosen-plaintext attacks and adaptive chosen-identity attacks; the full GS is resistant to chosen-ciphertext attacks and adaptive chosen-identity attacks.

Note that the length of the ciphertext of the GS HIBE scheme increases as the number of levels increases.

11.1.1 GS HIBE (Basic) Root Setup

The parameters needed for the root PKG are the same as those needed for the single-level IBE system: $GSHIBEBasicParams = (G_1, G_T, \hat{e}, n, P, s_0P, H_1, H_2)$ with a corresponding master secret s_0. The setup procedure for the Boneh-Franklin IBE (basic scheme) is also the root setup procedure for a GS HIBE system.

11.1.2 GS HIBE (Basic) Lower-Level Setup

Each lower-level PKG also has the parameters for the root PKG. The only additional parameter needed for each lower level PKG is the master secret for its level. For level t this parameter is s_t where s_t is a randomly chosen element of $\mathbb{Z}_p$.

11.1.3 GS HIBE (Basic) Extract

Suppose that a user has identity $ID = (ID_1, ID_2, \ldots, ID_k)$ in an l-level HIBE where $k \leq l$, and let $Q_{ID_i} = H_1(ID_1, ID_2, \ldots, ID_i)$. Then the private key $K = (K_0, K_1, \ldots K_{k-1})$ corresponding to this sequence of identities has k components. The first component of the private key is calculated as

$$K_0 = \sum_{i=1}^{l} s_{i-1} Q_{ID_i}$$

and the remaining $k - 1$ components are calculated as $K_i = s_i P$ for $1 \leq i \leq k - 1$.

11.1.4 GS HIBE (Basic) Encrypt

Suppose that we want to encrypt the message M to the identity $ID = (ID_1, ID_2, \ldots, ID_k)$ in an l-level HIBE where $k \leq l$. Let $g = \hat{e}(s_0P, Q_{ID_1})$. The sender picks a random r in $\mathbb{Z}_p$ and then calculates $k + 1$ components of the ciphertext $C = (V, U_0, U_2, \ldots U_k)$ which are given by the following:

$$V = M \oplus H_2(g^r)$$
$$U_0 = rP$$
$$U_i = rQ_{ID_i} \text{ for each } 2 \le i \le k$$

11.1.5 GS HIBE (Basic) Decrypt

When the recipient receives the ciphertext $C = (V, U_0, U_2, \ldots U_k)$ he recovers the message M by calculating

$$V \oplus H_2\left(\frac{\hat{e}(U_0, K_0)}{\prod_{i=2}^{l} \hat{e}(K_{i-1}, U_i)}\right) = V \oplus H_2\left(\frac{\hat{e}\left(rP, \sum_{i=1}^{l} s_{i-1} Q_{ID_i}\right)}{\prod_{i=2}^{l} \hat{e}\left(s_{i-1}P, rQ_{ID_i}\right)}\right)$$

$$= V \oplus H_2\left(\frac{\prod_{i=1}^{l} \hat{e}\left(rP, s_{i-1} Q_{ID_i}\right)}{\prod_{i=2}^{l} \hat{e}\left(s_{i-1}P, rQ_{ID_i}\right)}\right)$$

$$= V \oplus H_2\left(\frac{\prod_{i=1}^{l} \hat{e}\left(P, Q_{ID_i}\right)^{rs_{i-1}}}{\prod_{i=2}^{l} \hat{e}\left(P, Q_{ID_i}\right)^{rs_{i-1}}}\right)$$

$$= V \oplus H_2\left(\hat{e}\left(P, Q_{ID_i}\right)^{rs_0}\right) = V \oplus H_2(g^r)$$

$$= M \oplus H_2(g^r) \oplus H_2(g^r) = M$$

11.2 Example of a GS HIBE System

The following example illustrates the operation of Gentry and Silverman's HIBE system based on the Boneh-Franklin IBE. Suppose that the sender Alice wants to encrypt a message M to Bob using an HIBE with three subordinate levels in which Bob's identity has components ID_1, ID_2, and ID_3 for which we have

$$Q_{ID_1} = H_1(ID_1) = (128,\ 57)$$

$$Q_{ID_2} = H_1(ID_2) = (34,\ 108)$$

$$Q_{ID_3} = H_1(ID_3) = (33,\ 100)$$

11.2.1 GS HIBE (Basic) Root Setup

The setup for the root PKG is accomplished by generating the parameters $GSHIBEBasicParams = (G_1, G_T, \hat{e}, n, P, s_0 P, H_1, H_2)$ with a corresponding master secret s_0. The parameters used in this example are listed in Table 11.1.

11.2.2 GS HIBE (Basic) Lower-Level Setup

The setup for each of the subordinate PKG levels is accomplished by generating the master secrets for each level. The values used in this example are listed below in Table 11.1.

11.2.3 GS HIBE (Basic) Extraction of Private Key

Bob's private key has three components that are calculated as

$$\begin{aligned} K_0 &= \sum_{i=1}^{3} s_{i-1} Q_{ID_i} \\ &= s_0 Q_{ID_1} + s_1 Q_{ID_2} + s_2 Q_{ID_3} \\ &= 7(128,\ 57) + 3(34,\ 108) + 4(33,\ 100) \\ &= (113,\ 8) + (33,\ 100) + (128,\ 57) = (98,\ 58) \end{aligned}$$

$$K_1 = s_1 P = 3(98,\ 58) = (113,\ 8)$$

$$K_2 = s_2 P = 4(98,\ 58) = (34,\ 23)$$

Table 11.1
Parameters Used in Example of GS HIBE

Parameter	**Value**	**Comments**
l	3	Number of subordinate levels in HIBE
s_0	7	Root master secret
s_1	3	Master secret for subordinate level 1
s_2	4	Master secret for subordinate level 2
P	(98, 58)	$G_1 = \langle P \rangle$, $G_T = \langle \hat{e}(P, P) \rangle$
$s_0 P$	(33, 100)	

11.2.4 GS HIBE (Basic) Encryption

Suppose that Alice picks the random value $r = 6$ to use to encrypt the message M to Bob. She then calculates

$$g = \hat{e}\left(s_0 P,\ Q_{ID_i}\right) = \hat{e}((33,\ 100),\ (128,\ 57)) = 85 + 80i$$

so that

$$g^r = (85 + 80i)^6 = 49 + 73i$$

Alice than calculates the four components of the ciphertext as

$$\begin{aligned} V &= M \oplus H_2(g^r) = M \oplus H_2(49 + 73i) \\ U_0 &= rP = 6(98,\ 58) = (34,\ 108) \\ U_2 &= rQ_{ID_2} = 6(34,\ 108) = (113,\ 8) \\ U_3 &= rQ_{ID_3} = 6(33,\ 100) = (128,\ 74) \end{aligned}$$

11.2.5 GS HIBE (Basic) Decryption

After receiving the ciphertext $(V,\ U_0,\ U_2,\ U_3)$, Bob recovers the plaintext message M by calculating

$$V \oplus H_2\left(\frac{\hat{e}(U_0,\ K_0)}{\prod_{i=2}^{3} \hat{e}(K_{i-1},\ U_i)}\right)$$

$$V \oplus H_2\left(\frac{\hat{e}(U_0,\ K_0)}{\hat{e}(K_1,\ U_2)\hat{e}(K_2,\ U_3)}\right)$$

$$V \oplus H_2\left(\frac{39 + 104i}{(126 + 32i)(28 + 93i)}\right)$$

$$V \oplus H_2(49 + 73i) = M \oplus H_2(49 + 73i) \oplus H_2(49 + 73i) = M$$

11.3 HIBE Based on Boneh-Boyen IBE

Two different notations are often used for the Boneh-Boyen IBE algorithm. In most academic publications, the multiplicative notation is usually used, while in standards that define the implementation of pairing-based algorithms, the additive notation that is commonly used for elliptic curve operations is usually used. This section uses only the additive notation, but converting to the multiplicative notation should not be unduly difficult.

Suppose that we have a single-level Boneh-Boyen IBE scheme with parameters $BB_1\,BasicParamsAdditive = (G_1, G_T, \hat{e}, n, P, P_1, P_3, H_1, H_2, v)$ as defined in Section 9.1 and with a master secret α where we assume that $|G_1| = p$. The following sections describe how such a scheme can be extended to an l-level HIBE scheme using the technique described by Boneh, Boyen, and Goh (BBG) [4]. Because such an HIBE scheme will be based on the basic Boneh-Boyen scheme, it will be vulnerable to chosen-ciphertext attacks, but the extension of what follows to a scheme with chosen-ciphertext security can easily be accomplished by using the Fujisaki-Okamoto transform. The security of the resulting HIBE scheme depends on the difficulty of the BDHP. An adversary capable of decrypting such a system can also solve the BDHP; for a proof of this, see [5]. Assuming the BDHP is hard, the basic BBG scheme is resistant to chosen-plaintext attacks and adaptive chosen-identity attacks; the full BBG is resistant to chosen-ciphertext attacks and adaptive chosen-identity attacks.

The Boneh-Boyen IBE scheme that was described in Chapter 9 was created by limiting a HIBE construction to a single level of PKG. This HIBE construction also had the property that the length of the ciphertext increased as the number of levels in the HIBE increased. The HIBE construction that follows is also based on the Boneh-Boyen IBE scheme, but has the additional property that the length of the ciphertext is constant, neither increasing nor decreasing as the number of levels in the HIBE changes.

11.3.1 BBG HIBE (Basic) Setup

Suppose that we have a single-level Boneh-Boyen IBE scheme with parameters

$$BB_1\,BasicParamsAdditive = (G_1, G_T, \hat{e}, n, P, P_1, P_3, H_1, H_2, v)$$

To extend this system to an HIBE scheme we need additional randomly generated parameters $Q_1, Q_2, \ldots, Q_l$ that are each elements of G_1. This brings the parameters for the HIBE scheme to

$$BBGHIBEBasicParamsAdditive$$
$$= (G_1, G_T, \hat{e}, n, P, P_1, P_3, Q_1, Q_2, \ldots, Q_l, H_1, H_2, v)$$

11.3.2 BBG HIBE (Basic) Extract

To calculate the private key $D_{ID} = (D_1, D_2)$ for the identity $ID = (ID_1, ID_2, \ldots, ID_l)$, the root PKG randomly generates $r \in \mathbb{Z}_p$, calculates $q_{ID_i} = H_1(ID_1)$ for $1 \le i \le k$ and uses these values to calculate

$$D_1 = rP$$

and

$$D_2 = \alpha P_2 + r \sum_{i=1}^{k} q_{ID_i} Q_k$$

11.3.3 BBG HIBE (Basic) Encryption

To encrypt the message M to Bob where Bob has the identity $ID = (ID_1, ID_2, \ldots, ID_k)$ for any $k \le l$, Alice picks a random $s \in \mathbb{Z}_p$ and calculates the ciphertext $c = (c_0, C_1, C_2)$ where

$$c_0 = M \oplus H_2(v^s)$$
$$C_1 = sP$$

and

$$C_2 = s \sum_{i=1}^{k} q_{ID_k} Q_k$$

11.3.4 BBG HIBE (Basic) Decryption

To decrypt the ciphertext $c = (c_0, C_1, C_2)$ Bob calculates

$$c_0 \oplus H_2\left(\frac{\hat{e}(C_1, D_2)}{\hat{e}(D_1, C_2)}\right)$$

$$= c_0 \oplus H_2\left(\frac{\hat{e}\left(sP, \alpha P_2 + r\left(\sum_{i=1}^{k} q_{ID_i} Q_i + P_3\right)\right)}{\hat{e}\left(rP, s\left(\sum_{i=1}^{k} q_{ID_i} Q_i + P_3\right)\right)}\right)$$

$$= c_0 \oplus H_2(\hat{e}(sP, \alpha P_2)) = c_0 \oplus H_2(\hat{e}(P, P_2)^{\alpha s})$$

$$= c_0 \oplus H_2(\hat{e}(\alpha P, P_2)^s) = c_0 \oplus H_2(v^s)$$

$$= M \oplus H_2(v^s) \oplus H_2(v^s) = M$$

11.4 Example of a BBG HIBE System

The following example illustrates the operation of an HIBE system based on the Boneh-Boyen IBE using a technique developed by Boneh, Boyen, and Goh. Suppose that the sender Alice wants to encrypt a message M to Bob using a three-level HIBE in which Bob's identity has components ID_1, ID_2, and ID_3 for which we have

$$q_{ID_1} = H_1(ID_1) = 2$$

$$q_{ID_2} = H_1(ID_2) = 6$$

$$q_{ID_3} = H_1(ID_3) = 8$$

11.4.1 BBG HIBE (Basic) Setup

Suppose that we have a single-level Boneh-Boyen IBE system with parameters

$$BB_1 BasicParamsAdditive = (G_1, G_T, \hat{e}, n, P, P_1, P_3, H_1, H_2, v)$$

and that we pick additional points Q_1, Q_2, and Q_3 to create the parameters for the BBG HIBE system with the parameters shown in Table 11.2.

11.4.2 BBG HIBE (Basic) Extraction of Private Key

Suppose the PKG picks the random value $r = 5$, which it then determines the two components of Bob's private key (D_1, D_2) that correspond to the identity $ID = (ID_1, ID_2, D_3)$ by calculating

Table 11.2
Parameters Used in Example of BBG HIBE

Parameter	**Value**	**Comments**
l	3	Number of subordinate levels in HIBE
P	(98, 58)	$G_1 = \langle P \rangle$, $G_T = \langle \hat{e}(P, P) \rangle$
α	7	
$P_1 = \alpha P$	(33, 100)	
P_2	(113, 123)	
P_3	(98, 73)	
Q_1	(33, 100)	
Q_2	(33, 31)	
Q_3	(127, 74)	
$v = \hat{e}(P_1, P_2)$	$28 + 93i$	

Similarly,

$$e_2(x) = \frac{(x - x_1)(x - x_3)}{(x_2 - x_1)(x_2 - x_3)} = \frac{(x - 2)(x - 4)}{(3 - 2)(3 - 4)}$$
$$\equiv 10(x - 2)(x - 4) \pmod{11}$$

so that

$$e_2(0) = 10(-2)(-4) \equiv 3 \pmod{11}$$

and

$$e_3(x) = \frac{(x - x_1)(x - x_2)}{(x_3 - x_1)(x_3 - x_2)} = \frac{(x - 2)(x - 3)}{(4 - 2)(4 - 3)}$$
$$\equiv 6(x - 2)(x - 3) \pmod{11}$$

so that

$$e_3(0) = 6(-2)(-3) \equiv 3 \pmod{11}$$

The user then calculates his private key as

$$\begin{aligned} sQ_{ID} &= \sum_{i=1,2,3} e_i(0) y_i Q_{ID} \\ &= 6 \cdot (128, 57) + 3 \cdot (128, 74) + 3 \cdot (33, 100) \\ &= (98, 58) + (34, 23) + (98, 73) = (34, 23) \end{aligned}$$

which is equal to

$$sQ_{ID} = 5Q_{ID} = 5(98, 58) = (34, 23)$$

Any three shares of the master secret will also reconstruct the same private key sQ_{ID}. So the user will also be able to reconstruct the same value of sQ_{ID} by using any three of the five PKGs listed in Table 11.3.

References

[1] Horwitz, J., and B. Lynn, "Toward Hierarchical Identity-Based Encryption," *Proceedings of EUROCRYPT 2002*, Amsterdam, the Netherlands, April 28–May 2, 2002, pp. 466–481.

$$D_1 = rP = 5(98, 58) = (34, 23)$$

and

$$\begin{aligned} D_2 &= \alpha P_2 + r\left(q_{ID_1} Q_1 + q_{ID_2} Q_2 + q_{ID_3} Q_3 + P_3\right) \\ &= 7(113, 123) + 5[2(128, 57) + 6(33, 31) + 8(127, 74) + (98, 73)] \\ &= (98, 58) \end{aligned}$$

11.4.3 BBG HIBE (Basic) Encryption

Suppose that Alice picks the random value $r = 5$ which she then uses to encrypt the message M to Bob by calculating the three components of the ciphertext (c_0, C_1, C_2) as

$$\begin{aligned} c_0 &= M \oplus H_2(v^s) = M \oplus H_2(126 + 32i) \\ C_1 &= sP = 9(98, 58) = (128, 74) \\ C_2 &= s\left(q_{ID_1} Q_1 + q_{ID_2} Q_2 + q_{ID_3} Q_3 + P_3\right) \\ &= 9[2(128, 57) + 6(33, 31) + 8(127, 74) + (98, 73)] = O \end{aligned}$$

11.4.4 BBG HIBE (Basic) Decryption

To decrypt the ciphertext (c_0, C_1, C_2) Bob calculates

$$\begin{aligned} c_0 \oplus H_2\left(\frac{\hat{e}(C_1, D_2)}{\hat{e}(D_1, C_2)}\right) &= c_0 \oplus H_2\left(\frac{126 + 32i}{1}\right) \\ &= M \oplus H_2(126 + 32i) \oplus H_2(126 + 32i) = M \end{aligned}$$

11.5 Master Secret Sharing

Shamir's secret sharing [2] provides the basis for sharing an IBE master secret among n PKGs from which a user will need to receive t shares to calculate his private key. This technique encodes a master secret as a coefficient of a polynomial of degree $t - 1$. Each PKG has a point (x_i, y_i) that satisfies this polynomial, so that a user with t of these points can uniquely determine the coefficients of the polynomial and thus his private key while any $t - 1$ PKGs that collude will be unable to determine the same private key.

Suppose that a master PKG wants to create n shares of a Boneh-Franklin master secret s so that any t of these shares can be used to determine an IBE private key. To do this, he picks $t - 1$ random coefficents to determine the polynomial

$$f(x) = s + a_1 x + \ldots + a_{t-1} x^{t-1}$$

in which the master secret is used as the constant coefficient of the polynomial and we have that $f(0) = s$.

The master PKG then randomly generates n values x_i for $1 \leq i \leq n$ and distributes the pair $(x_i, y_i) = (x_i, f(x_i))$ to the ith PKG. When a user requests a share of a private key from PKG number i for identity Q_{ID}, the PKG responds with the pair $(x_i, y_i Q_{ID})$. From a set of t such pairs a user can uniquely calculate his private key sQ_{ID}. He does this by determining the value of $sQ_{ID} = f(0)\, Q_{ID}$ using Lagrange interpolation.

Because we have that

$$f(x) = \sum_i e_i(x) y_i$$

we have that

$$f(x) Q_{ID} = \sum_i e_i(x) y_i Q_{ID}$$

so that

$$sQ_{ID} = f(0) Q_{ID} = \sum_i e_i(0) y_i Q_{ID}$$

and thus a user who receives t pairs of the form $(x_i, y_i Q_{ID})$ can calculate the Lagrange coefficients $e_i(0)$ and then use these to calculate his private key sQ_{ID}. Similar constructions are possible for other IBE algorithms.

11.6 Master Secret Sharing Example

Suppose that we have an IBE system that uses the Boneh-Franklin scheme in which we want a user to have to get any three components out of a possible five that will allow him to calculate his private key sQ_{ID}, and that the master PKG has the master secret $s = 5$ which is encoded as the constant coefficient in the polynomial $f(x) = x^2 + 2x + 5$. To implement Shamir secret sharing among five PKGs, the master PKG can create and distribute the elements shown in Table 11.3, where each of the values of x_i are chosen randomly.

Table 11.3
Setup for Shamir Secret Sharing for Three Out of Five PKGs

PKG Number (i)	x_i	$y_i = f(x_i)$
1	2	2
2	3	9
3	4	7
4	8	8
5	9	5

Suppose that our IBE scheme uses operations of the elliptic curve $E/\mathbb{F}_{131}: y^2 = x^3 + 1$ and that a user with identity $Q_{ID} = (98, 58)$ gets components from PKGs numbered one through three and wants to calculate his private key from the shared secrets that he receives. He will receive the components from the three PKGs that he has selected that are shown in Table 11.4.

To calculate his private key as

$$sQ_{ID} = \sum_{i=1,2,3} e_i(0) y_i Q_{ID}$$

the user then needs to calculate the values of $e_i(0)$ which he finds by first calculating the Lagrange polynomials $e_i(x)$. He then finds that

$$e_1(x) = \frac{(x - x_2)(x - x_3)}{(x_1 - x_2)(x_1 - x_3)} = \frac{(x-3)(x-4)}{(2-3)(2-4)}$$
$$\equiv 6(x-3)(x-4) \pmod{11}$$

so that

$$e_1(0) = 6(-3)(-4) \equiv 6 \pmod{11}$$

Table 11.4
Shares of Private Key Received by User

PKG Number	x_i	$y_i Q_{ID}$
1	2	$2Q_{ID} = 2(98, 58) = (128, 57)$
2	3	$9Q_{ID} = 9(98, 58) = (128, 74)$
3	4	$7Q_{ID} = 7(98, 58) = (33, 100)$

$$D_1 = rP = 5(98,\ 58) = (34,\ 23)$$

and

$$\begin{aligned} D_2 &= \alpha P_2 + r\left(q_{ID_1} Q_1 + q_{ID_2} Q_2 + q_{ID_3} Q_3 + P_3\right) \\ &= 7(113,\ 123) + 5[2(128,\ 57) + 6(33,\ 31) + 8(127,\ 74) + (98,\ 73)] \\ &= (98,\ 58) \end{aligned}$$

11.4.3 BBG HIBE (Basic) Encryption

Suppose that Alice picks the random value $r = 5$ which she then uses to encrypt the message M to Bob by calculating the three components of the ciphertext $(c_0,\ C_1,\ C_2)$ as

$$\begin{aligned} c_0 &= M \oplus H_2(v^s) = M \oplus H_2(126 + 32i) \\ C_1 &= sP = 9(98,\ 58) = (128,\ 74) \\ C_2 &= s\left(q_{ID_1} Q_1 + q_{ID_2} Q_2 + q_{ID_3} Q_3 + P_3\right) \\ &= 9[2(128,\ 57) + 6(33,\ 31) + 8(127,\ 74) + (98,\ 73)] = O \end{aligned}$$

11.4.4 BBG HIBE (Basic) Decryption

To decrypt the ciphertext $(c_0,\ C_1,\ C_2)$ Bob calculates

$$\begin{aligned} c_0 \oplus H_2\left(\frac{\hat{e}(C_1,\ D_2)}{\hat{e}(D_1,\ C_2)}\right) &= c_0 \oplus H_2\left(\frac{126 + 32i}{1}\right) \\ &= M \oplus H_2(126 + 32i) \oplus H_2(126 + 32i) = M \end{aligned}$$

11.5 Master Secret Sharing

Shamir's secret sharing [2] provides the basis for sharing an IBE master secret among n PKGs from which a user will need to receive t shares to calculate his private key. This technique encodes a master secret as a coefficient of a polynomial of degree $t - 1$. Each PKG has a point $(x_i,\ y_i)$ that satisfies this polynomial, so that a user with t of these points can uniquely determine the coefficients of the polynomial and thus his private key while any $t - 1$ PKGs that collude will be unable to determine the same private key.

Suppose that a master PKG wants to create n shares of a Boneh-Franklin master secret s so that any t of these shares can be used to determine an IBE private key. To do this, he picks $t-1$ random coefficents to determine the polynomial

$$f(x) = s + a_1 x + \ldots + a_{t-1} x^{t-1}$$

in which the master secret is used as the constant coefficient of the polynomial and we have that $f(0) = s$.

The master PKG then randomly generates n values x_i for $1 \leq i \leq n$ and distributes the pair $(x_i, y_i) = (x_i, f(x_i))$ to the ith PKG. When a user requests a share of a private key from PKG number i for identity Q_{ID}, the PKG responds with the pair $(x_i, y_i Q_{ID})$. From a set of t such pairs a user can uniquely calculate his private key sQ_{ID}. He does this by determining the value of $sQ_{ID} = f(0)\,Q_{ID}$ using Lagrange interpolation.

Because we have that

$$f(x) = \sum_i e_i(x) y_i$$

we have that

$$f(x) Q_{ID} = \sum_i e_i(x) y_i Q_{ID}$$

so that

$$sQ_{ID} = f(0) Q_{ID} = \sum_i e_i(0) y_i Q_{ID}$$

and thus a user who receives t pairs of the form $(x_i, y_i Q_{ID})$ can calculate the Lagrange coefficients $e_i(0)$ and then use these to calculate his private key sQ_{ID}. Similar constructions are possible for other IBE algorithms.

11.6 Master Secret Sharing Example

Suppose that we have an IBE system that uses the Boneh-Franklin scheme in which we want a user to have to get any three components out of a possible five that will allow him to calculate his private key sQ_{ID}, and that the master PKG has the master secret $s = 5$ which is encoded as the constant coefficient in the polynomial $f(x) = x^2 + 2x + 5$. To implement Shamir secret sharing among five PKGs, the master PKG can create and distribute the elements shown in Table 11.3, where each of the values of x_i are chosen randomly.

Table 11.3
Setup for Shamir Secret Sharing for Three Out of Five PKGs

PKG Number (i)	x_i	$y_i = f(x_i)$
1	2	2
2	3	9
3	4	7
4	8	8
5	9	5

Suppose that our IBE scheme uses operations of the elliptic curve $E/\mathbb{F}_{131}$: $y^2 = x^3 + 1$ and that a user with identity $Q_{ID} = (98, 58)$ gets components from PKGs numbered one through three and wants to calculate his private key from the shared secrets that he receives. He will receive the components from the three PKGs that he has selected that are shown in Table 11.4.

To calculate his private key as

$$sQ_{ID} = \sum_{i=1,2,3} e_i(0) y_i Q_{ID}$$

the user then needs to calculate the values of $e_i(0)$ which he finds by first calculating the Lagrange polynomials $e_i(x)$. He then finds that

$$\begin{aligned} e_1(x) &= \frac{(x - x_2)(x - x_3)}{(x_1 - x_2)(x_1 - x_3)} = \frac{(x - 3)(x - 4)}{(2 - 3)(2 - 4)} \\ &\equiv 6(x - 3)(x - 4) \pmod{11} \end{aligned}$$

so that

$$e_1(0) = 6(-3)(-4) \equiv 6 \pmod{11}$$

Table 11.4
Shares of Private Key Received by User

PKG Number	x_i	$y_i Q_{ID}$
1	2	$2Q_{ID} = 2(98, 58) = (128, 57)$
2	3	$9Q_{ID} = 9(98, 58) = (128, 74)$
3	4	$7Q_{ID} = 7(98, 58) = (33, 100)$

Similarly,

$$e_2(x) = \frac{(x - x_1)(x - x_3)}{(x_2 - x_1)(x_2 - x_3)} = \frac{(x - 2)(x - 4)}{(3 - 2)(3 - 4)}$$
$$\equiv 10(x - 2)(x - 4) \pmod{11}$$

so that

$$e_2(0) = 10(-2)(-4) \equiv 3 \pmod{11}$$

and

$$e_3(x) = \frac{(x - x_1)(x - x_2)}{(x_3 - x_1)(x_3 - x_2)} = \frac{(x - 2)(x - 3)}{(4 - 2)(4 - 3)}$$
$$\equiv 6(x - 2)(x - 3) \pmod{11}$$

so that

$$e_3(0) = 6(-2)(-3) \equiv 3 \pmod{11}$$

The user then calculates his private key as

$$sQ_{ID} = \sum_{i=1,2,3} e_i(0) y_i Q_{ID}$$
$$= 6 \cdot (128, 57) + 3 \cdot (128, 74) + 3 \cdot (33, 100)$$
$$= (98, 58) + (34, 23) + (98, 73) = (34, 23)$$

which is equal to

$$sQ_{ID} = 5Q_{ID} = 5(98, 58) = (34, 23)$$

Any three shares of the master secret will also reconstruct the same private key sQ_{ID}. So the user will also be able to reconstruct the same value of sQ_{ID} by using any three of the five PKGs listed in Table 11.3.

References

[1] Horwitz, J., and B. Lynn, "Toward Hierarchical Identity-Based Encryption," *Proceedings of EUROCRYPT 2002*, Amsterdam, the Netherlands, April 28–May 2, 2002, pp. 466–481.

[2] Gentry, C., and A. Silverberg, "Hierarchical ID-Based Cryptography," *Proceedings of ASIACRYPT 2002*, Queenstown, New Zealand, December 1–5, 2002, pp. 548–566.

[3] Boyen, X., "General Ad Hoc Encryption from Exponent Inversion IBE," *Proceedings of EUROCRYPT 2007*, Barcelona, Spain, May 20–24, 2007, pp. 394–411.

[4] Boneh, D., X. Boyen, and E. Goh, "Hierarchical Identity-Based Encryption with Constant Size Ciphertext," *Proceedings of EUROCRYPT 2005*, Aarhus, Denmark, May 22–26, pp. 440–456.

[5] Shamir, A., "How to Share a Secret," *Communications of the ACM*, Vol. 22, No. 1, 1979, pp. 612–613.

12

Calculating Pairings

With the one exception of the Cocks IBE scheme that is described in Chapter 7, the operation of all IBE schemes rely on the properties of a pairing. Calculating the value of a pairing is typically the most computationally expensive part of implementing such algorithms and it may be necessary to carefully optimize the calculation of pairings to make them practical.

This chapter discusses several aspects of this. Some elliptic curves are suitable for implementing pairings while others are not. The curves that are suitable for such use are called "pairing-friendly" curves, and finding pairing-friendly ordinary curves is an active area of research. The structure of finite fields also provides some shortcuts that may be used to speed pairing calculations when some factors become irrelevant after the final exponentiation that is used to make the Tate pairing unique. By carefully reusing intermediate results, it is possible to calculate the product of more than one pairings more efficiently than calculating each of the pairings separately, a fact that is particularly useful in the implementation of both HIBE systems and the Boneh-Boyen IBE scheme. Finally, an alternative to Miller's algorithm for calculating the Tate pairing that is not based on manipulating divisors is also discussed.

12.1 Pairing-Friendly Curves

As discussed in Chapter 3, a typical elliptic curve $E/\mathbb{F}_q$ provides a structure unsuitable for calculating a pairing because the embedding degree of subgroups of $E(\mathbb{F}_q)$ of large prime order is typically too high to make calculating a pairing practical. To provide a structure suitable for implementing pairing-based algorithms, we want the following properties:

1. The existence of a subgroup of $E(\mathbb{F}_q)$ of large prime order p.
2. A low embedding degree of $E(\mathbb{F}_q)$.

The first of these conditions is easy to define carefully: the desired security parameters of a system will determine the necessary order of G_1 . Defining a low embedding degree requires the creation of a somewhat arbitrary threshold, however. Although an embedding degree $k < (\log q)^2$ is low enough to make the calculation of discrete logarithms in $\mathbb{F}_{q^k}$ efficient in a theoretical sense, a subgroup with such an embedding degree can still provide an impractical structure for implementing a pairing. A more practical requirement is that the embedding degree of G_1 with respect to p is less than $(\log_2 p)/8$, where the constant $(\log_2 p)/8$ is chosen somewhat arbitrarily, although it attempts to reflect a rough consensus amongst implementers of pairing-based algorithms. This provides the motivation for the following definition.

Definition 12.1

An elliptic curve $E/\mathbb{F}_q$ is *pairing-friendly* if we have that

1. There is a subgroup of $E(\mathbb{F}_q)$ of a suitably large prime order p.
2. The embedding degree of $E(\mathbb{F}_q)$ with respect to p is less than $(\log_2 p)/8$.

Note that if $E/\mathbb{F}_q$ is supersingular and $E(\mathbb{F}_q)$ has a subgroup of the necessary order then $E/\mathbb{F}_q$ is automatically pairing-friendly because we must have $k \leq 6$ for the embedding degree of $E(\mathbb{F}_q)$. Finding pairing-friendly ordinary curves, on the other hand, is an active area of research, but enough progress has been made to provide enough curves to allow the relatively efficient implementation of pairing-based cryptography at the most commonly used levels of bit strength. Among these alternatives, some choices are more efficient that others, however. Existing techniques for generating pairing-friendly ordinary curves use a variant of the technique for generating elliptic curve groups of a known order that are called the complex multiplication (CM) algorithm, the details of which are beyond the scope of this book. Generating suitable elliptic curves using the CM algorithm [1] is based on the following property, in which the integer D is the CM discriminant of the resulting curve and the integer t represents its trace.

Property 12.1 (Atkin and Morain [2])

Let q be an odd prime such that $4q = t^2 + Ds^2$ for integers s, t, and D. Then there is an elliptic curve $E/\mathbb{F}_q$ with $\#E(\mathbb{F}_q) = q + 1 - t$.

An elliptic curve can be constructed with these properties if and only if the following conditions hold [3], none of which pose a problem for generating ordinary curves for use in pairing-based algorithms.

1. q is a prime or prime power.
2. p is a prime.
3. p divides $q + 1 - t$.
4. $p \mid (q^k - 1)$ but $p \nmid (q^i - 1)$ for $i \leq i < k$.
5. $4q = t^2 + Ds^2$ for integers D and s.

The general strategy for finding pairing-friendly ordinary curves has the following steps, the details of which vary depending on the embedding degree that is required. Details of the algorithms for finding curves with particular embedding degrees may be found in [4–9], and are beyond the scope of this book.

1. Fix an embedding degree k and find integers t, p, and q such that $E/\mathbb{F}_q$ has trace t, $E(\mathbb{F}_q)$ has a subgroup of large prime order p and embedding degree k.
2. Use the CM algorithm [1] to find the explicit form of $E/\mathbb{F}_q$.

Table 12.1 lists types of ordinary curves that are created using this strategy that have proven to be particularly useful in attaining standard levels of bit security while allowing relatively efficient implementations.

12.1.1 Relative Efficiency of Parameters of Pairing-Friendly Curves

One parameter that is often used to compare the relative efficiency of parameters of a pairing-based algorithm is the size of the finite field $\mathbb{F}_q$ relative to p, the size of the prime-order subgroup. This parameter is denoted by ρ, perhaps for *relative* efficiency, and is defined to be

$$\rho = \frac{\log q}{\log p}$$

Table 12.1
Useful Types of Ordinary Curves

Type of Construction	Embedding Degree	Reference
MNT (Miyaji, Nakabayashi and Tanako)	$k = 3, 4, 6$	[4]
Freeman	$k = 10$	[5]
BN (Baretto-Naehrig)	$k = 12$	[6]
BW (Brezing-Weng)	$18 \nmid k$	[7]

so that

$$\frac{\log q^k}{\log p} = \rho \cdot k$$

In general, choices of parameters with small values of ρ provide the opportunity for faster elliptic curve operations and thus may be preferred over choices of parameters with larger values of ρ, although this should not be taken as a rigid design principle as other trade-offs may be more important than the additional speed that faster elliptic curve operations can provide. In practice, for example, if ρ is close to 1 it may be difficult to find a value of p which is a Solinas prime, and the additional speed in the pairing calculation from having p be a Solinas prime may more than make up for the slightly slower elliptic curve operations that may be required for a larger value of ρ. For $\rho = 1$, ideal values of p, q, and k that can be used to attain standard levels of bit strength are shown in Table 12.2.

Current research, however, has not yet found curves that meet all of the requirements of Table 12.2. The closest fit to the ideal values that is currently possible using known curves is shown in Table 12.3.

12.2 Eliminating Irrelevant Factors

Some factors that occur in the calculation of the Tate pairing are guaranteed to reduce to a value to 1 after the final exponentiation that is used to create a unique value from the pairing, and eliminating such irrelevant factors can make the calculation of the Tate pairing much more efficient.

Table 12.2
Ideal Parameters to Attain Standard Bit-Strength Levels for $\rho = 1$ Using Ordinary Curves

Bit Strength	Size of p	Embedding Degree k	Size of q^k
80	171	6	1,026
112	228	9	2,052
128	256	12	3,072
192	384	20	7,680
256	512	30	15,360

Table 12.3
Best-Known Parameters to Attain Standard Bit-Strength Levels Using Ordinary Curves

Bit Strength	Size of p	ρ	Embedding Degree k	Size of q^k	Construction
80	171	1	6	1,026	MNT
112	224	1	10	2,240	Freeman
128	256	1	12	3,072	BN
192	384	10/9	19	8,113	BW
256	512	15/14	29	15,921	BW

12.2.1 Eliminating Random Components

The Tate pairing $e(P, Q)$ where P is a point of order n is calculated as $e(P, Q) = f_P(A_Q)$, where f_P is a rational function with $div(f_P)$ equivalent to the divisor $n(P) - n(O)$ and A_Q is a divisor equivalent to $(Q) - (O)$. In the simple version of the Tate pairing that was presented in Chapter 4, we avoided the problems of dealing with evaluating f_P at the point O by evaluating f_P at the divisor $(Q + R) - (R)$ instead of at $(Q) - (O)$.

Another strategy [9] to avoid having to deal with the point infinity is to use a divisor equivalent to $n(P) - n(O)$, perhaps using $n(P + R) - n(R)$ to calculate f_P', where

$$div(f_P') = n(P + R) - n(R)$$

where R is a randomly chosen point in $E(\mathbb{F}_q)$, and use f_P' instead of f_P to calculate $e(P, Q)$.

From the form $div(f_P')$ we can see that the poles and zeroes of f_P' avoid the point at infinity, making it a possible candidate for use in calculating the Tate pairing. It turns out, however, that using such a random point to create an equivalent divisor is actually not needed due to the way in which the final exponentiation eliminates some components of $f_P'(A_Q)$.

Suppose that $p \mid (q^k - 1)$. We would like to be able to use Fermat's little theorem to find terms that we can ignore because they will be eliminated by a final exponentiation when we find that

$$x^{(q^k - 1)/p} = 1$$

Fortunately this turns out to be true in the cases useful to implementing pairing-based algorithms.

Note that if $d \mid k$ we can write

$$q^k - 1 = (q^d - 1) \sum_{i=0}^{k/d-1} q^{i \cdot d}$$

If $k > 1$ is the embedding degree of some group G_1 of order p then we must have $p \nmid (q^d - 1)$ (otherwise the embedding degree would be no more than d) so that

$$p \left| \sum_{i=0}^{k/d-1} q^{i \cdot d} \right.$$

and thus

$$(q^d - 1) \left| \frac{q^k - 1}{p} \right.$$

or that

$$\frac{q^k - 1}{p} = m(q^d - 1)$$

for some integer m. Then we can appeal to Fermat's little theorem to find that factors of the form

$$x^{(q^k-1)/p} = x^{(q^d-1)m} = 1$$

reduce to the value of 1 after a final exponentiation, so that they can be dropped from some calculations without changing the final value.

Now f_P' is a rational function with neither a zero nor pole at the point O, so if the point P has coordinates in $\mathbb{F}_q$ then $f_P'(O)$ does also. Thus, $f_P'(O)$ is a factor what will reduce to the value of 1 after a final exponentiation by $(q^k - 1)/p$ so we can omit it from calculations without introducing any error and we can calculate the reduced Tate pairing as

$$e(P, Q)^{(q^k-1)/p} = (f_P'(A_Q))^{(q^k-1)/p} = f_P'((Q) - (O))$$

$$= \left(\frac{f_P'(Q)}{f_P'(O)}\right)^{(q^k-1)/p} = f_P'(Q)^{(q^k-1)/p}$$

Suppose that $R \in E(\mathbb{F}_q)$ with $R \notin \{O, -P, Q, Q - P\}$. Then $(P + R) - (R)$ is equivalent to $(P) - (O)$ because they differ by the divisor of some rational function, say

$$(P + R) - (R) = (P) - (O) + div(g)$$

so that

$$\begin{aligned} div(f'_P) &= p((P + R) - (R)) = p((P) - (O) + div(g)) \\ &= div(f_P) + p \cdot div(g) \end{aligned}$$

or that $f'_P = f_P g^P$.

Since Q not a pole or zero of either f'_P or f_P, then $g(Q) \in \mathbb{F}^*_{q^k}$, so we can write

$$f'_P(Q)^{(q^k - 1)/p} = f_P(Q)^{(q^k - 1)/p} g(Q)^{q^k - 1} = f_P(Q)^{(q^k - 1)/p}$$

because Fermat's little theorem guarantees that

$$g(Q)^{q^k - 1} = 1$$

So after the final exponentiation there is essentially no difference between f'_P and f_P, and we can ignore any of the terms involving the random point R in Miller's algorithm, giving the more efficient version of it that is defined by Algorithm 12.1, which uses the same notation in Algorithm 4.1.

Algorithm 12.1: SimplifiedTatePairing (simplified Miller's algorithm for computing the Tate pairing)

INPUT: Elliptic curve $E/\mathbb{F}_q$, $P \in E(\mathbb{F}_q)[n]$ with $n = \sum_{i=0}^{t} b_i 2^i$, $Q \in E(\mathbb{F}_{q^k})$

OUTPUT: $e(P, Q)$

1. $f \leftarrow 1$, $t \leftarrow \lfloor \log_2 n \rfloor$, $S \leftarrow P$
2. For $i \leftarrow t - 1$ down to 0
3. $f \leftarrow f^2 \dfrac{u_{S,S}(Q)}{v_{2,S}(Q)}$
4. $S \leftarrow 2S$
5. If $b_i = 1$
6. $f \leftarrow f \dfrac{u_{S,P}(Q)}{v_{S+P}(Q)}$
7. $S \leftarrow S + P$
8. Return f

Example 12.1

Suppose that we have the elliptic curve $E/\mathbb{F}_{11} : y^2 = x^3 + x$. Let $P = (5, 8) \in E(\mathbb{F}_{11})[3]$ and let $Q = (4, 3i) \in E(\mathbb{F}_{11^2})$. Using (4.3) we find that

$$f_P(x, y) = y + 9x + 2$$

where

$$div(f_P) = 3(P) - 3(O)$$

so that

$$f_P(Q) = 5 + 3i$$

which gives

$$f_P(Q)^{(q^k - 1)/p} = (5 + 3i)^{40} = 5 + 3i$$

for the reduced pairing.

12.2.2 Eliminating Extension Field Divisions

In some cases, it is possible to replace the extension field division that happen in steps 3 and 6 of Algorithm 12.1. In the case where the embedding degree k is even, it is possible to replace these divisions with a complex conjugation in a way that will result in the correct result after the final exponentiation [10]. This can be very beneficial because inversions are typically very expensive operations in a large finite field. The basis for this is to consider the field $\mathbb{F}_{q^k}$ as an extension of degree 2 of $\mathbb{F}_{q^d}$ where $d = k/2$, so that elements of $\mathbb{F}_{q^k}$ can be represented as $a + ib$ where a and b are elements of $\mathbb{F}_{q^d}$.

Expanding $(a + ib)^{q^d}$ as

$$(a + ib)^{q^d} = \sum_{k=0}^{q^d} \binom{q^d}{k} a^{q^d - k}(ib)^k$$

we see that most of the terms are equal to zero modulo q so that we have

$$(a + ib)^{q^d} = a - ib$$

so that we have that

$$\begin{aligned} \left(\frac{1}{a + ib}\right)^{q^d - 1} &= \frac{a + ib}{(a + ib)^{q^d - 1}} \\ &= \frac{a + ib}{a - ib} = \frac{(a - ib)^{q^d}}{a - ib} = (a - ib)^{q^d - 1} \end{aligned}$$

And since we can write the final exponentiation after a Tate pairing as

$$x^{(q^k-1)/p} = \left(x^{q^d-1}\right)^{(q^k-1)/p}$$

we see that we can replace the extension field divisions in steps 3 and 6 by complex conjugation, which is equivalent to division in the extension field after the final exponentiation is applied. This suggests the modification to Miller's algorithm that is shown in Algorithm 12.2.

Algorithm 12.2: SimplifiedTatePairingConjugation (simplified Miller's algorithm for computing the Tate pairing replacing extension field divisions with complex conjugation)

INPUT: Elliptic curve $E/\mathbb{F}_q$, $P \in E(\mathbb{F}_q)[n]$ with $n = \sum_{i=0}^{t} b_i 2^i$, $Q \in E(\mathbb{F}_{q^k})$

OUTPUT: $e(P, Q)$

1. $f \leftarrow 1$, $t \leftarrow \lfloor \log_2 n \rfloor$, $S \leftarrow P$
2. For $i \leftarrow t-1$ down to 0
3. $f \leftarrow f^2 \cdot u_{S,S}(Q) \cdot \overline{v_{2,S}(Q)}$
4. $S \leftarrow 2S$
5. If $b_i = 1$
6. $f \leftarrow f \cdot u_{S,P}(Q) \cdot \overline{v_{S+P}(Q)}$
7. $S \leftarrow S + P$
8. Return f

12.2.3 Denominator Elimination

In either the basic algorithm for the Tate pairing (Algorithm 4.1) or the more efficient version shown above (Algorithm 12.1), the denominators that appear in Miller's algorithm are all terms of the form $v_P(Q)$ for some point P, where $v_P(Q) = x_Q - x_P$. If we have that the x-coordinates of both P and Q are elements of $\mathbb{F}_q$, then their difference is also an element of $\mathbb{F}_q$ and will be eliminated by a final exponentiation. If this happens, then the calculation of the Tate pairing can be further simplified to the version shown in Algorithm 12.3, which further simplifies Algorithm 12.1.

Algorithm 12.3: SimplifiedTatePairingWithDenomElim (simplified Miller's algorithm for computing the Tate pairing using denominator elimination)

INPUT: Elliptic curve $E/\mathbb{F}_q$, $P \in E(\mathbb{F}_q)[n]$ with $n = \sum_{i=0}^{t} b_i 2^i$, $Q \in E(\mathbb{F}_{q^k})$

OUTPUT: $e(P, Q)$

1. $f \leftarrow 1$, $t \leftarrow \lfloor \log_2 n \rfloor$, $S \leftarrow P$
2. For $i \leftarrow t - 1$ down to 0
3. $f \leftarrow f^2 \cdot u_{S,S}(Q)$
4. $S \leftarrow 2S$
5. If $b_i = 1$
6. $f \leftarrow f \cdot u_{S,P}(Q)$
7. $S \leftarrow S + P$
8. Return f.

Unlike the elimination of the random component that produces Algorithm 12.1, denominator elimination only works in special cases, those in which we can guarantee that the x-coordinate of the input Q to be an element of $\mathbb{F}_q$. This will happen, for example, in the case where the supersingular curve $E/\mathbb{F}_q : y^2 = x^3 + x$ is used, and we calculate $\hat{e}(P, Q) = e(P, \phi(Q))^{(q^k - 1)/p}$ where ϕ is the distortion map given by $\phi(x, y) = (-x, iy)$. In this case, the x-coordinate of the output of the distortion map is an element of $\mathbb{F}_q$, so denominator elimination can be used. In the case of the supersingular curve $E/\mathbb{F}_q : y^2 = x^3 + 1$, on the other hand, where we have a distortion map of the form $\phi(x, y) = (\xi x, y)$ where $\xi^3 = 1$, $\xi \neq 1$, we do not have the x-coordinate of the output of the distortion map being an element of $\mathbb{F}_q$, so denominator elimination cannot be used.

12.3 Calculating the Product of Pairings

Calculating the product of pairings can be useful in two important cases. Products of pairings are required in the implementation of many HIBE schemes, and because we can write

$$\frac{e(P_1, Q_1)}{e(P_2, Q_2)} = e(P_1, Q_1)\,e(P_2, -Q_2)$$

the same technique that will allow the efficient calculation of the product of pairings can also be used to calculate the ratio of pairings, which is required in the Boneh-Boyen IBE scheme.

To efficiently calculate the product of pairings of the form

$$\prod_{i=1}^{n} e(P_i, Q_i)$$

we assume that all of the values P_i are elements of the same order. This guarantees that the loop index variable i in Algorithm 12.1 is shared by each of the calculations of $e(P_i, Q_i)$ so that we can combine some of the operations that are required in the calculation of each of the separate pairings [9–11].

In particular, the accumulation steps that take place in steps 3 and 6 of Algorithm 12.1 can be combined into a single accumulation that returns the product of the pairings. Once this value is calculated, a single final exponentiation is then required.

In an important special case, the computational efficiency gained by combining these operations makes calculating the ratio of two pairings, like is required in the Boneh-Boyen IBE algorithm, approximately 20% slower than calculating a single pairing instead of twice as slow.

Algorithm 12.4: ProductOfPairings (simplified Miller's algorithm for computing the product of Tate pairings)

INPUT: Elliptic curve $E/\mathbb{F}_q$, $P_1, P_2, \ldots P_m \in E(\mathbb{F}_q)[n]$ with $n = \sum_{i=0}^{t} b_i 2^i$, $Q_1, Q_2, \ldots Q_m \in E(\mathbb{F}_{q^k})$

OUTPUT: $\prod_{i=1}^{n} e(P_i, Q_i)$

1. $f \leftarrow 1$, $t \leftarrow \lfloor \log_2 n \rfloor$, $S_1 \leftarrow P_1$, $S_2 \leftarrow P_2, \ldots S_m \leftarrow P_m$
2. For $i \leftarrow t - 1$ down to 0
3. $f \leftarrow f^2 \prod_{i=1}^{m} \frac{u_{S_i, S_i}(Q_i)}{v_{2, S_i}(Q_i)}$
4. $S_1 \leftarrow 2S_1$, $S_2 \leftarrow 2S_2, \ldots, S_m \leftarrow 2S_m$
5. If $b_i = 1$
6. $f \leftarrow f \prod_{i=1}^{m} \frac{u_{S_i, P_i}(Q_i)}{v_{S_i + P_i}(Q_i)}$
7. $S_1 \leftarrow 2S_1 + P_1$, $S_2 \leftarrow 2S_2 + P_2, \ldots, S_m \leftarrow S_m + P_m$
8. Return f

12.4 The Shipsey-Stange Algorithm

Although most research to date on efficient implementations of the Tate pairing have focused on optimizing Miller's algorithm, there has been an alternative to Miller's algorithm that has been recently discovered that provides a way to calculate the Tate pairing without requiring any manipulation of divisors. This algorithm is due to Katherine Stange [12], and uses the properties of elliptic nets to create an algorithm for calculating the Tate pairing.

An *elliptic net* is a function that satisfies the following recursion

$$\begin{aligned}
&W(p+q+s)\,W(p-q)\,W(r+s)\,W(r)\\
&+W(q+r+s)\,W(q-r)\,W(p+s)\,W(p)\\
&+W(r+p+s)\,W(r-p)\,W(q+s)\,W(q)=0
\end{aligned}$$

Elliptic nets are closely related to elliptic curves, and can be defined in terms of the same $\wp$ function that underlies an elliptic curve. Stange's remarkable result was that it is possible to calculate the Tate pairing for $P \in E(\mathbb{F}_q)[n]$ with and $Q \in E(\mathbb{F}_{q^k})$ as

$$e(P, Q) = \frac{W(s+np+q)\,W(s)}{W(s+np)\,W(s+q)}$$

where all of the initial conditions of the elliptic net can be calculated from either the coefficients a and b of the elliptic curve $E/\mathbb{F}_q : y^2 = x^3 + ax + b$ or from the points $P = (x_P, y_P)$ and $Q = (x_Q, y_Q)$. This can be done as follows. First calculate three constants A, B, and C as

$$A = \frac{1}{x_P - x_Q} \tag{12.1}$$

$$B = \frac{1}{(2x_P - x_Q)(x_P - x_Q)^2 - (y_P + y_Q)^2} \tag{12.2}$$

$$C = \frac{1}{2y_P} \tag{12.3}$$

Then determine the initial conditions of two sequences $\{c_i\}$ and $\{d_i\}$ as

$$c_{-2} = -2y_P \tag{12.4}$$

$$c_{-1} = -1 \tag{12.5}$$

$$c_0 = 0 \tag{12.6}$$

$$c_1 = 1 \tag{12.7}$$

$$c_2 = 2y_P \tag{12.8}$$

$$c_3 = 3x_P^4 + 6ax_P^2 + 12bx_P - a^2 \tag{12.9}$$

$$c_4 = 4y_P\left(x_P^6 + 5ax_P^4 + 20bx_P^3 - 5a^2x_P^2 - 4abx_P - 8b^2 - a^3\right) \tag{12.10}$$

and

$$d_0 = 1 \tag{12.11}$$

$$d_1 = 1 \tag{12.12}$$

$$d_2 = (2x_P - x_Q) - \left(\frac{y_Q - y_P}{x_Q - x_P}\right)^2 \tag{12.13}$$

Additional terms of the sequences $\{c_i\}$ and $\{d_i\}$ can then be calculated using the recursions

$$c_{2k-1} = c_{2k+1}c_{k-1}^3 - c_{k-2}c_k^3 \tag{12.14}$$

$$c_{2k} = C\left(c_k c_{k+2} c_{k-1}^2 - c_k c_{k-2} c_{k+1}^2\right) \tag{12.15}$$

and

$$d_{2k-1} = d_{k+1}d_{k-1}c_{k-1}^2 - d_k^2 c_{k-2} c_k \tag{12.16}$$

$$d_{2k} = d_{k+1}d_{k-1}c_k^2 = d_k^2 c_{k-1} c_{k+1} \tag{12.17}$$

$$d_{2k+1} = A(d_{k+1}d_{k-1}c_{k+1}^2 - d_k^2 c_k c_{k+2} \tag{12.18}$$

$$d_{2k+2} = B(d_{k+1}d_{k-1}c_{k+2}^2 - d_k^2 c_{k+1} c_{k+3} \tag{12.19}$$

Once the values c_{n+1} and d_{n+1} have been calculated, it is then possible to calculate the value of the Tate pairing as

$$e(P, Q) = \frac{d_{n+1}}{c_{n+1}}$$

Example 12.2

Suppose that we have the elliptic curve $E/\mathbb{F}_{11} : y^2 = x^3 + x$. Let $P = (5, 8) \in E(\mathbb{F}_{11})[3]$ so that $x_P = 5$ and $y_P = 8$, and let $Q = (4, 3i) \in E(\mathbb{F}_{11^2})$ so that $x_Q = 4$ and $y_Q = 3i$. This gives the following constants:

$$A = 1$$

$$B = 9 + 6i$$

$$C = 9$$

and the following initial conditions for the elliptic net:

$$c_{-2} = 6$$

$$c_{-1} = -1$$

$$c_0 = 0$$

$$c_1 = 1$$

$$c_2 = 5$$

$$c_3 = 0$$

$$c_4 = 10$$

$$d_0 = 1$$

$$d_1 = 1$$

$$d_2 = 3 + 4i$$

$$d_3 = 9 + i$$

$$d_4 = 5 + 3i$$

Because the order of the point P is so low, we can immediately calculate the value of

$$e(P, Q) = \frac{d_4}{c_4} = \frac{5 + 3i}{10} = 6 + 8i$$

which gives the value of

$$\hat{e}(P, Q) = (6 + 8i)^{(11^2 - 1)/3} = 5 + 3i$$

for the reduced pairing, the same result as found in Example 12.1.

Rachel Shipsey [13] invented a double-and-add technique for calculating the values of recursions like (12.14), (12.15), and (12.16) through (12.19). This technique gives the Shipsey-Stange algorithm for calculating the Tate pairing using elliptic nets which is defined in Algorithm 12.5. The Shipsey-Stange algorithm is less efficient at calculating the Tate pairing than optimized versions of Miller's algorithm are, but future research may close this gap and make the algorithm more useful.

Algorithm 12.5: TateShipseyStange (Shipsey-Stange algorithm for the Tate pairing using elliptic nets)
INPUT: Elliptic curve $E/\mathbb{F}_q : y^2 = x^3 + ax + b$, $P \in E(\mathbb{F}_q)[n]$ with $n = \sum_{i=0}^{t} b_i 2^i$, $Q \in E(\mathbb{F}_{q^k})$
OUTPUT: $e(P, Q)$

1. $k \leftarrow 1$, $t \leftarrow \lfloor \log_2 n \rfloor$
2. Calculate A, B, C using (12.1) through (12.2)
3. Calculate $c_{-2}, c_{-1}, \ldots c_4$ using (12.4) through (12.10)
4. Calculate d_0, d_1, d_2 using (12.11) through (12.13)
5. For $i \leftarrow t - 1$ down to 0
6. If $b_i = 0$ then
7. Calculate $c_{2k-3}, \ldots, c_{2k+4}$ using (12.14) and (12.15)
8. Calculate $d_{2k-1}, d_{2k}, d_{2k+1}$ using (12.16) through (12.19)
9. $k \leftarrow 2k$
10. else
11. Calculate $c_{2k-2}, \ldots, c_{2k+5}$ using (12.14) and (12.15)
12. Calculate $d_{2k}, d_{2k+1}, d_{2k+2}$ using (12.16) through (12.19)
13. $k \leftarrow 2k + 1$
14. Return d_{r+1} / c_{r+1}

12.5 Precomputation

In many calculations of pairings, the value of P in $\hat{e}(P, Q)$ is relatively fixed. In the Boneh-Franklin IBE system, for example, if we need to calculate

$\hat{e}(sP, rQ_{ID})$, where sP is part of the public parameters of the system, which will rarely change. Because we calculate the value of the pairing as $e(P, Q) = f_P(Q)$, if the value of the point P is fixed then the functions u and v that are used in calculating the value of the pairing, like in step 3 of Algorithm 12.1, are also fixed, so we can calculate the values needed to evaluate u and v once, saving significant computational effort.

With the value of the point P is fixed, the order n of the point P is also fixed, so that the iteration on the binary expansion of n is also fixed, so that the functions of P that are calculated in the double-and-add iteration of the Tate pairing, like the values of S that are calculated in steps 4 and 7 of Algorithm 12.1 are also fixed. Calculating these values once and reusing them will also save significant computational effort in evaluating the Tate pairing.

References

[1] IEEE Standard Number 1363-2000, "Standard Specifications for Public-Key Cryptography," 2000.

[2] Atkin, A., and F. Morain, "Elliptic Curves and Primality Proving," *Mathematics of Computation*, Vol. 61, No. 203, 1993, pp. 29–68.

[3] Lay, G., and H. Zimmer, "Constructing Elliptic Curves with Given Group Order over Large Finite Fields," *Proceedings of the First International Symposium on Algorithmic Number Theory*, Ithaca, NY, May 6–9, 1994, pp. 250–263.

[4] Miyaji, A., M. Nakabayashi, and S. Tanako, "New Explicit Constructions of Elliptic Curve Traces for FR-Reduction," *IEICE Transactions on Fundamentals*, Vol. E84-A, No. 5, 2001, pp. 1234–1243.

[5] Freeman, D., "Constructing Pairing-Friendly Elliptic Curves with Embedding Degree 10," *Proceedings of the 4th Algorithmic Number Theory Symposium*, Leiden, the Netherlands, July 2–7, 2000, pp. 452–465.

[6] Baretto, P., and M. Naehrig, "Pairing-Friendly Elliptic Curves of Prime Order," *Proceedings of the 12th Annual Workshop on Selected Areas in Cryptography*, Kingston, Canada, August 11–23, 2005, pp. 319–331.

[7] Brezing, F., and A. Weng, "Elliptic Curves Suitable for Pairing-Based Cryptography," *Designs, Codes and Cryptography*, Vol. 37, No. 1, 2005, pp. 133–141.

[8] Baretto, P., B. Lynn, and M. Scott, "Constructing Elliptic Curves with Prescribed Embedding Degrees," *Proceedings of the 3rd Conference on Security in Networks*, Amalfi, Italy, September 12–13, 2002, pp. 263–273.

[9] Baretto, P., H. Kim, B. Lynn, and M. Scott, "Efficient Algorithms for Pairing-Based Cryptosystems," *Proceedings of CRYPTO 2002*, Santa Barbara, CA, August 18–22, 2002, pp. 23–36.

[10] Kobayashi, T., K. Aoki, and H. Imai, "Efficient Algorithms for the Tate Pairing," *IEICE Transactions on Fundamentals*, Vol. E89-A, No. 1, 2006, pp. 134–143.

[11] Scott, M., "Computing the Tate Pairing," *Proceedings of the Cryptographers' Track at the RSA Conference 2005*, San Jose, CA, February 13–17, 2005, pp. 293–304.

[12] Stange, K., "The Tate Pairing Via Elliptic Nets," *Proceedings of the 1st International Conference on Pairing-Based Cryptography*, Tokyo, Japan, July 2–4, 2007, pp. 329–384.

[13] Shipsey, R., "Elliptic Divisibility Sequences," Ph.D. thesis, University of London, 2000.

Appendix: Useful Test Data

Values Useful for Testing Pairing Calculations

The following values are provided to help test software that implements the Tate pairing. They can also be used to help manually calculate the encryption and decryption algorithms described in Chapters 8, 9, 10, and 11.

A.1 Points on $E/\mathbb{F}_{131} : y^2 = x^3 + 1$

For the elliptic curve $E/\mathbb{F}_{131} : y^2 = x^3 + 1$ and $P = (98, 58) \in E(\mathbb{F}_{131})[11]$, we have that $\phi(x, y) = (\xi x, y)$, where $\xi = 65 + 112i$, is a distortion map for finite points in $\langle P \rangle$. The elements of $\langle P \rangle$, the value of the distortion map at the points of $\langle P \rangle$, as well as the values $\hat{e}(P, P)^n$, where $\hat{e}(P, Q) = e(P, \phi(Q))^{1560}$ are listed here.

n	nP	$\phi(nP)$	$\hat{e}(P, P)^n$
1	(98, 58)	$(82 + 103i, 58)$	$28 + 93i$
2	(128, 57)	$(67 + 57i, 57)$	$126 + 99i$
3	(113, 8)	$(9 + 80i, 8)$	$85 + 80i$
4	(33, 31)	$(49 + 28i, 31)$	$49 + 58i$
5	(34, 23)	$(114 + 9i, 23)$	$39 + 24i$
6	(34, 108)	$(114 + 9i, 108)$	$39 + 107i$
7	(33, 100)	$(49 + 28i, 100)$	$49 + 73i$
8	(113, 123)	$(9 + 80i, 123)$	$85 + 51i$
9	(128, 74)	$(67 + 57i, 74)$	$126 + 32i$
10	(98, 73)	$(82 + 103i, 73)$	$28 + 38i$
11	O	O	1

A.2 Points on $E/\mathbb{F}_{131}: y^2 = x^3 + x$

For the elliptic curve $E/\mathbb{F}_{131}: y^2 = x^3 + 1$ and $P = (55, 45) \in E(\mathbb{F}_{131})[11]$, we have that $\phi(x, y) = (130 \cdot x, i \cdot y)$, where $\xi = 65 + 112i$, is a distortion map for finite points in $\langle P \rangle$. The elements of $\langle P \rangle$, the value of the distortion map at the points of $\langle P \rangle$, as well as the values $\hat{e}(P, P)^n$, where $\hat{e}(P, Q) = e(P, \phi(Q))^{1560}$ are listed here.

n	nP	$\phi(nP)$	$\hat{e}(P, P)^n$
1	(55, 45)	(76, 45i)	126 + 32i
2	(60, 33)	(71, 33i)	49 + 73i
3	(27, 45)	(104, 45i)	39 + 24i
4	(49, 86)	(82, 86i)	85 + 80i
5	(121, 13)	(10, 13i)	28 + 93i
6	(121, 118)	(10, 118i)	28 + 38i
7	(49, 45)	(82, 45i)	85 + 51i
8	(27, 86)	(104, 86i)	39 + 107i
9	(60, 98)	(71, 98i)	49 + 58i
10	(55, 86)	(76, 86i)	126 + 99i
11	O	O	1

A.3 Rational Functions of Divisors for $E/\mathbb{F}_{11}: y^2 = x^3 + 1$

For the elliptic curve $E/\mathbb{F}_{11}: y^2 = x^3 + 1$ we have that $\#E(\mathbb{F}_{11}) = 12$. Each of the finite elements of $E(\mathbb{F}_{11})$ are listed next along with the rational function $f_P(x, y)$ such that $div(n(P) - n(O)) = div(f_P(x, y))$ for a point P of order n.

Point	*Order*	$f_P(x, y)$
(9, 12)	12	$\dfrac{(y+3x+3)^2(y+4x+6)^4(y+8x+3)^4}{(x+1)(x+6)^4(x+9)^4}$
(2, 8)	6	$\dfrac{(y+x+1)^2(y+2x+10)^2}{x^2(x+1)}$
(5, 4)	4	$\dfrac{(y+3x+3)^2}{x+1}$
(0, 10)	3	$y+1$
(7, 6)	12	$\dfrac{(y+3x+3)^2(y+6x+7)^4(y+7x)^4}{(x+1)(x+6)^4(x+9)^4}$

(10, 0)	2	$x + 1$
(7, 5)	12	$\dfrac{(y + 4x)^2 (y + 5x + 4)^4 (y + 8x + 8)^4}{(x + 1)(x + 6)^4 (x + 9)^4}$
(0, 1)	3	$y + 10$
(5, 7)	4	$\dfrac{(y + 8x + 8)^2}{x + 1}$
(2, 3)	6	$\dfrac{(y + 9x + 1)^2 (y + 10x + 10)^2}{x^2 (x + 1)}$
(9, 9)	12	$\dfrac{(y + 8x + 8)^2 (y + 7x + 5)^4 (y + 3x + 8)^4}{(x + 1)(x + 6)^4 (x + 9)^4}$

A.4 Rational Functions of Divisors for Selected Points on $E/\mathbb{F}_{11} : y^2 = x^3 + x$

For the elliptic curve $E/\mathbb{F}_{11} : y^2 = x^3 + x$ we have that $\#E(\mathbb{F}_{131}) = 132$. Each of the finite elements of $E(\mathbb{F}_{131})[11]$ are listed next along with the rational function $f_P(x, y)$ such that $div(11(P) - 11(O)) = div(f_P(x, y))$ for a point P.

Point	*Order*	$f_P(x, y)$
(7, 8)	12	$\dfrac{(y + 8x)^2 (y + 9x + 6)^4 (y + 10x + 10)^4}{x(x + 1)^4 (x + 2)^4}$
(9, 1)	6	$\dfrac{(y + 6x)^2 (y + 10x + 8)^2}{x(x + 6)^2}$
(10, 8)	4	$\dfrac{(y + 8x)^2}{x}$
(5, 3)	3	$y + 2x + 9$
(8, 6)	12	$\dfrac{(y + 8x)^2 (y + 7x + 4)^4 (y + 5x + 9)^4}{x(x + 1)^4 (x + 2)^4}$
(0, 0)	2	x
(8, 5)	12	$\dfrac{(y + 3x)^2 (y + 4x + 7)^4 (y + 6x + 2)^4}{x(x + 1)^4 (x + 2)^4}$
(5, 8)	3	$y + 9x + 2$
(10, 3)	4	$\dfrac{(y + 3x)^2}{x}$

(9, 10)	6	$\dfrac{(y+5x)^2(y+x+3)^2}{x(x+6)^2}$
(7, 3)	12	$\dfrac{(y+3x)^2(y+2x+5)^4(y+x+1)^4}{x(x+1)^4(x+2)^4}$

A.5 Rational Functions of Divisors for Selected Points on $E/\mathbb{F}_{131} : y^2 = x^3 + 1$

For the elliptic curve $E/\mathbb{F}_{131} : y^2 = x^3 + 1$ we have that $\#E(\mathbb{F}_{131}) = 132$. Each of the finite elements of $E(\mathbb{F}_{131})[11]$ are listed next along with the rational function $f_P(x, y)$ such that $div(n(P) - n(O)) = div(f_P(x, y))$ for a point of order n.

$$P = (98, 58) \in E(\mathbb{F}_{131})[11]$$

(98, 58)	$\dfrac{(y+54x+21)(y+67x+57)^2(y+113x+3)^4(y+17x+125)^4}{(x+3)^2(x+97)^4(x+98)^4}$
(128, 57)	$\dfrac{(y+18x+128)(y+83x+61)^2(y+110x+17)^2(y+17x+125)^4}{(x+18)^2(x+33)^2(x+98)^4}$
(113, 8)	$\dfrac{(y+110x+7)(y+47x+52)^2(y+64x+74)^2(y+103x+12)^4}{(x+33)^2(x+97)^4(x+98)^4}$
(33, 31)	$\dfrac{(y+114x+6)(y+8x+98)^2(y+28x+119)^2(y+110x+7)^4}{(x+3)^2(x+97)^2(x+18)^4}$
(34, 23)	$\dfrac{(y+103x+112)(y+12x+93)^2(y+18x+128)^2(y+67x+57)^4}{(x+3)^2(x+18)^2(x+33)^4}$
(34, 108)	$\dfrac{(y+28x+119)(y+113x+3)^2(y+119x+38)^2(y+64x+74)^4}{(x+3)^2(x+18)^2(x+33)^4}$
(33, 100)	$\dfrac{(y+17x+125)(y+123x+33)^2(y+103x+12)^2(y+21x+124)^4}{(x+3)^2(x+97)^2(x+18)^4}$
(113, 123)	$\dfrac{(y+21x+124)(y+84x+79)^2(y+57x+67)^2(y+28x+119)^4}{(x+33)^2(x+97)^4(x+98)^2}$
(128, 74)	$\dfrac{(y+113x+3)(y+48x+70)^2(y+21x+124)^2(y+114x+6)^4}{(x+18)^2(x+33)^2(x+98)^4}$
(98, 73)	$\dfrac{(y+64x+74)(y+77x+110)^2(y+114x+6)^4(y+18x+128)^4}{(x+3)^2(x+97)^4(x+98)^4}$

About the Author

Luther Martin is a security architect at Voltage Security in Palo Alto, California. He has published numerous articles on the topics of information security and risk management, is the technical editor of the IEEE P1363.3 standard for identity-based encryption, and is the principal author of the IETF standards that define identity-based encryption algorithms and their use in encrypting e-mail. Mr. Martin holds an M.S. in mathematics from the University of Cincinnati and an M.S. in electrical engineering from The Johns Hopkins University.

Index

Recent Titles in the Artech House Information Security and Privacy Series

Rolf Oppliger, Series Editor

Bluetooth Security, Christian Gehrmann, Joakim Persson and Ben Smeets

Computer Forensics and Privacy, Michael A. Caloyannides

Computer and Intrusion Forensics, George Mohay, et al.

Defense and Detection Strategies against Internet Worms, Jose Nazario

Demystifying the IPsec Puzzle, Sheila Frankel

Developing Secure Distributed Systems with CORBA, Ulrich Lang and Rudolf Schreiner

Electric Payment Systems for E-Commerce, Second Edition, Donal O'Mahony, Michael Peirce, and Hitesh Tewari

Evaluating Agile Software Development: Methods for Your Organization, Alan S. Koch

Implementing Electronic Card Payment Systems, Cristian Radu

Implementing the ISO/IEC 27001 Information Security Management System Standard, Edward Humphreys

Implementing Security for ATM Networks, Thomas Tarman and Edward Witzke

Information Hiding Techniques for Steganography and Digital Watermarking, Stefan Katzenbeisser and Fabien A. P. Petitcolas, editors

Internet and Intranet Security, Second Edition, Rolf Oppliger

Introduction to Identity-Based Encryption, Luther Martin

Java Card for E-Payment Applications, Vesna Hassler, Martin Manninger, Mikail Gordeev, and Christoph Müller

Multicast and Group Security, Thomas Hardjono and Lakshminath R. Dondeti

Non-repudiation in Electronic Commerce, Jianying Zhou

Outsourcing Information Security, C. Warren Axelrod

Privacy Protection and Computer Forensics, Second Edition, Michael A. Caloyannides

Role-Based Access Control, Second Edition, David F. Ferraiolo, D. Richard Kuhn, and Ramaswamy Chandramouli

Secure Messaging with PGP and S/MIME, Rolf Oppliger

Security Fundamentals for E-Commerce, Vesna Hassler

Security Technologies for the World Wide Web, Second Edition, Rolf Oppliger

Techniques and Applications of Digital Watermarking and Content Protection, Michael Arnold, Martin Schmucker, and Stephen D. Wolthusen

User's Guide to Cryptography and Standards, Alexander W. Dent and Chris J. Mitchell

For further information on these and other Artech House titles, including previously considered out-of-print books now available through our In-Print-Forever® (IPF®) program, contact:

Artech House
685 Canton Street
Norwood, MA 02062
Phone: 781-769-9750
Fax: 781-769-6334
e-mail: artech@artechhouse.com

Artech House
46 Gillingham Street
London SW1V 1AH UK
Phone: +44 (0)20 7596-8750
Fax: +44 (0)20 7630-0166
e-mail: artech-uk@artechhouse.com

Find us on the World Wide Web at:
www.artechhouse.com